T. Kitahara Collection

ROBOTS

Tin Toy Dreams

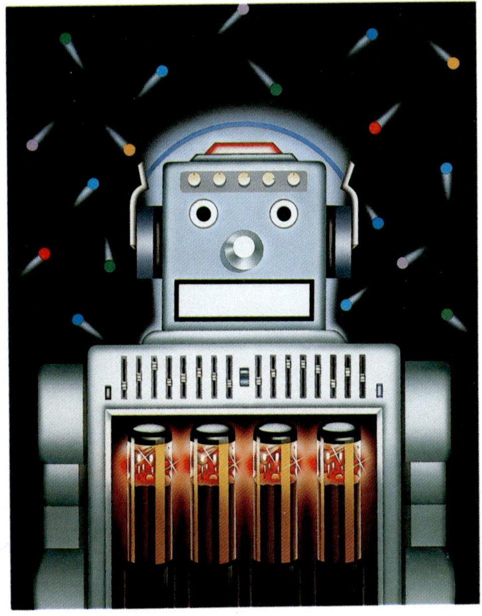

By Teruhisa Kitahara

AF530973

Chronicle Books · San Francisco

First published in the United States 1985 by Chronicle Books.

Copyright © 1983 by Shinko Music Publishing Co., Ltd. All rights reserved. No part of this book may be reproduced in any form without written permission from the publisher.

First published in Japan by Shinko Music Publishing Co., Ltd. Printed in Japan by Dai Nippon Printing Co., Ltd., Tokyo.

Library of Congress Cataloging in Publication Data

Kitahara, Teruhisa.
Robots: tin toys.

Rev. ed. of: Tin toy robots. 1983.
1. Tin toys–Japan–Catalogs.
2. Robots–Catalogs. 3. Toys, Mechanical–Japan–Catalogs.
4. Kitahara, Teruhisa–Art collections–Catalogs. 5. Tin toys–Private collections–Japan–Catalogs. I. Kitahara, Teruhisa. Tin toy robots. II. Title.
NK8454.K57 1985 688.7'28
84-23313 ISBN 0-87701-355-1

Chronicle Books
One Hallidie Plaza
San Francisco, CA 94102

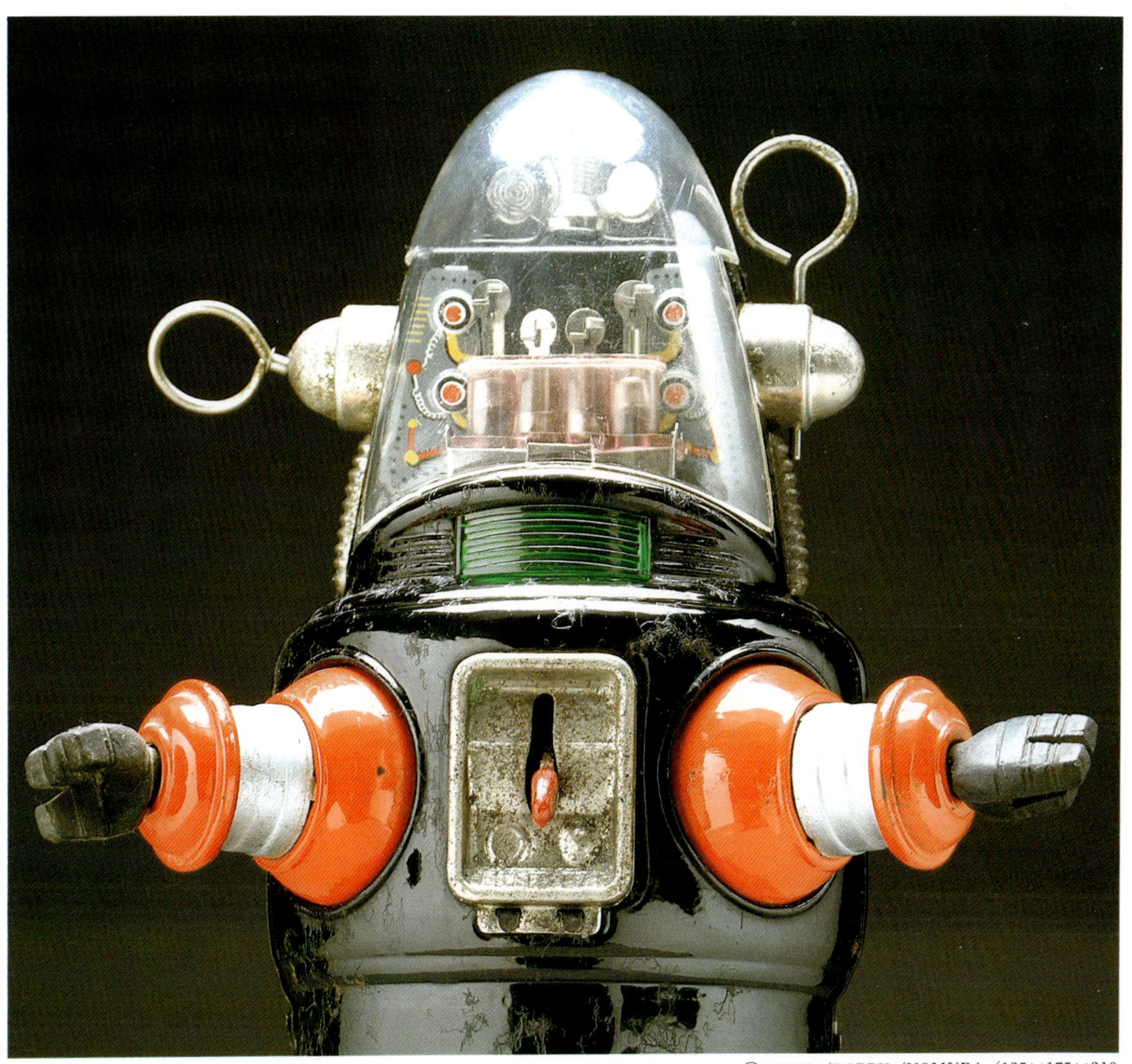

PB 293

① 1950'S／ROBBY／NOMURA／135×175×310

NUMBER／DECADE／NAME／MAKER／SIZE: depth × width × height(mm)

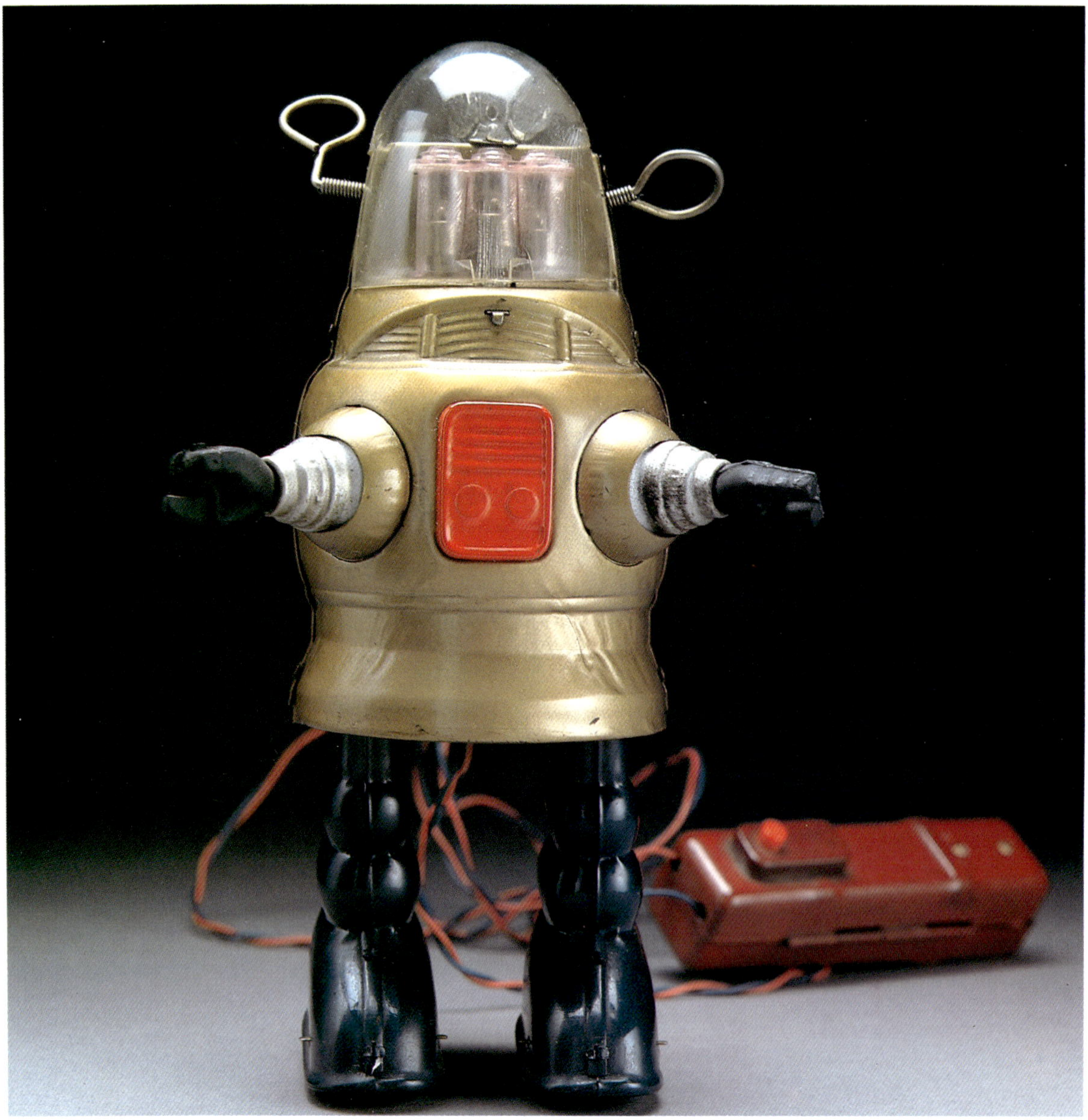

②③ 1950'S／ROBBY／NOMURA／95×125×215

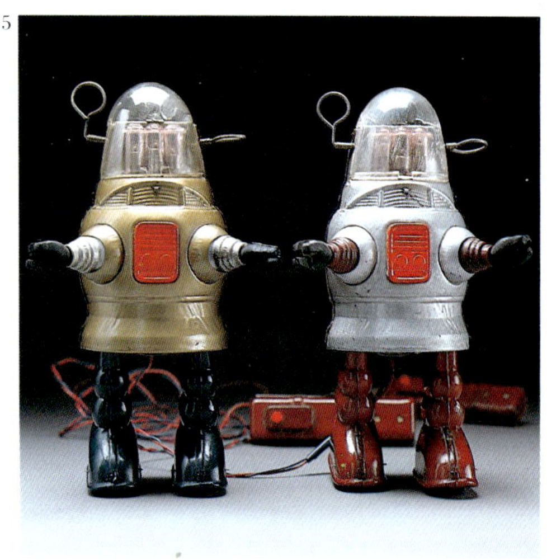

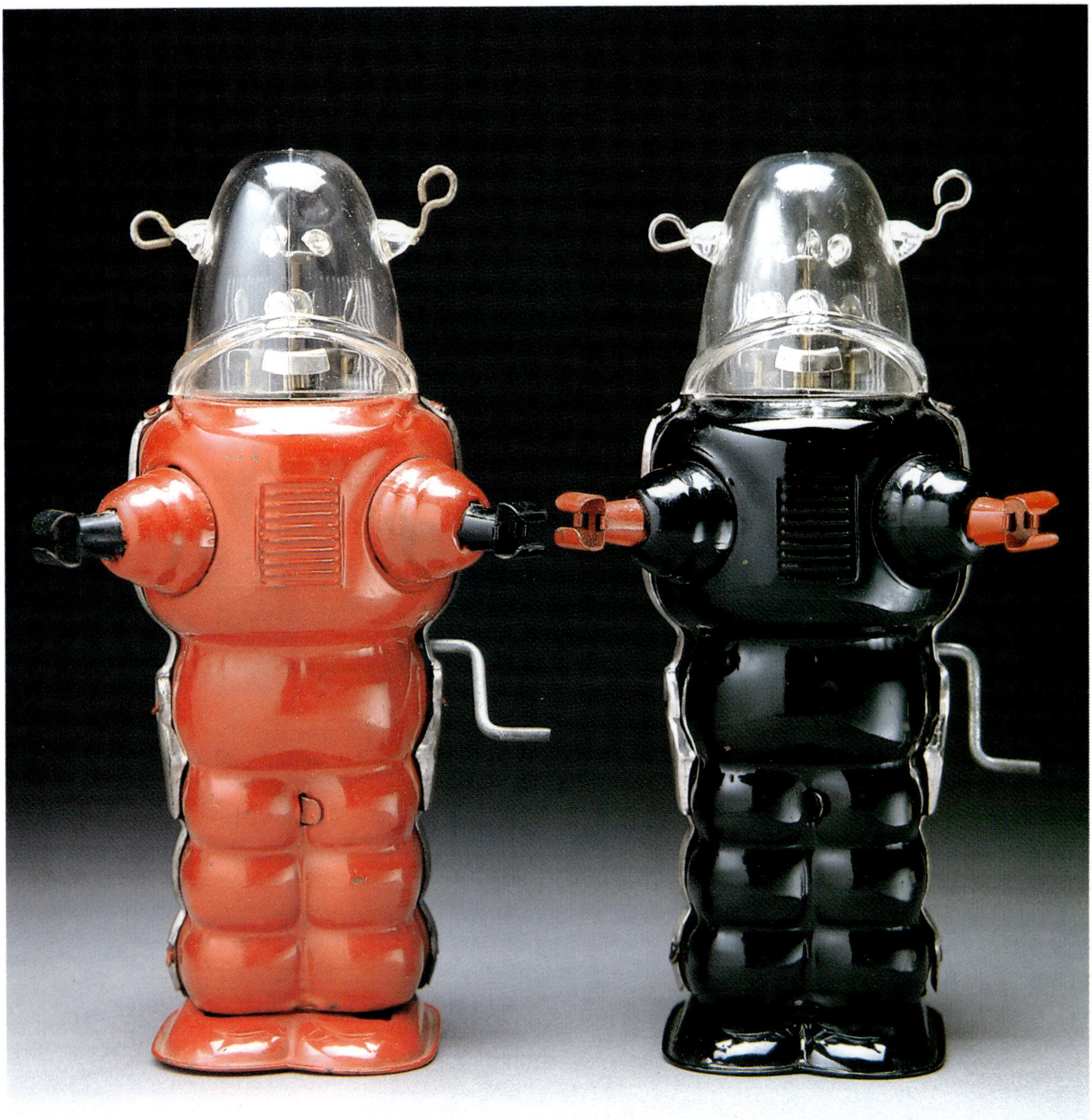

④⑤ 1950'S／ROBBY／YOSHIYA／65×92×160

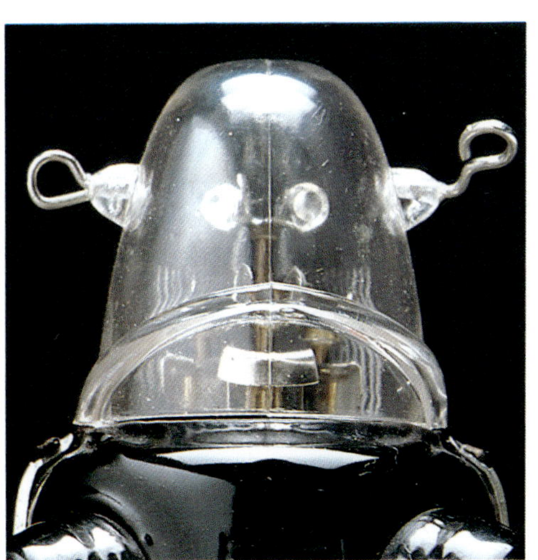

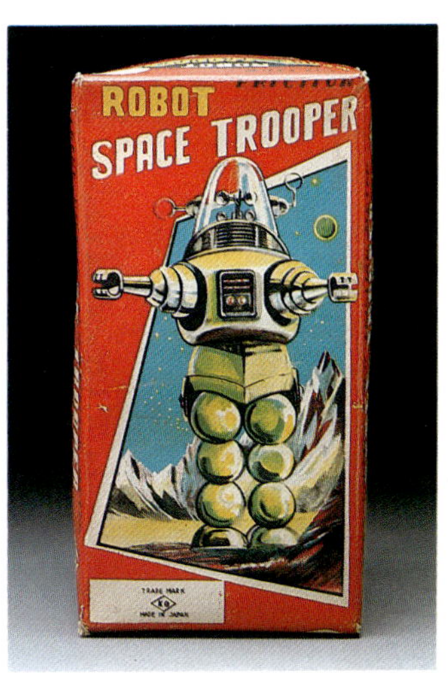

CASE ATTACHED

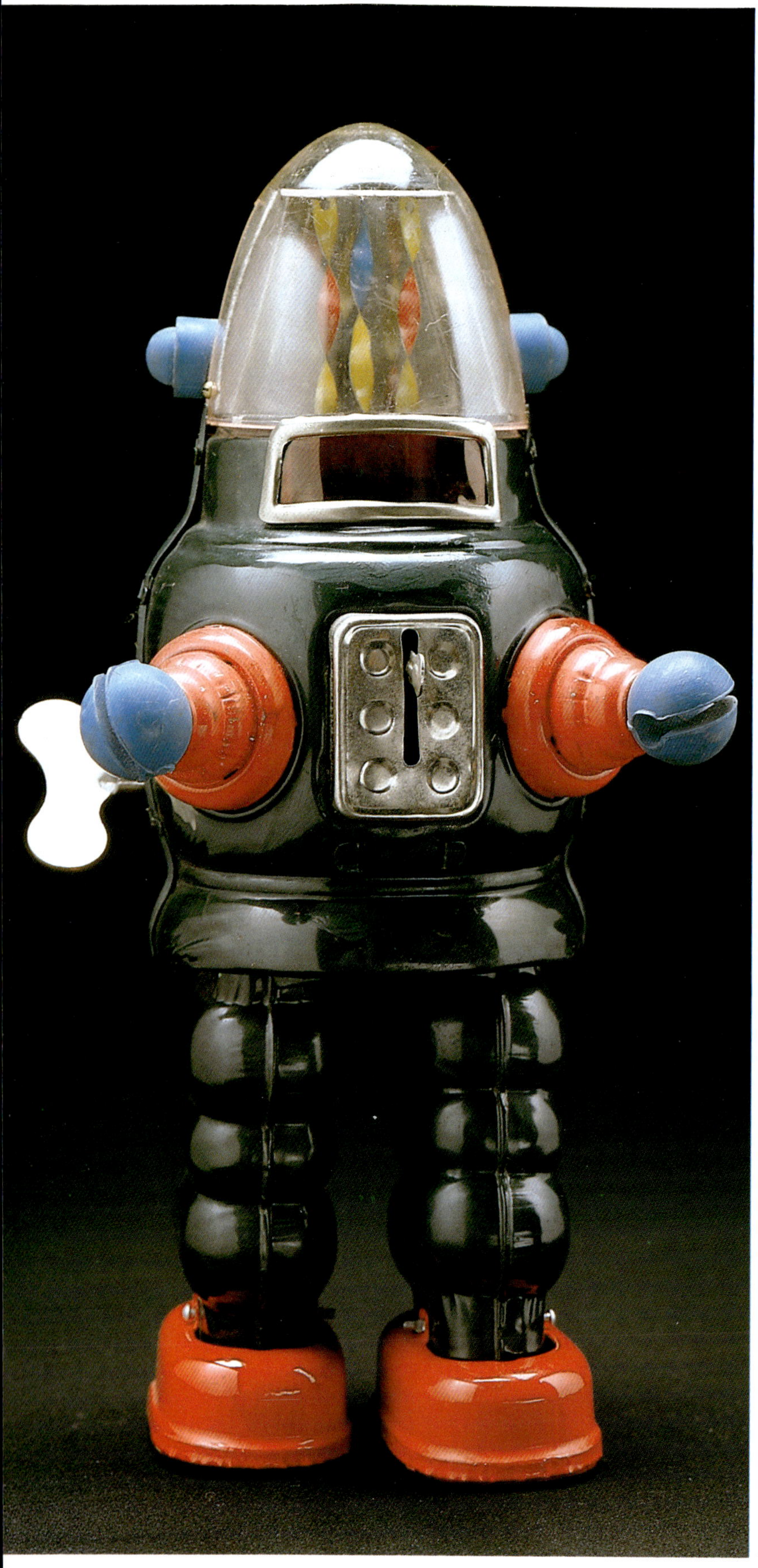

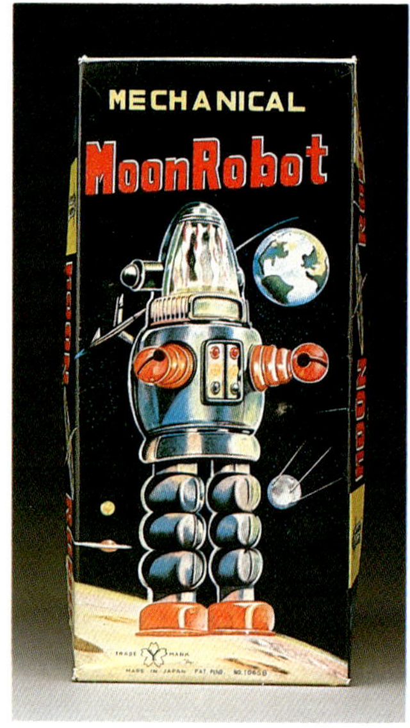

CASE ATTACHED

⑥ 1950'S／MOON ROBOT／YONEZAWA／110×125×260

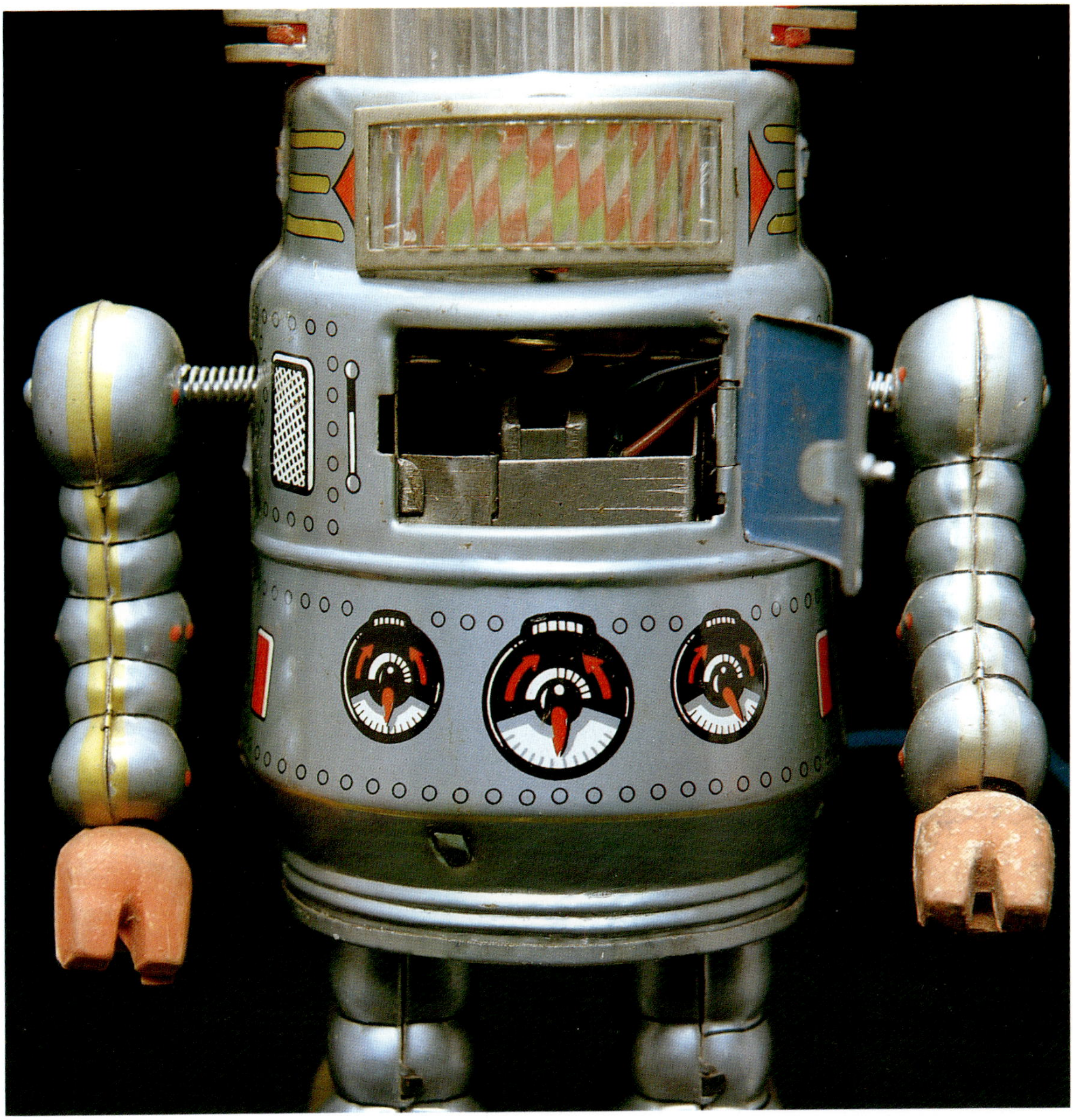

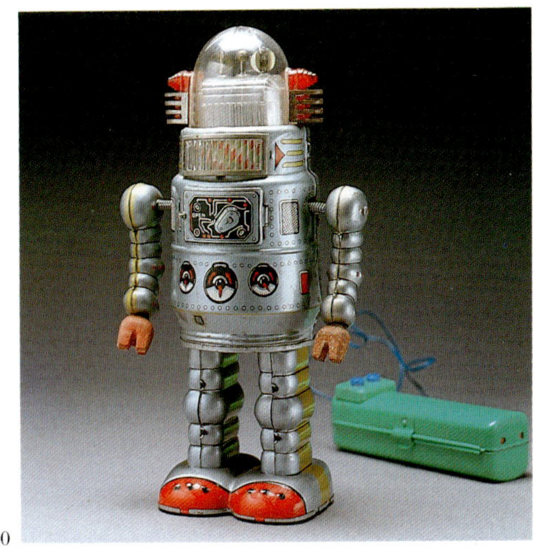

⑦ 1950'S／ROBOT／UNKNOWN／75×125×230

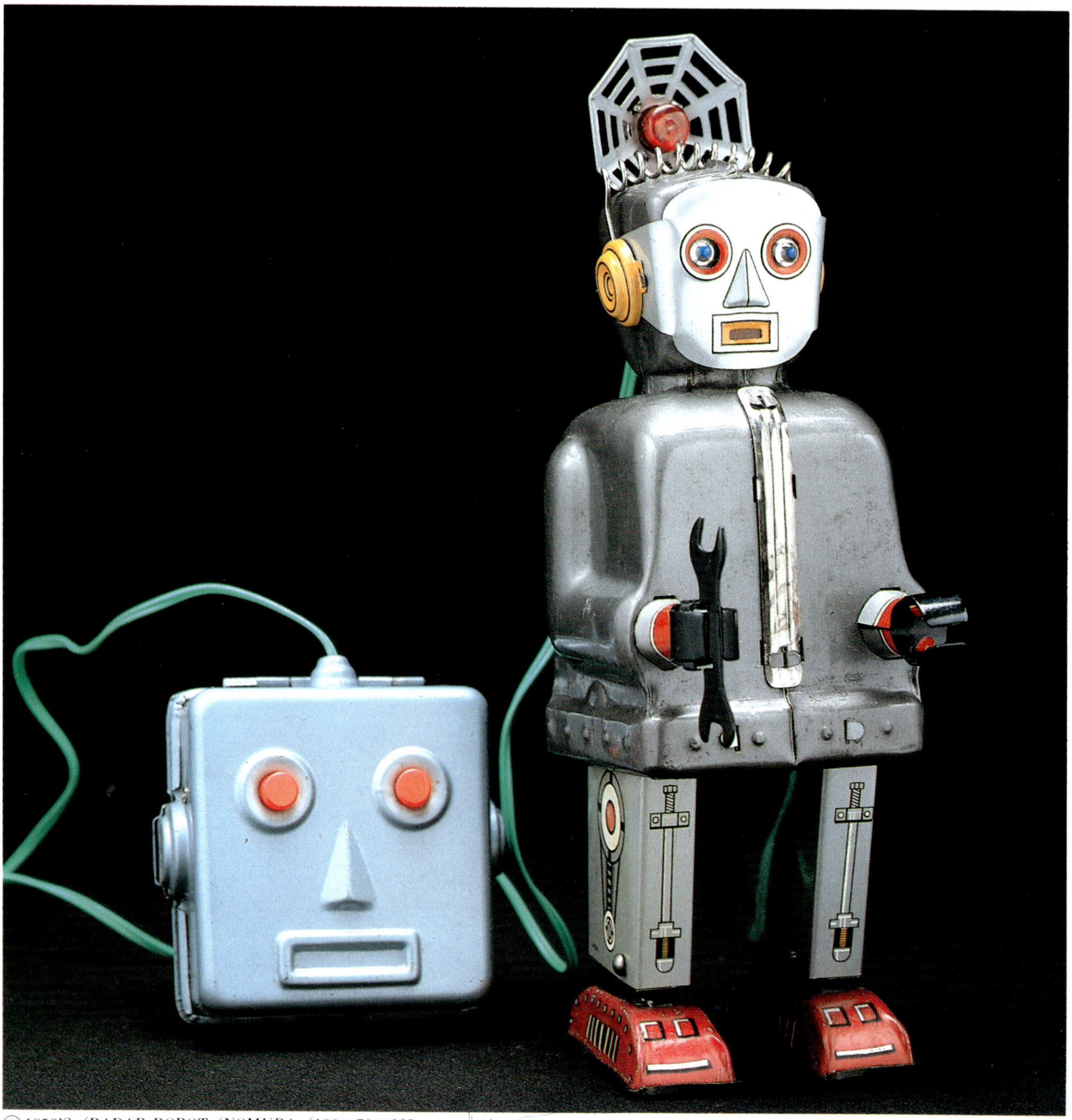

⑧ 1950'S／RADAR ROBOT／NOMURA／100×70×225

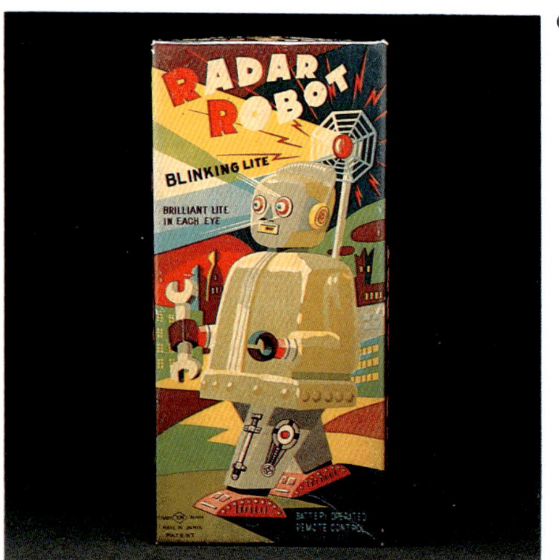

CASE ATTACHED

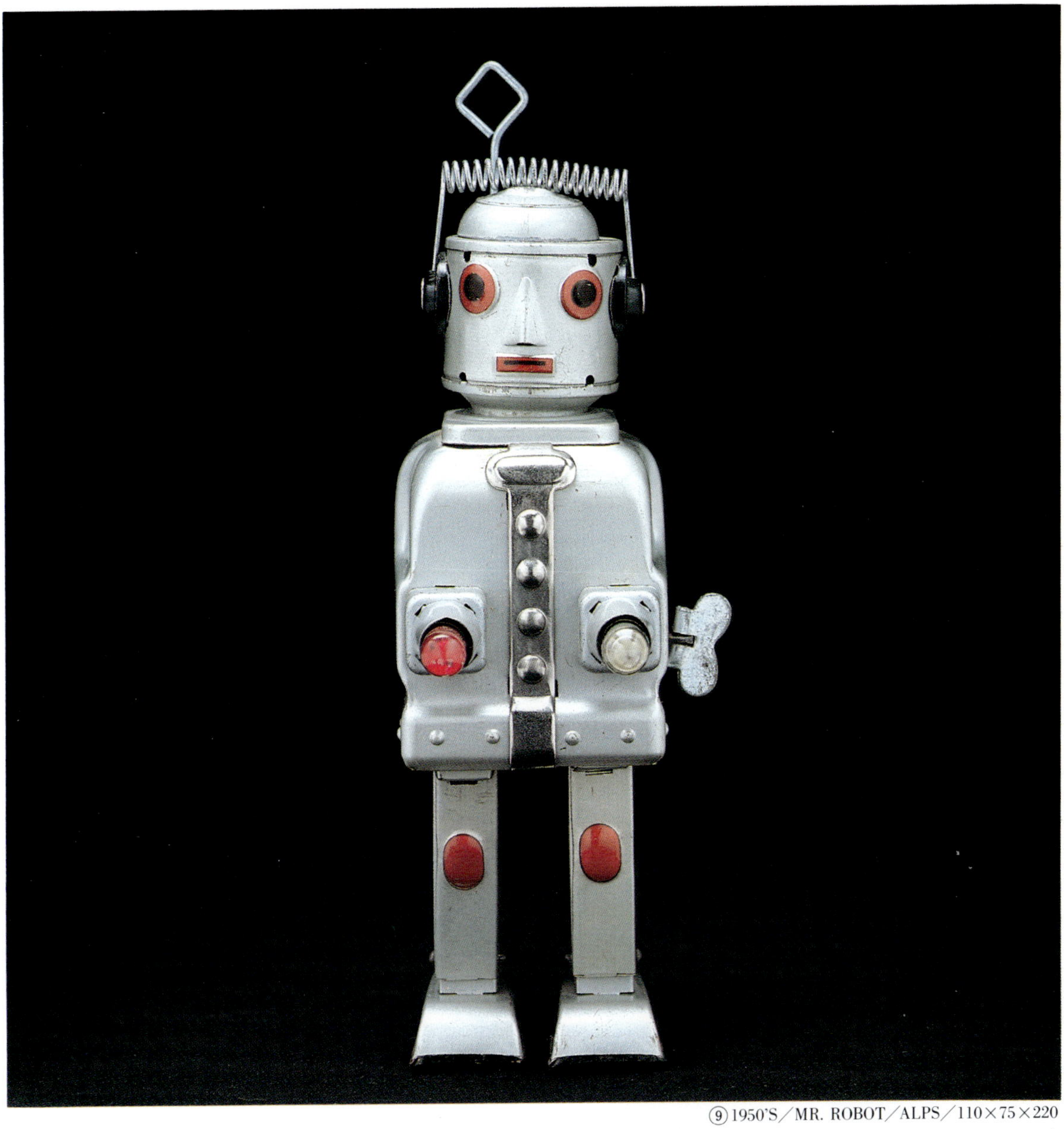

⑨ 1950'S／MR. ROBOT／ALPS／110×75×220

CASE ATTACHED

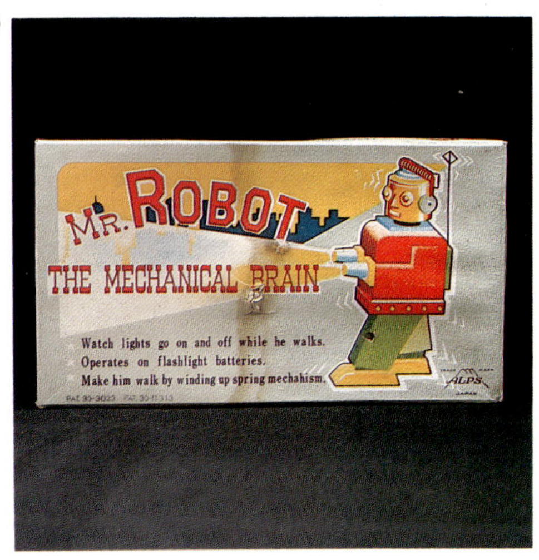

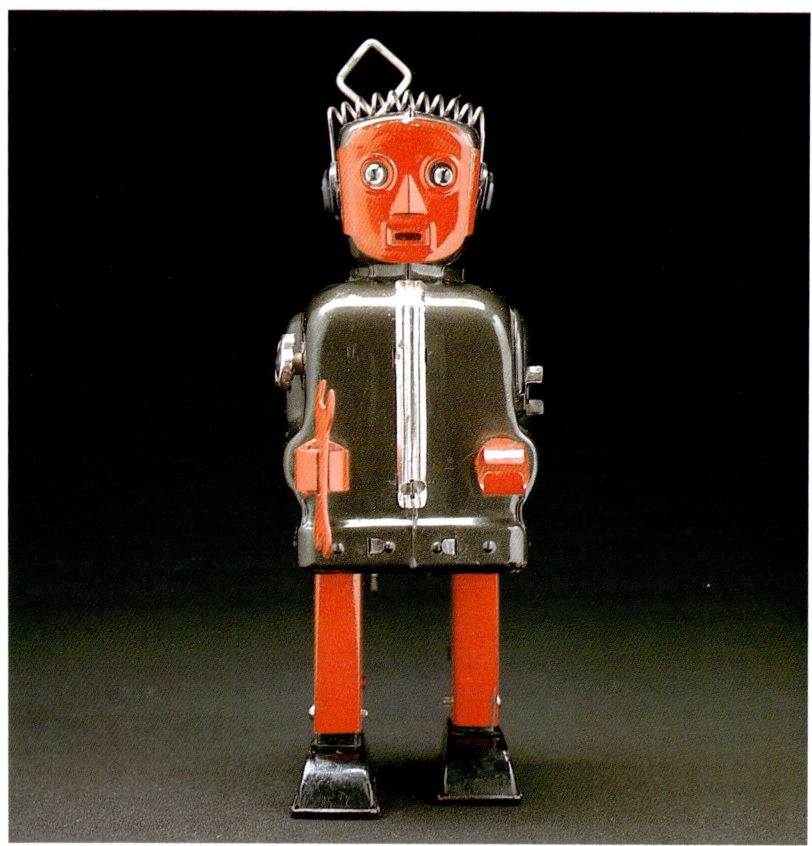

⑩ 1950'S／ZOOMER THE ROBOT／NOMURA／100×70×190

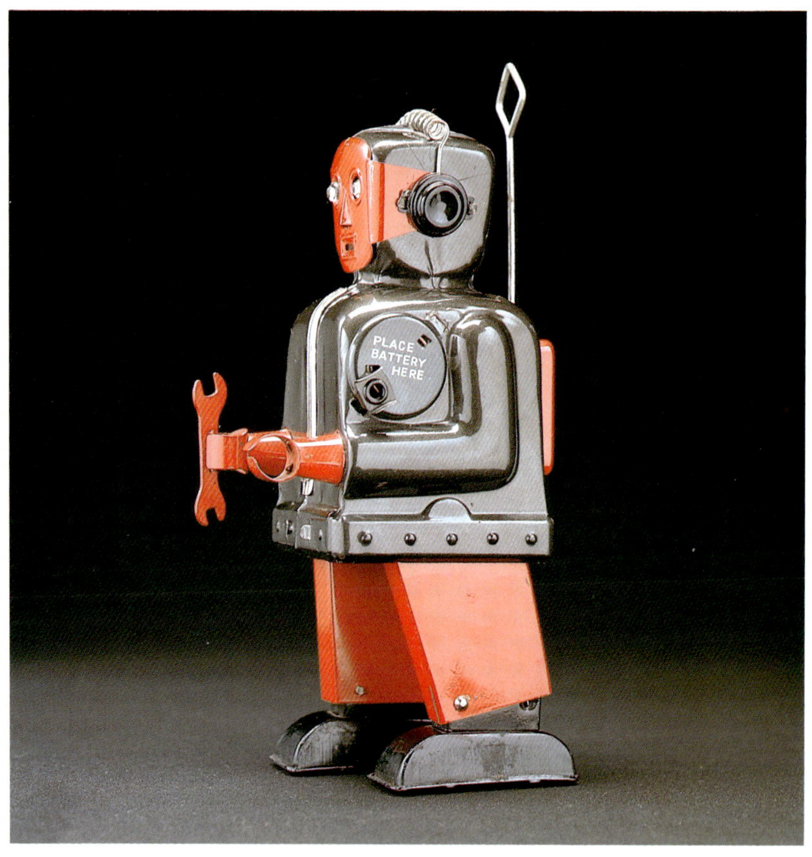

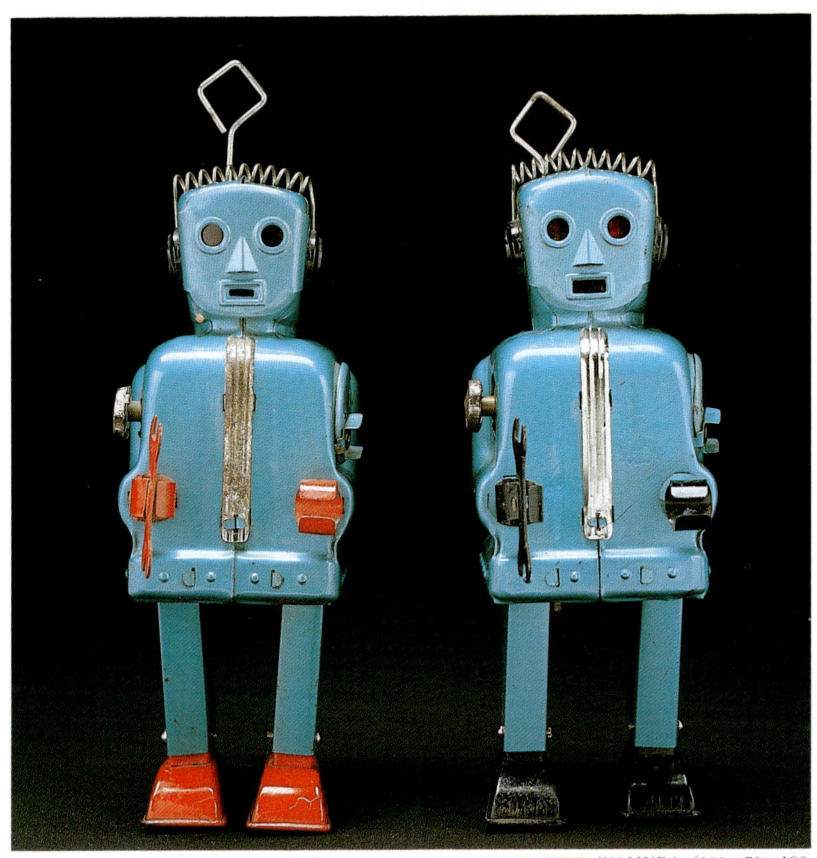

⑪⑫ 1950'S／ZOOMER THE ROBOT／NOMURA／100×70×190

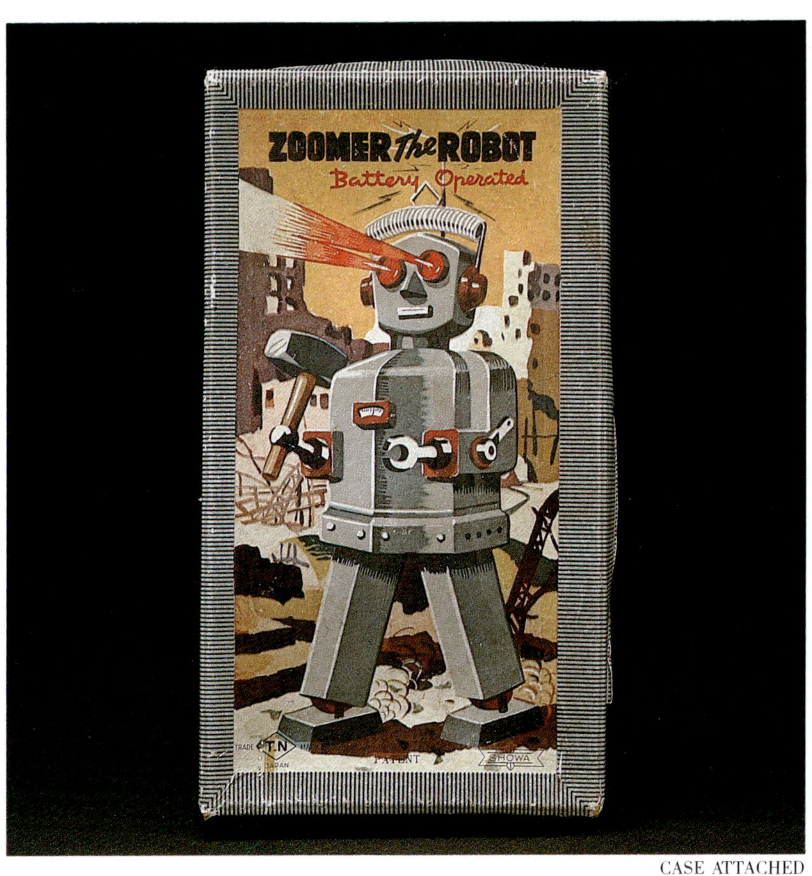

CASE ATTACHED

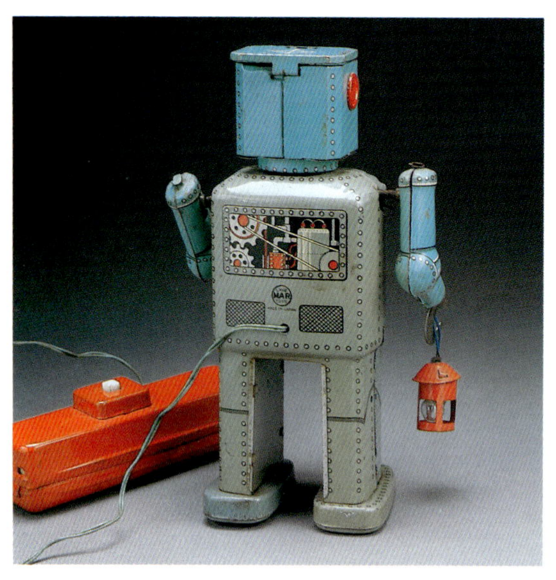

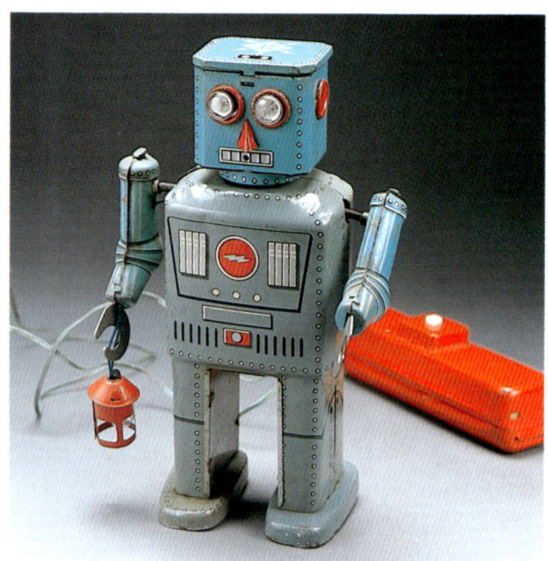

⑬ 1950'S／ROBOT WITH LANTERN／LINE MAR／90×115×200

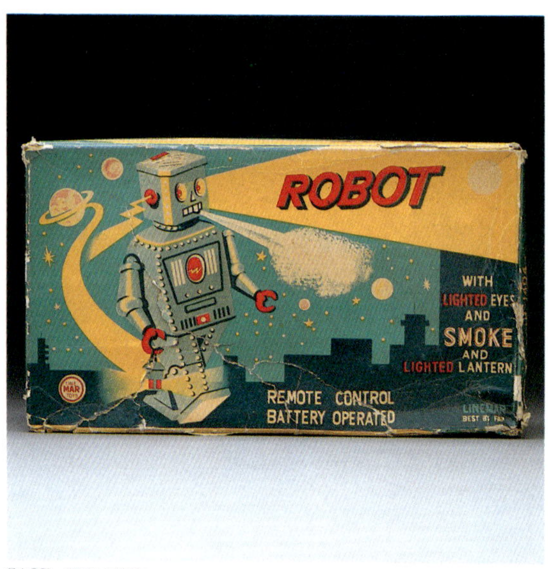

CASE ATTACHED

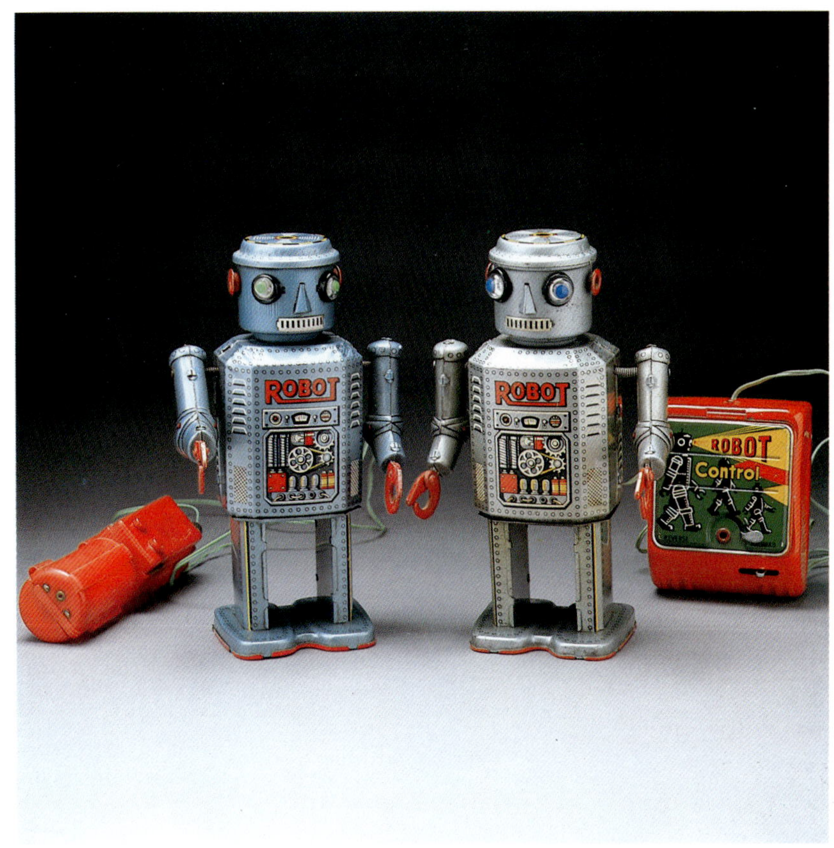

⑭⑮ 1950'S／ROBOT／MASUDAYA／65×110×190

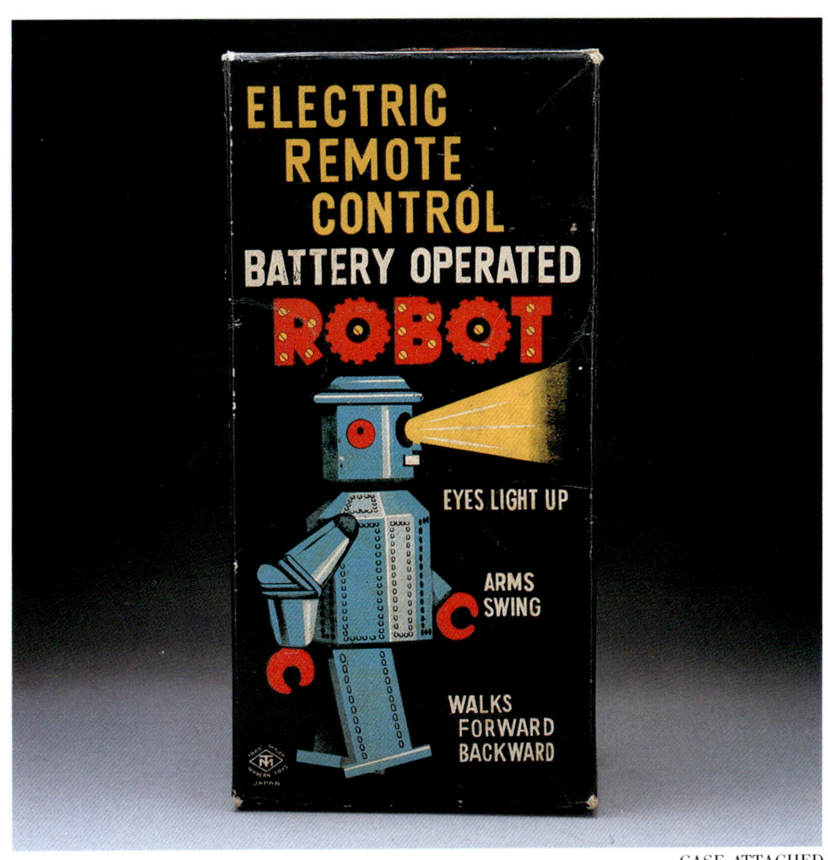

CASE ATTACHED

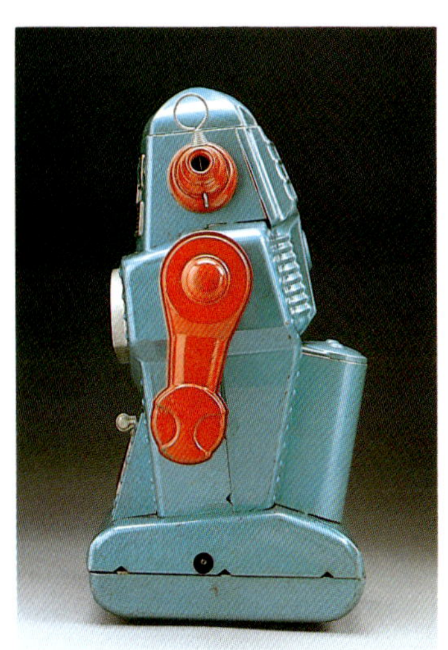

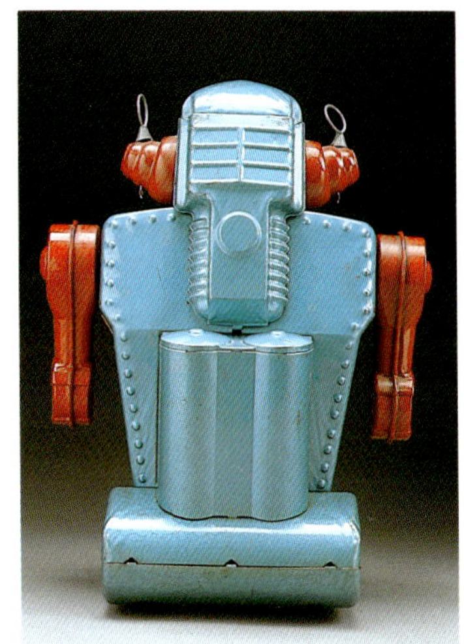

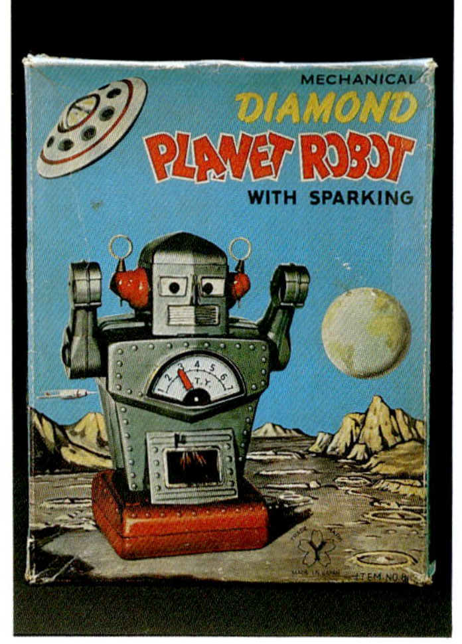

CASE ATTACHED

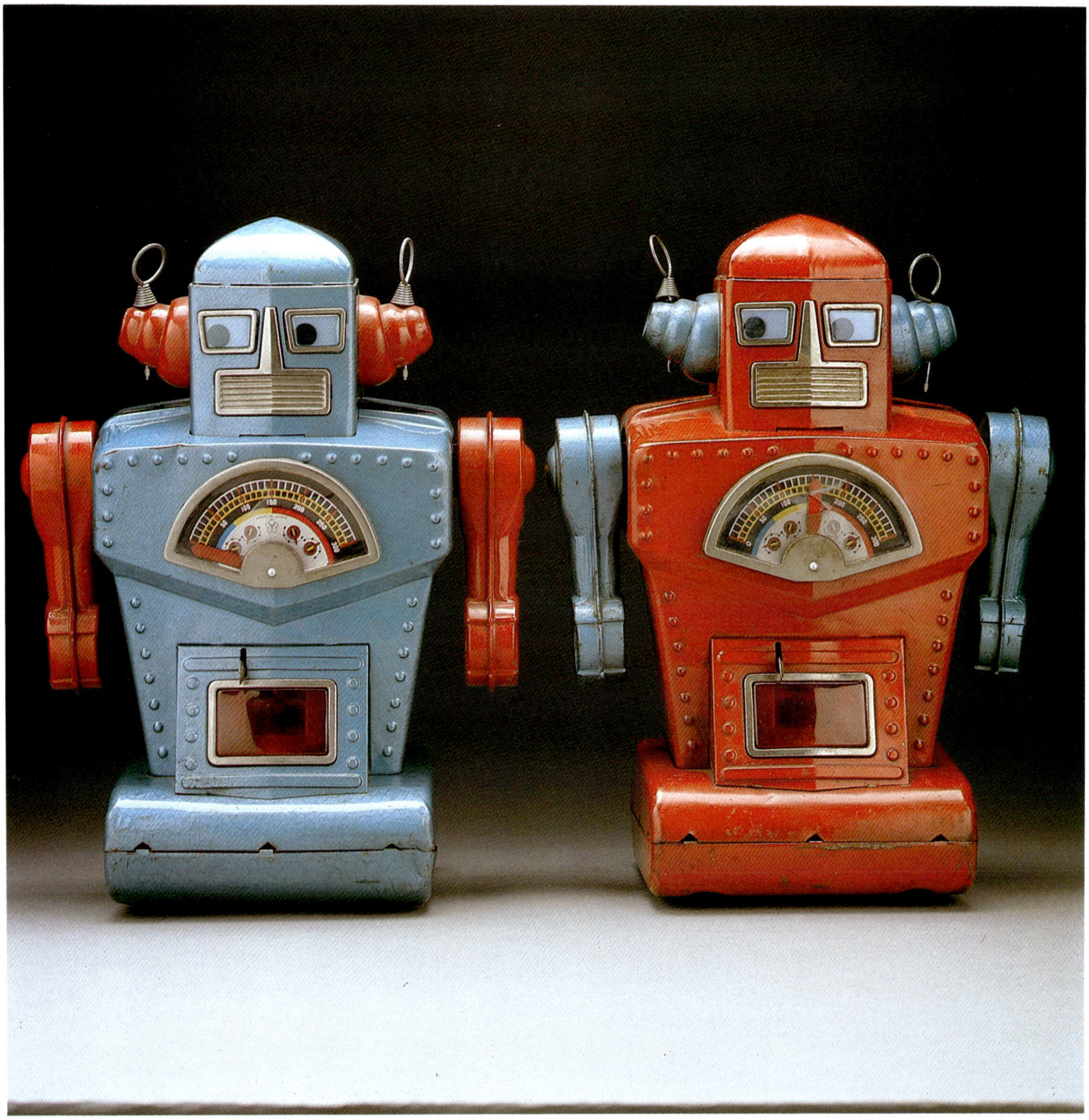

⑯⑰1950'S／DIAMOND PLANET ROBOT／YONEZAWA／140×200×260

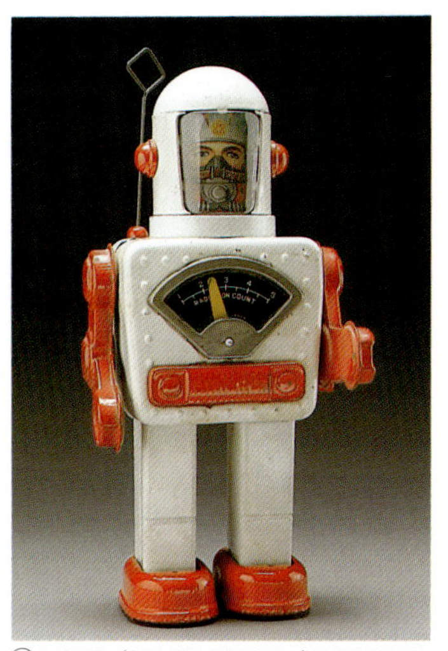

⑱ 1950'S／SPACE SCOUT／YONEZAWA
／100×115×240

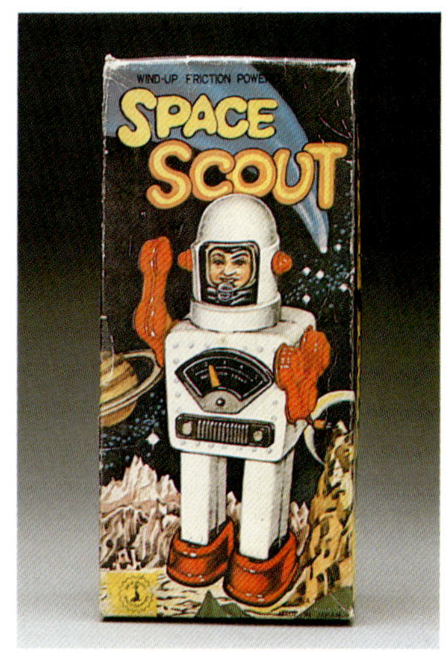

CASE ATTACHED

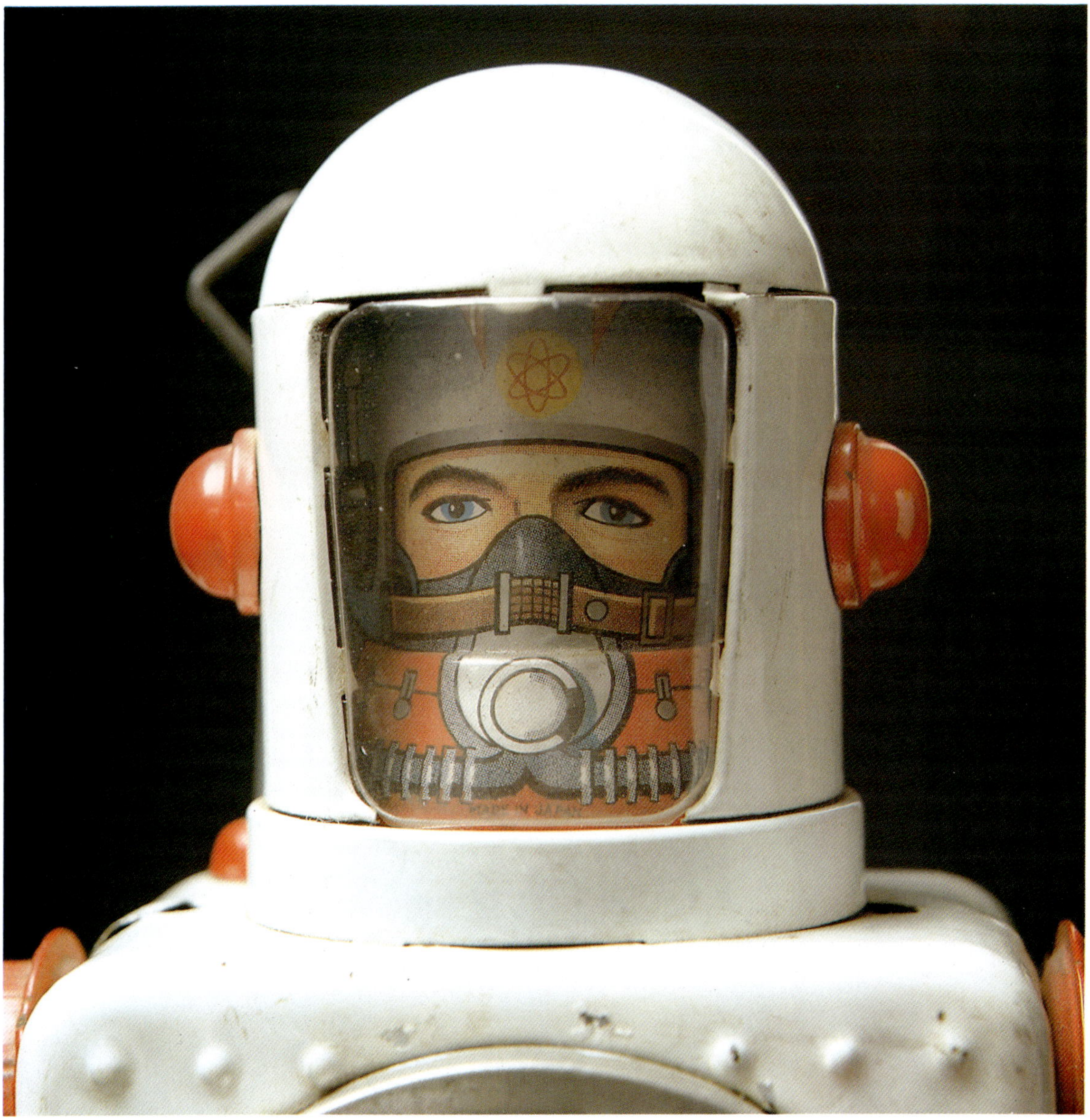

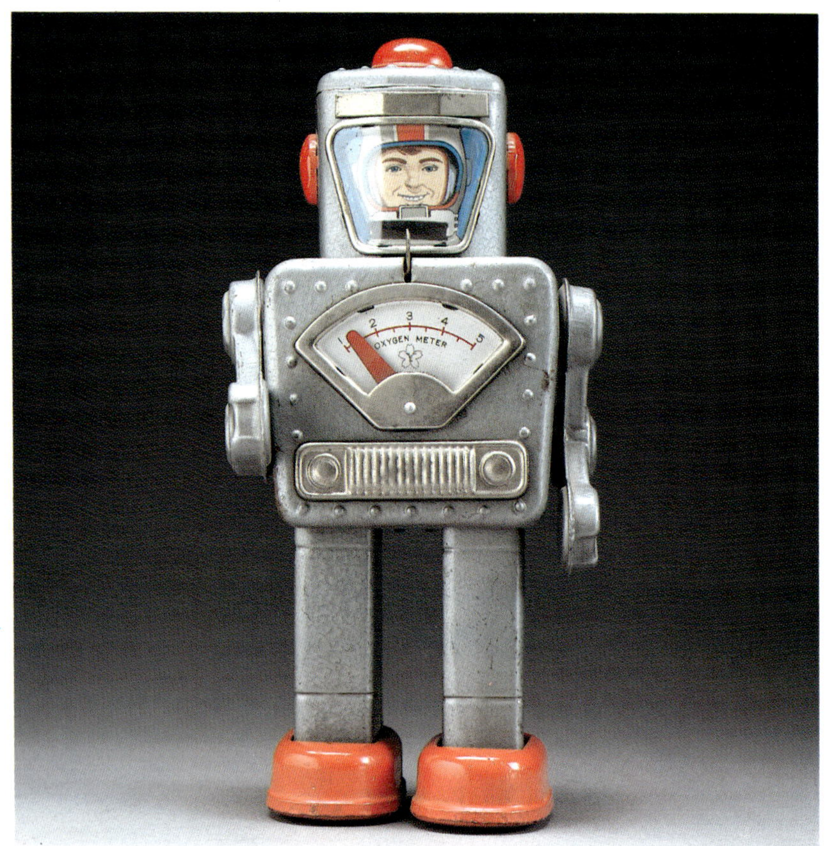

⑲ 1950'S／SPACE EXPLORER／YONEZAWA／70×120×230

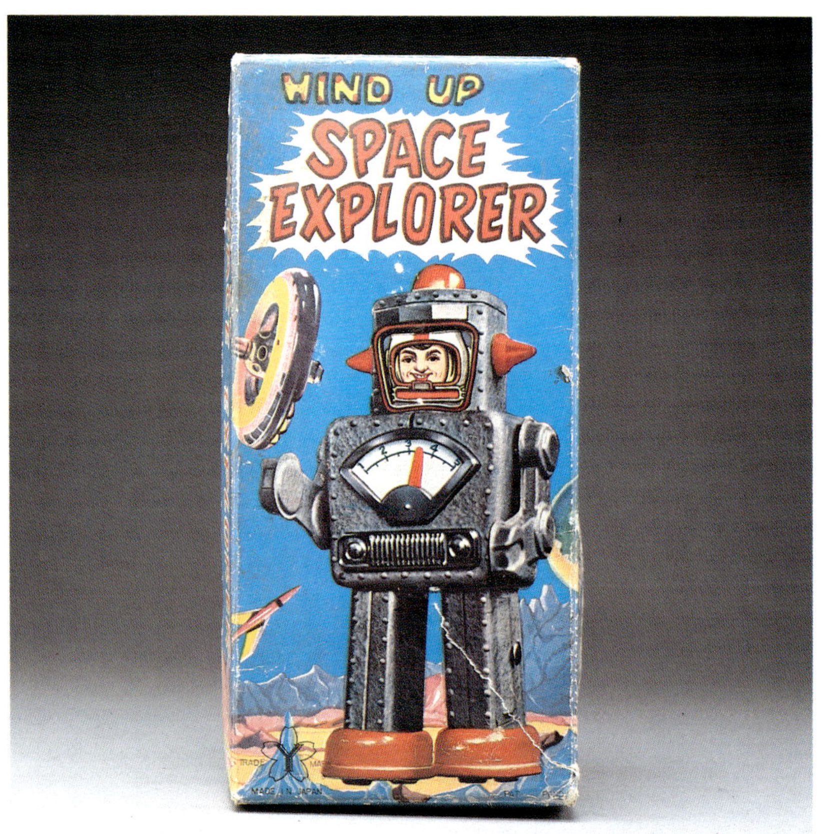

CASE ATTACHED

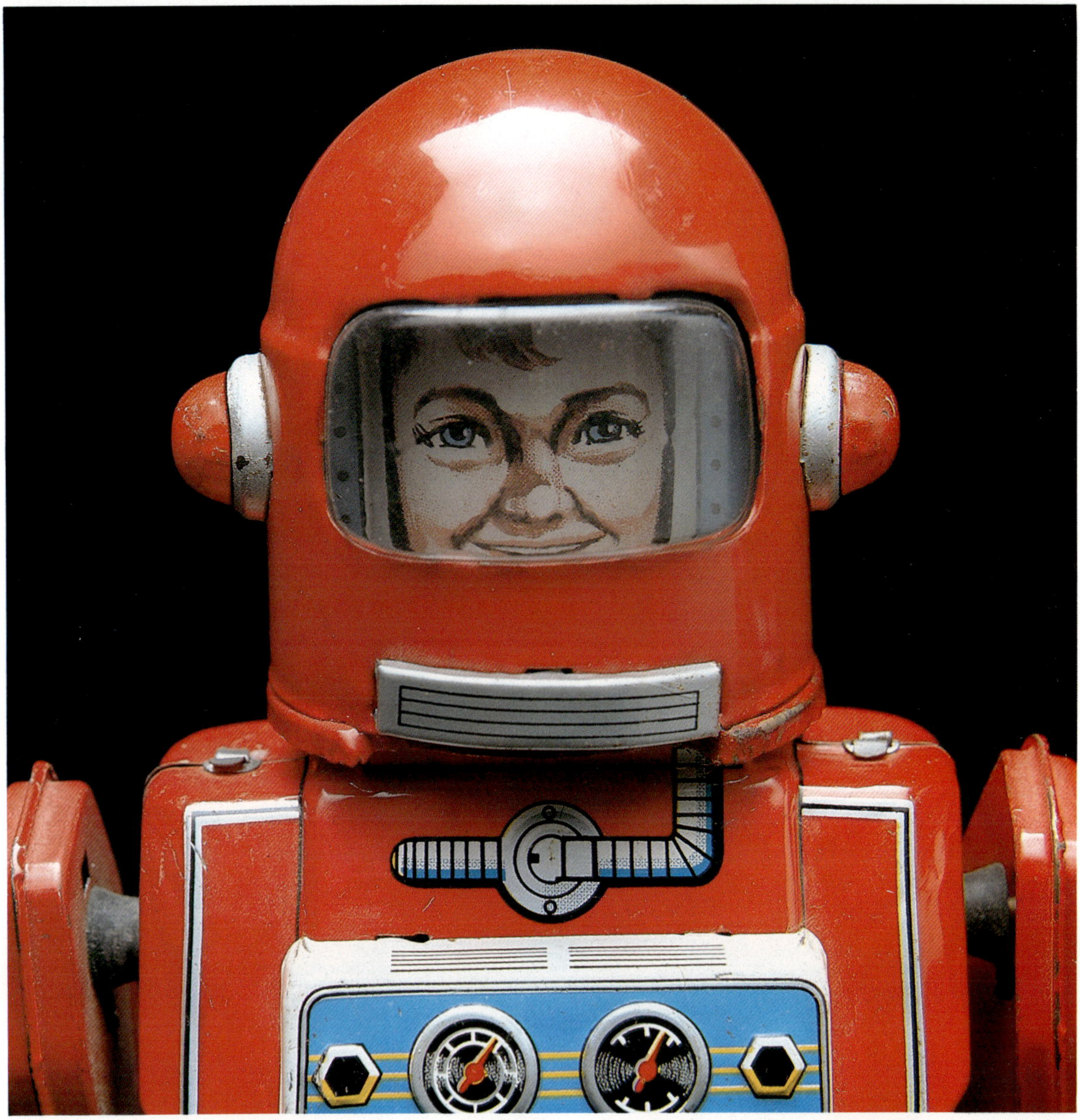

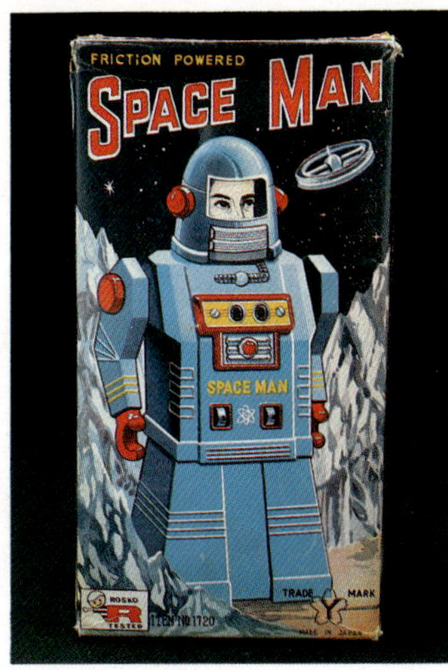

CASE ATTACHED

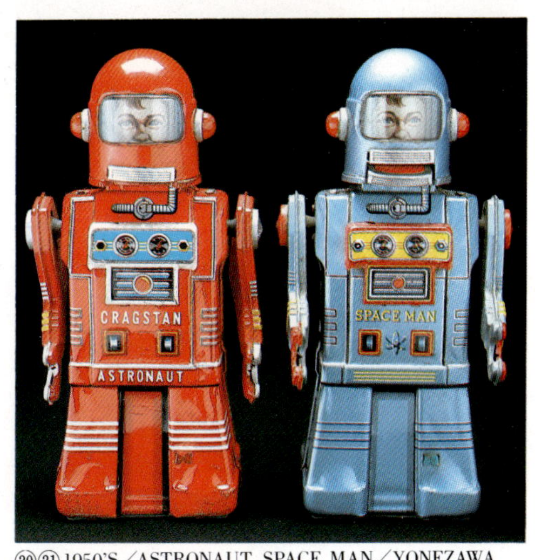

⑳㉑ 1950'S／ASTRONAUT, SPACE MAN／YONEZAWA ／95×125×240

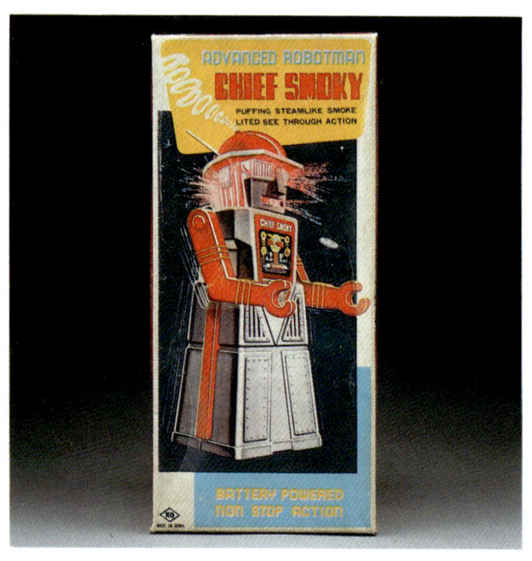

CASE ATTACHED

㉒ 1950'S／CHIEF SMOKY／YOSHIYA／110×140×295

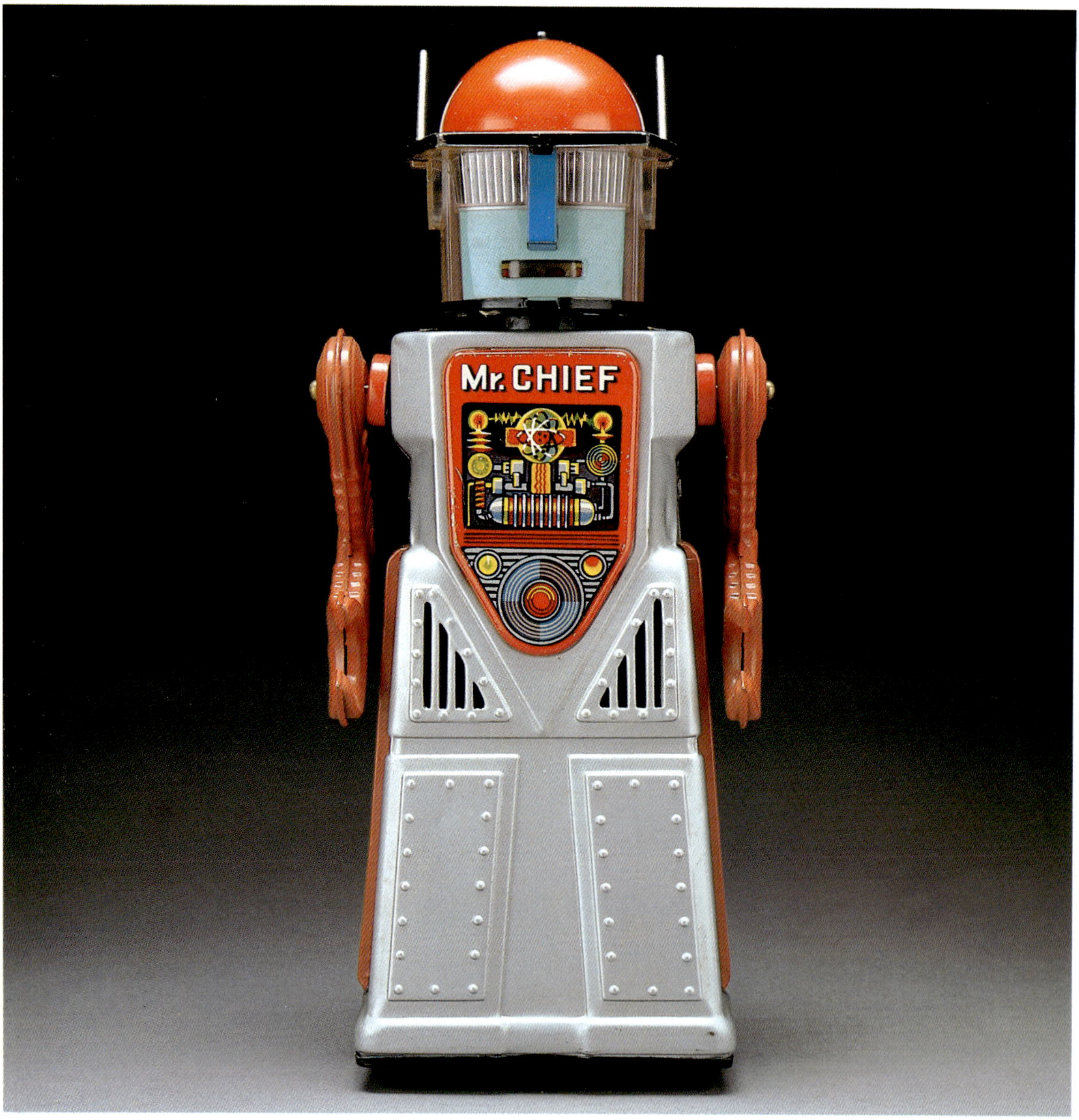

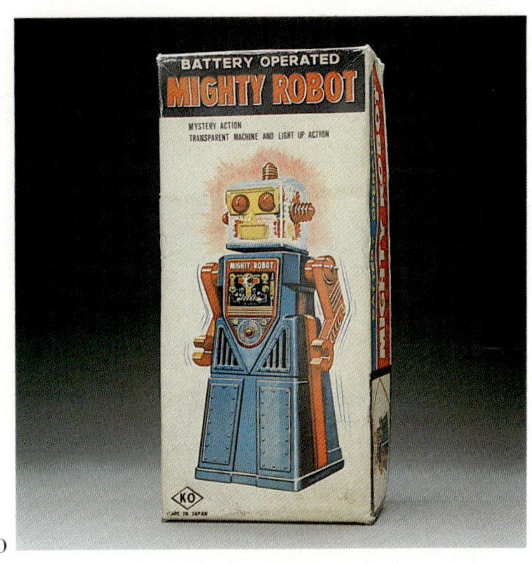

CASE ATTACHED

㉓1960'S／MIGHTY ROBOT／YOSHIYA／110×150×300

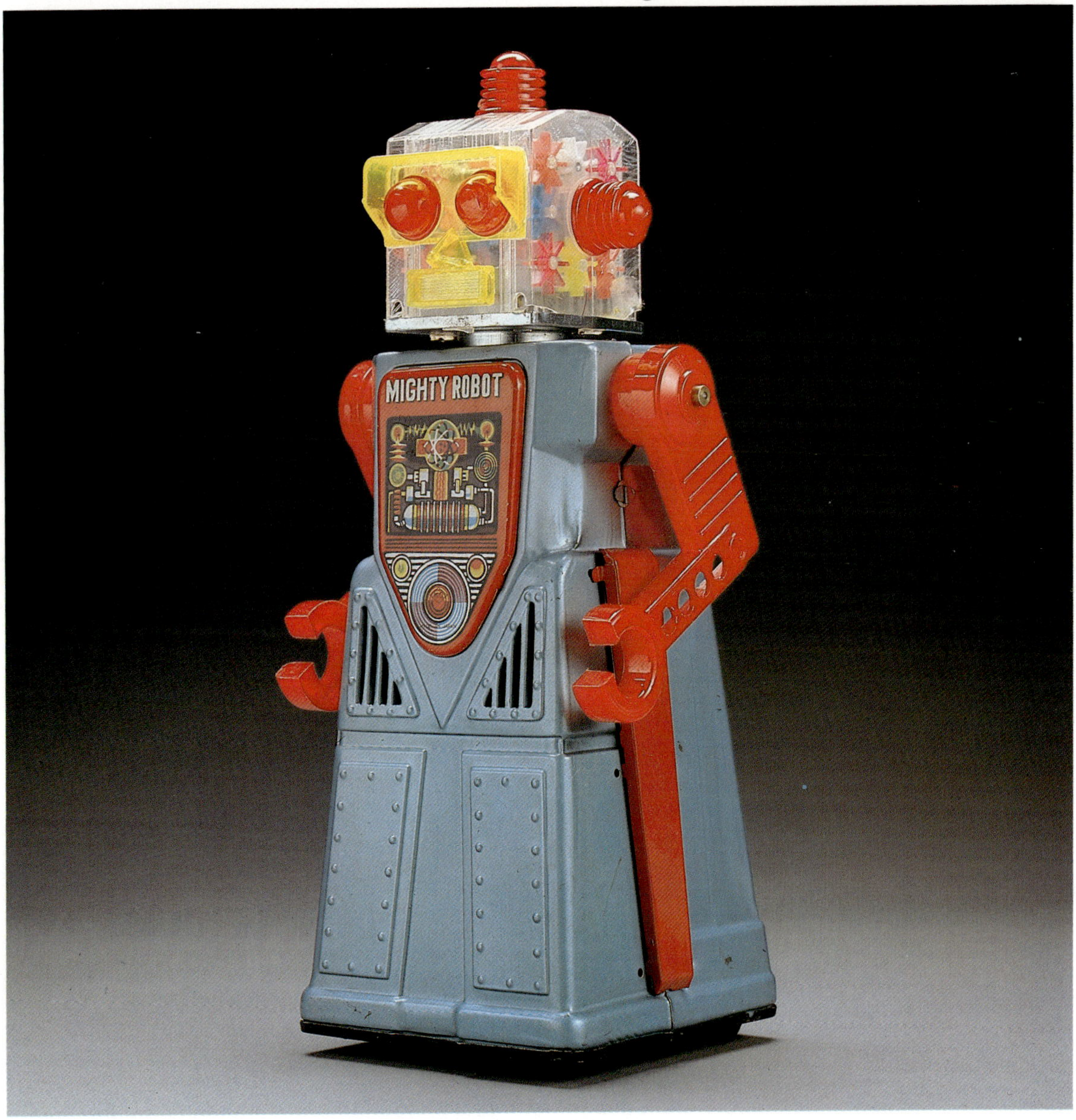

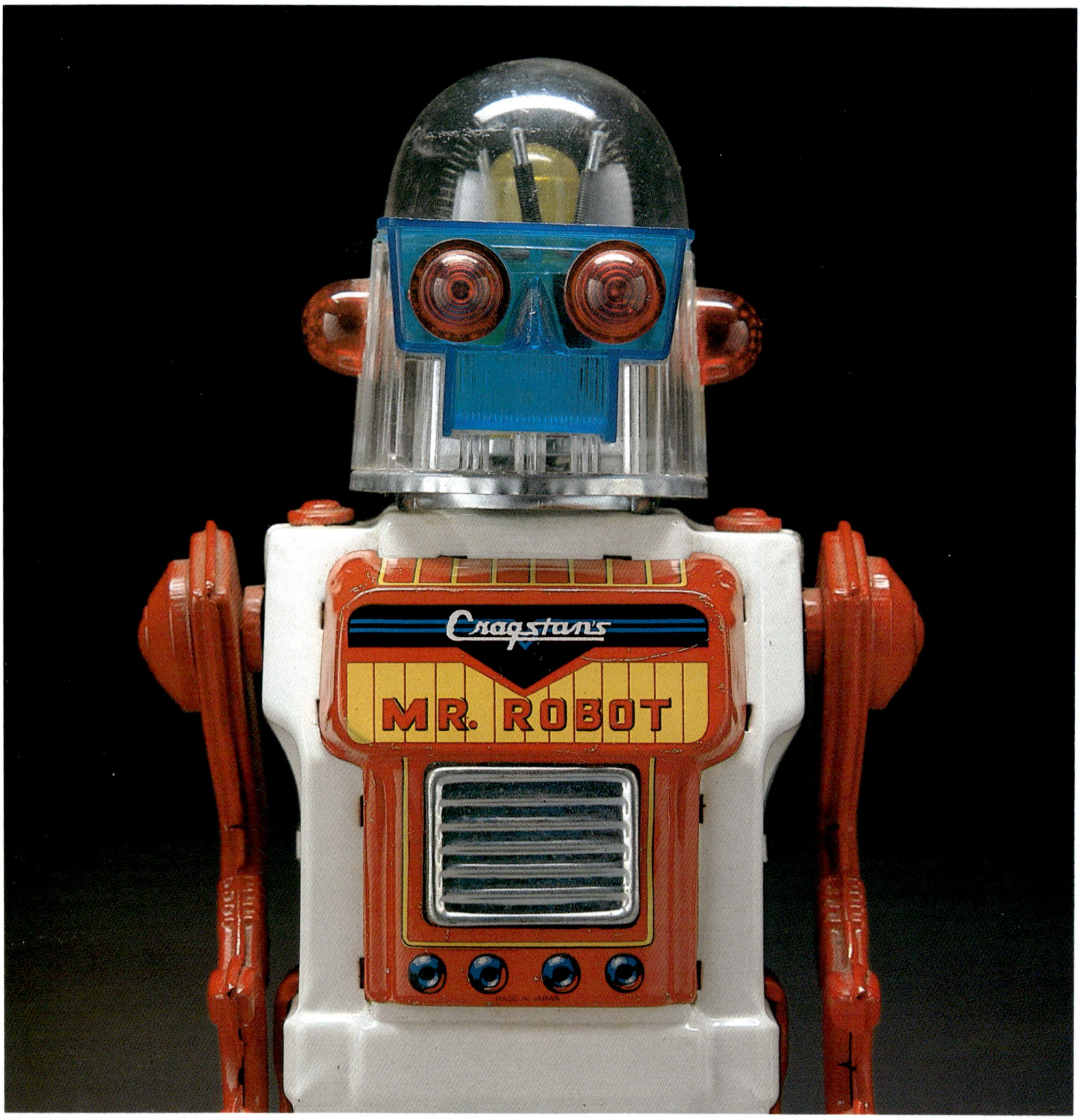

㉔1950'S／MR. ROBOT／YONEZAWA／115×155×275

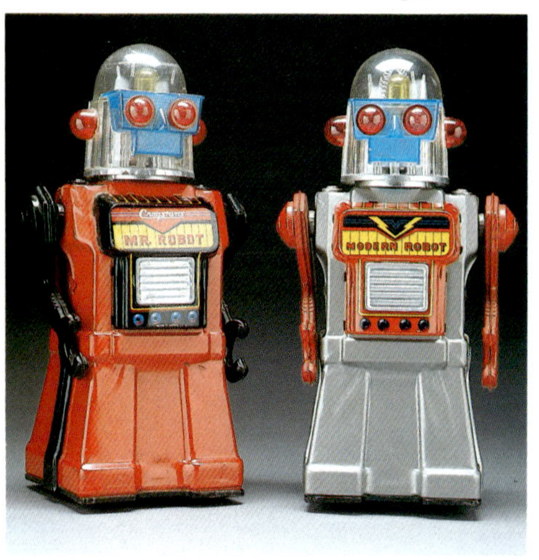

㉕㉖1950'S／MR. ROBOT／YONEZAWA／115×155×275

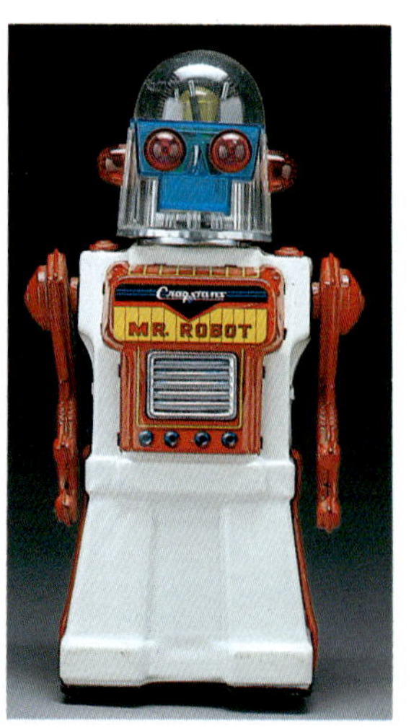

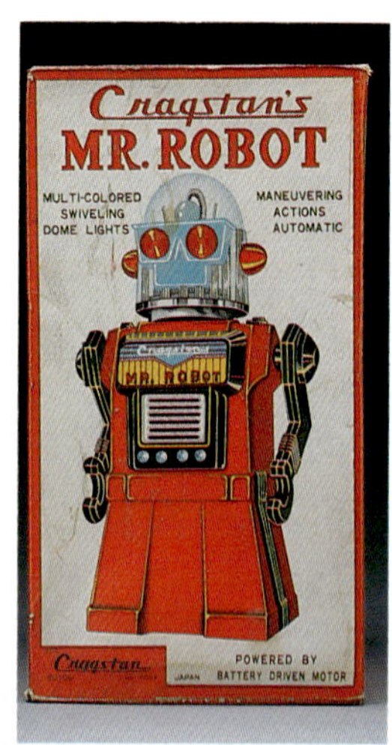

CASE ATTACHED

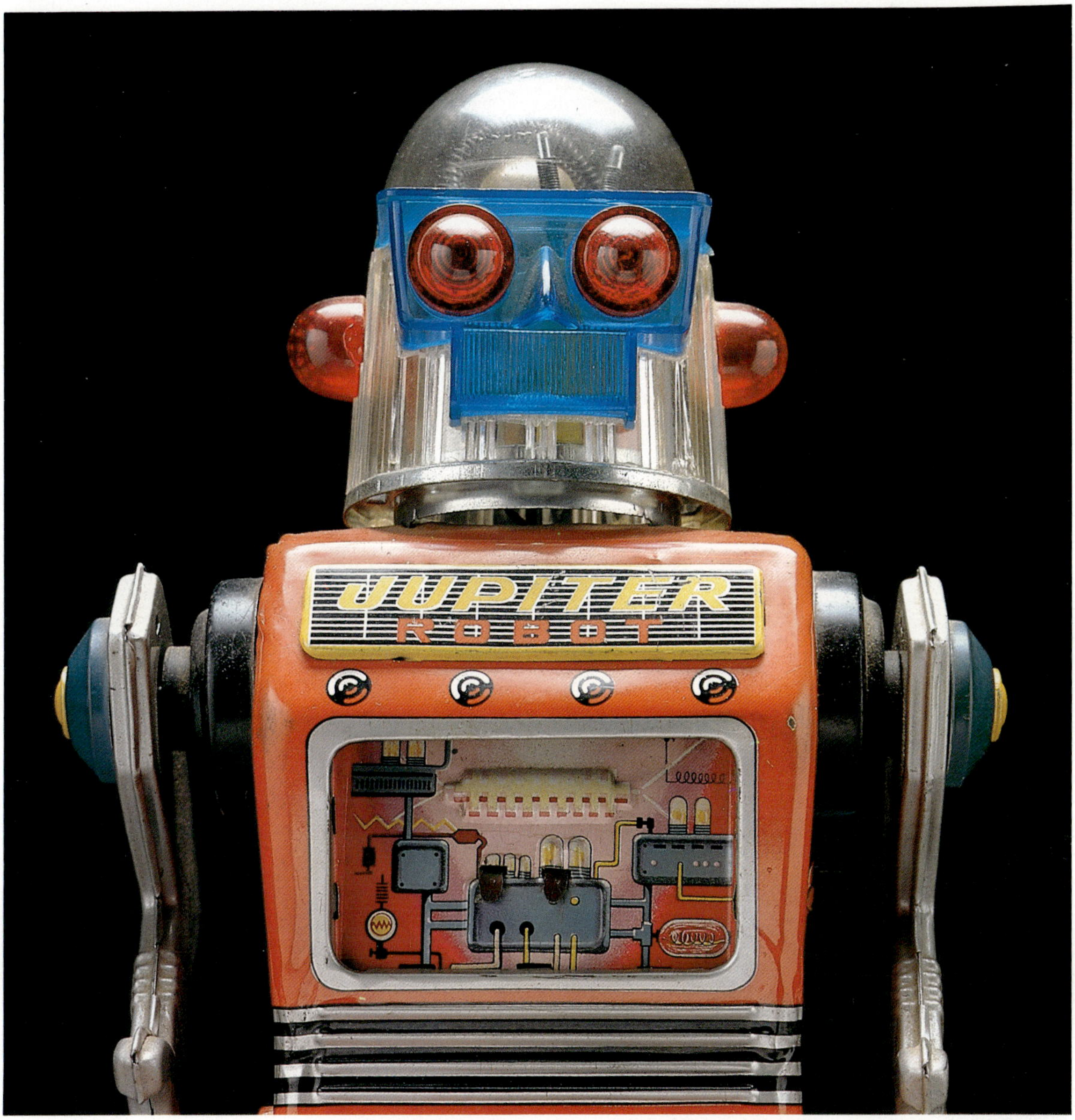

㉗ 1950'S／JUPITER ROBOT／YONEZAWA／120×170×325

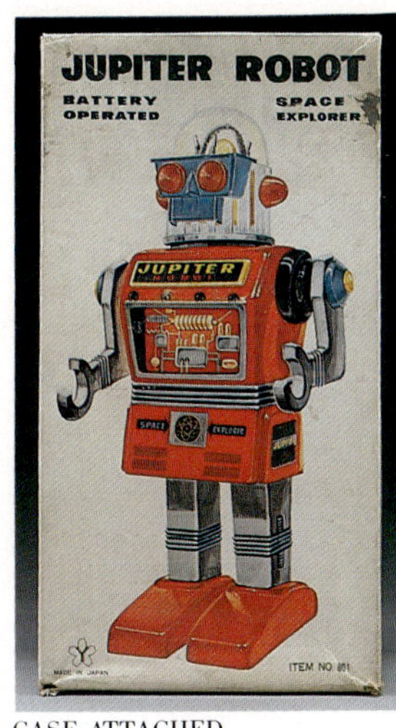

CASE ATTACHED

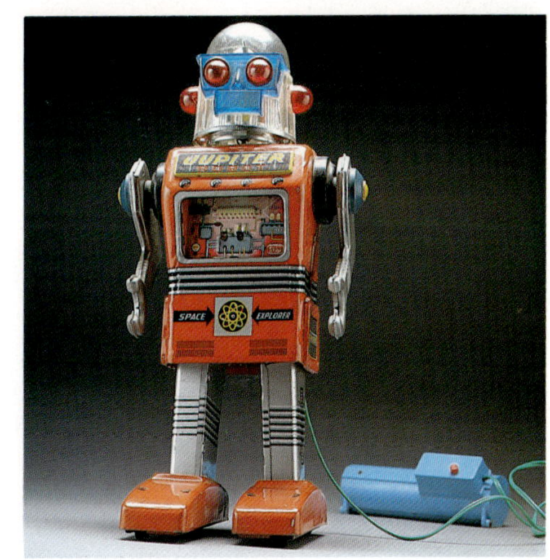

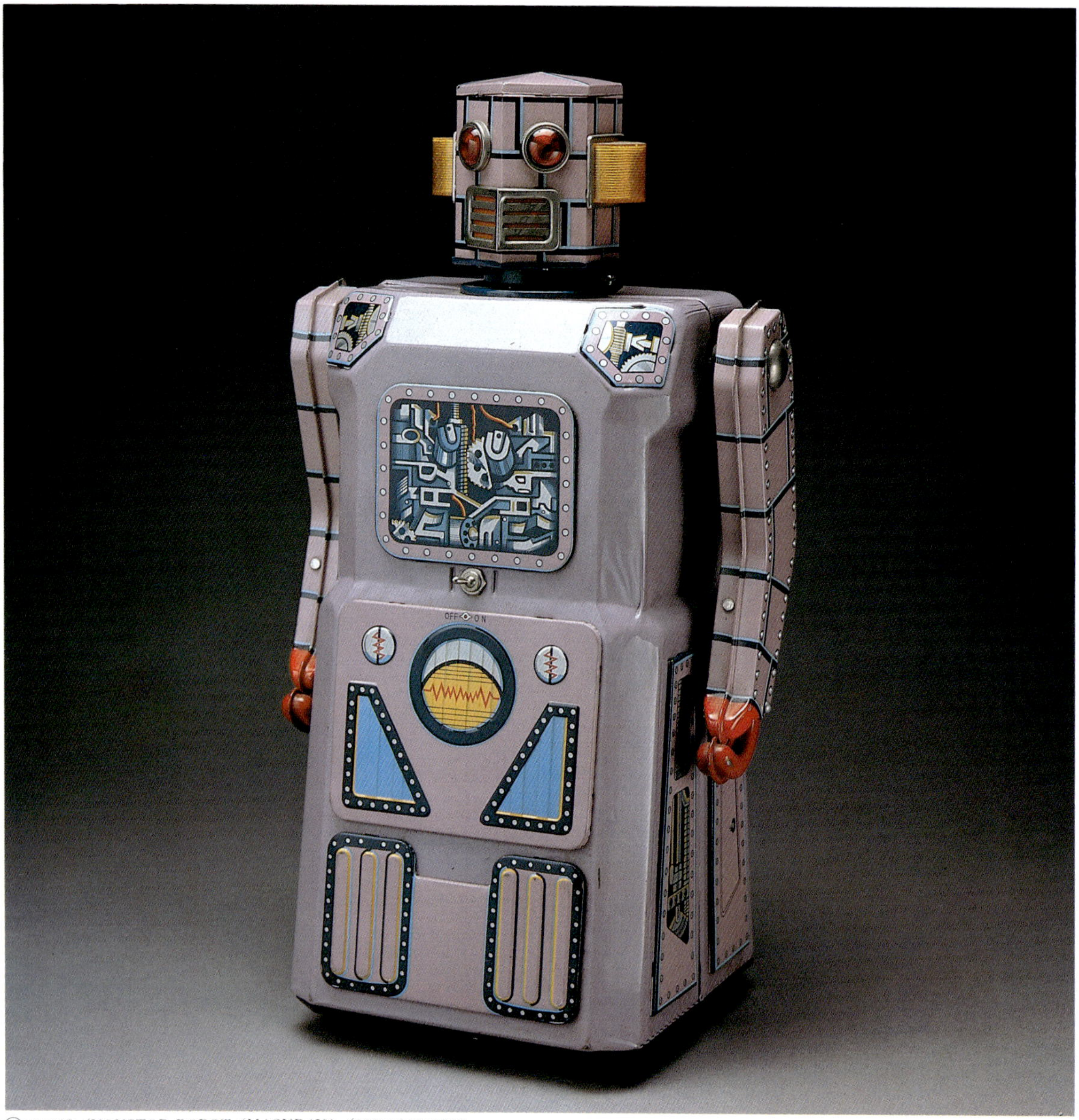

㉘1950'S／NONSTOP ROBOT／MASUDAYA／155×210×370

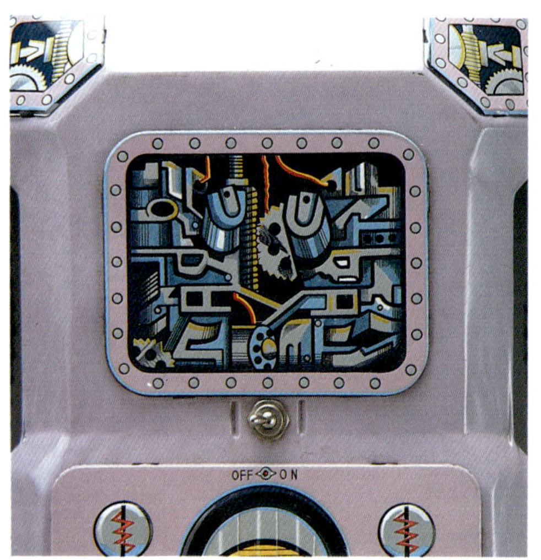

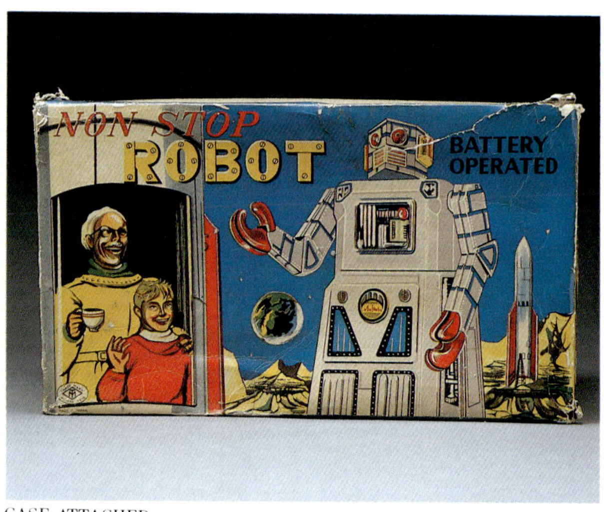

CASE ATTACHED

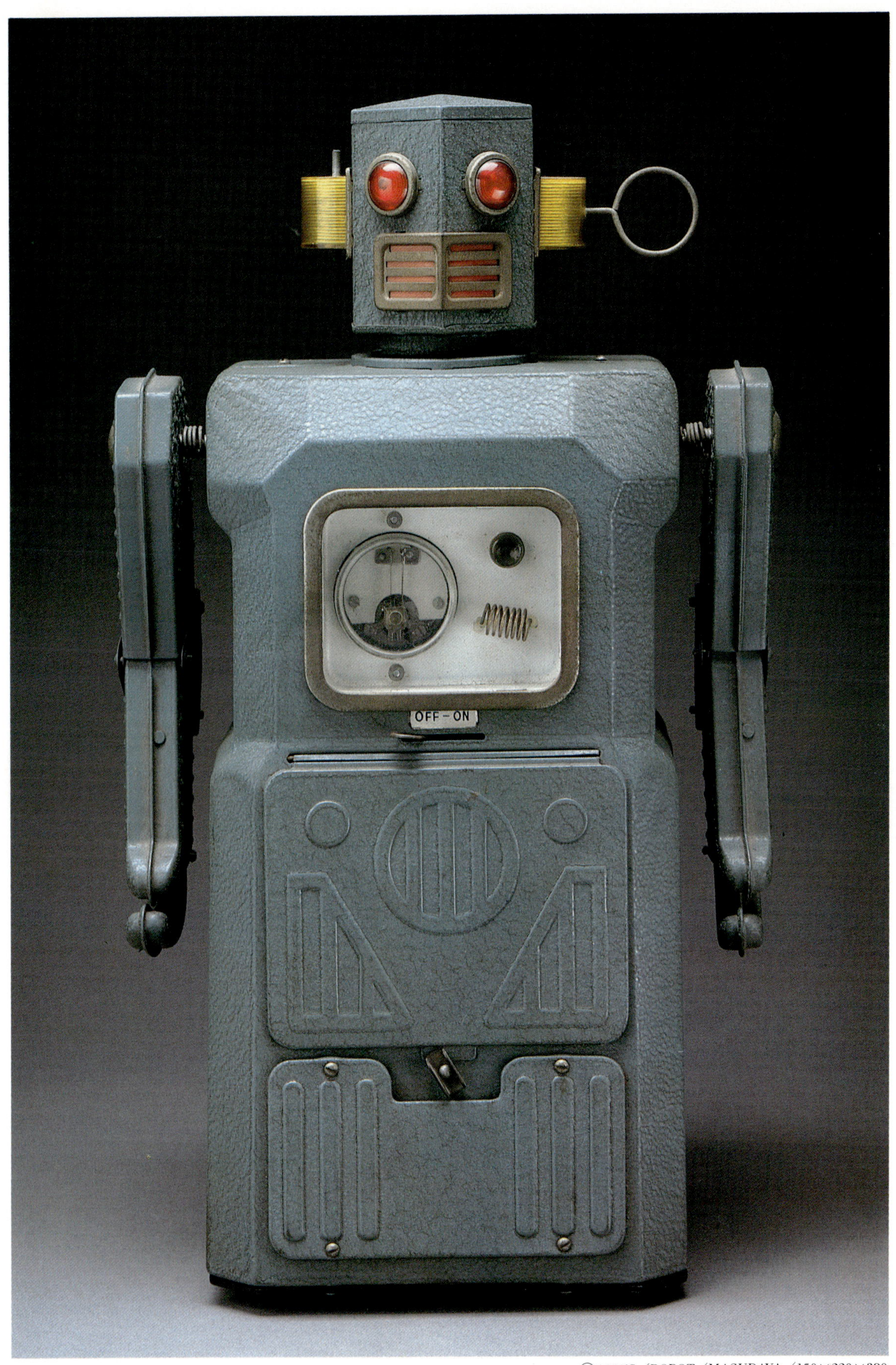

㉙ 1950'S／ROBOT／MASUDAYA／150×220×380

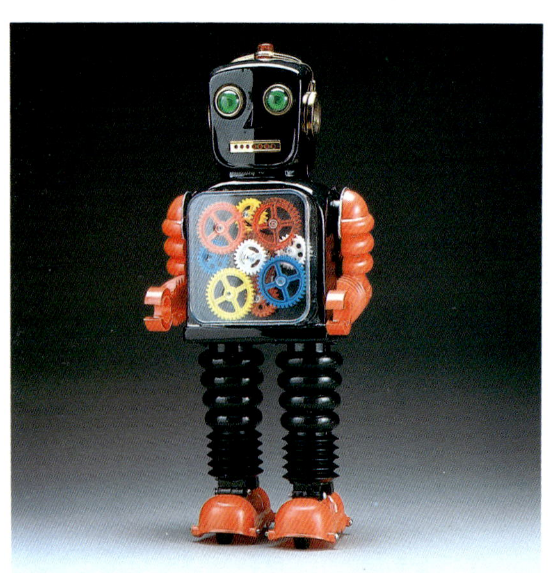

㉚ 1960'S／GEAR ROBOT／TAIYO／135×155×370

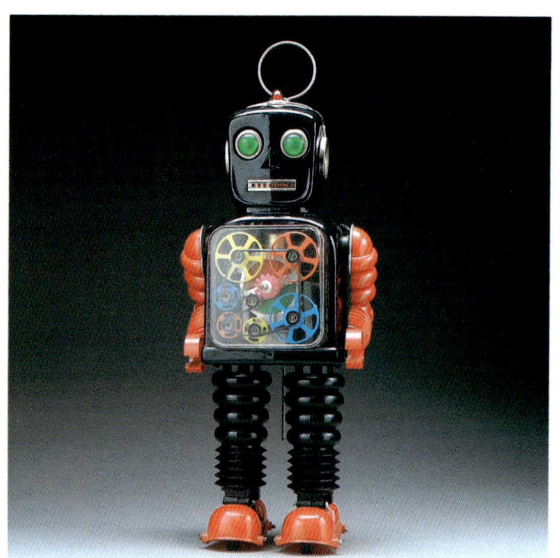

㉛ 1960'S／GEAR ROBOT／TAIYO／135×155×370

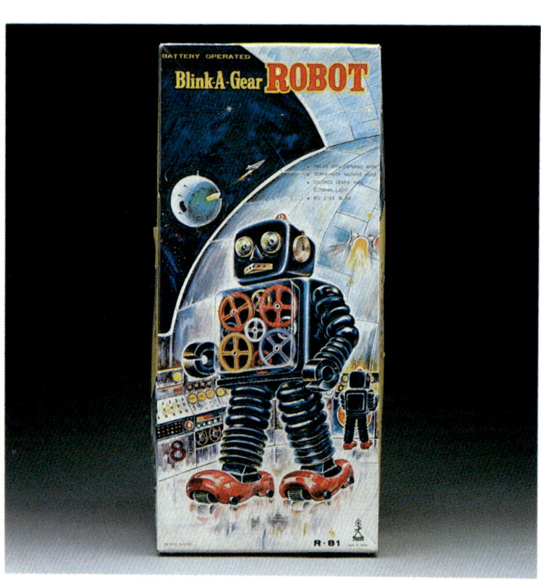

CASE ATTACHED

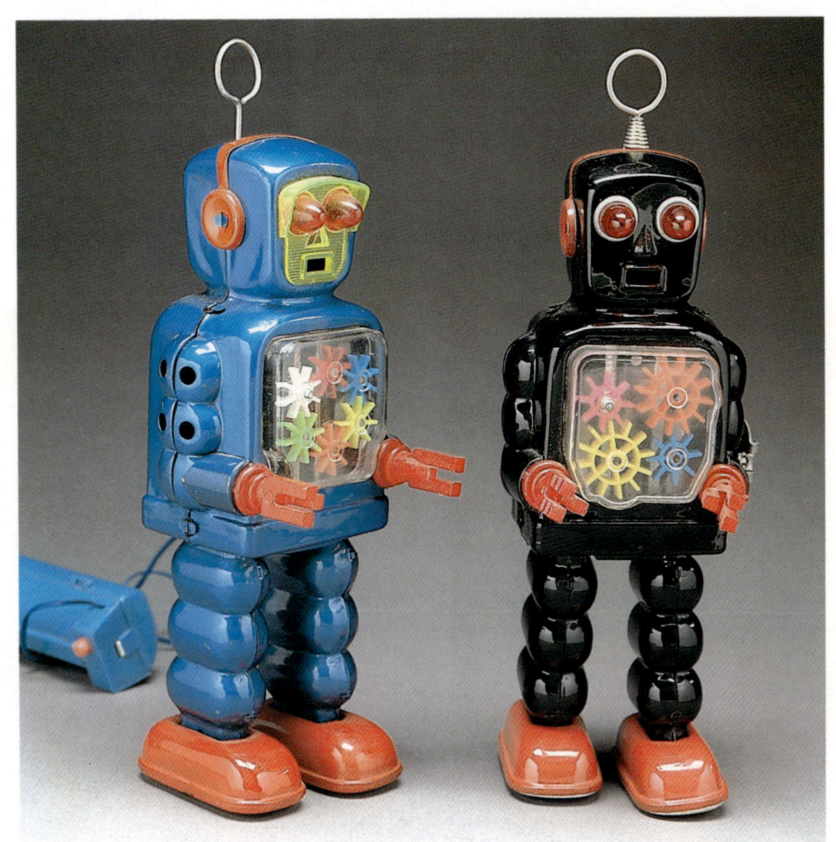

㉜㉝ 1960'S／GEAR ROBOT／YOSHIYA／90×85×255

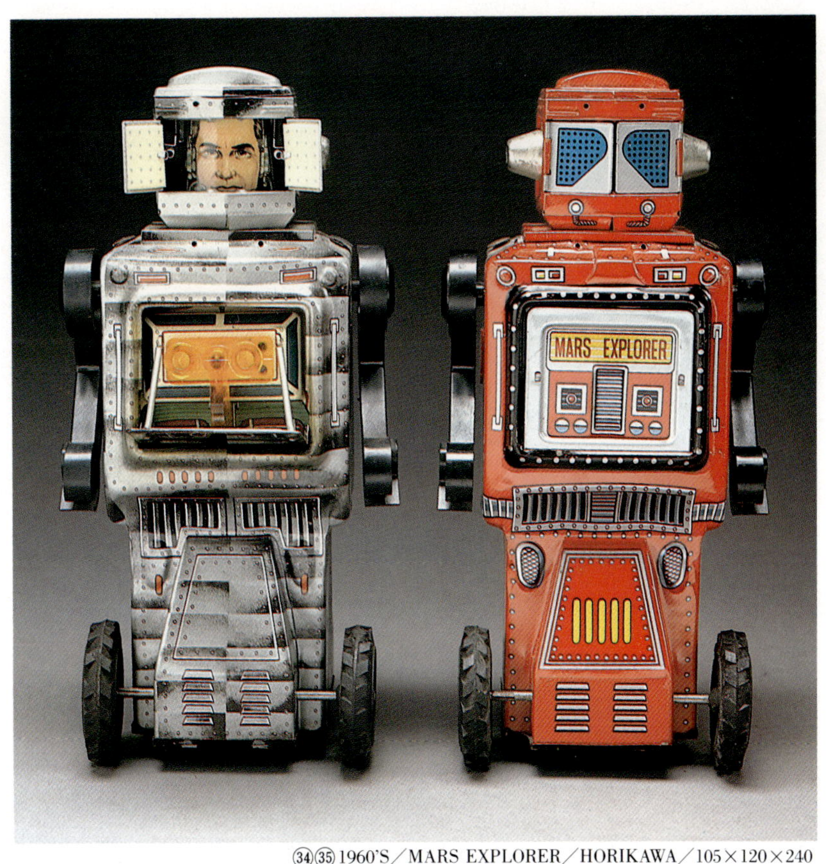

㉞㉟ 1960'S／MARS EXPLORER／HORIKAWA／105×120×240

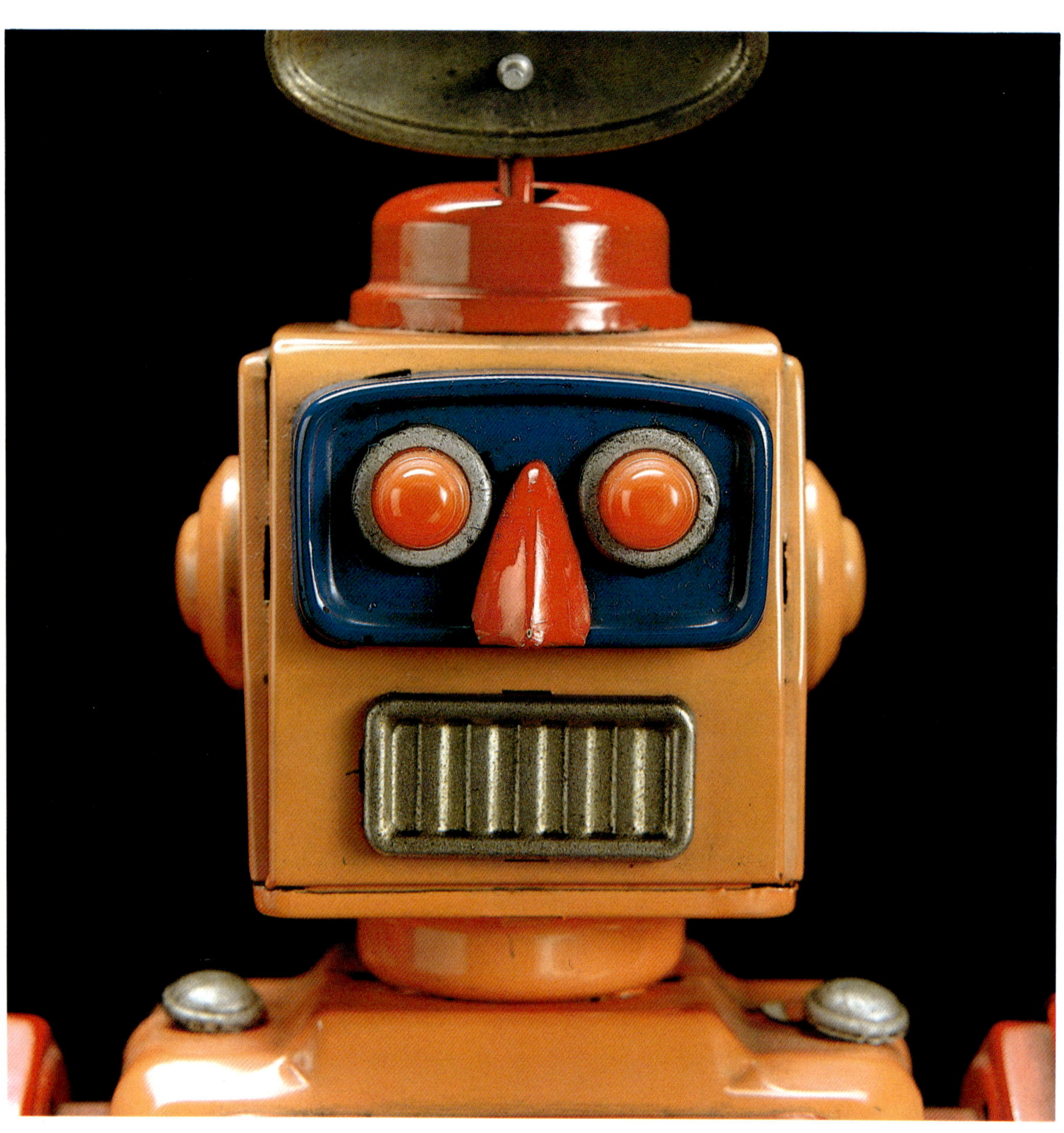

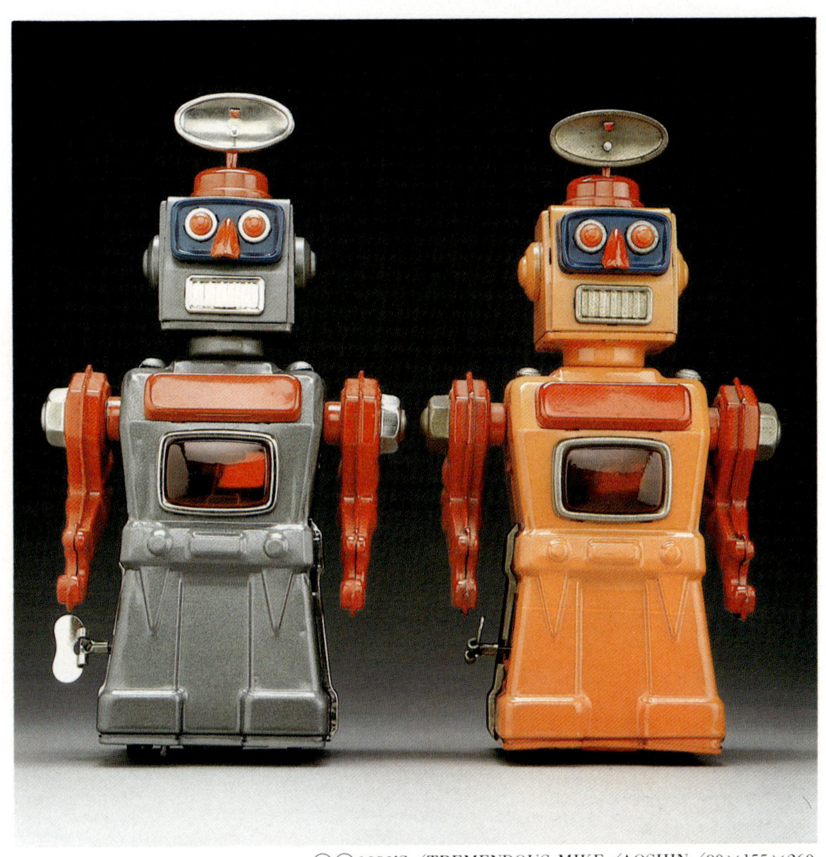

㊱㊲ 1950'S／TREMENDOUS MIKE／AOSHIN／90×155×260

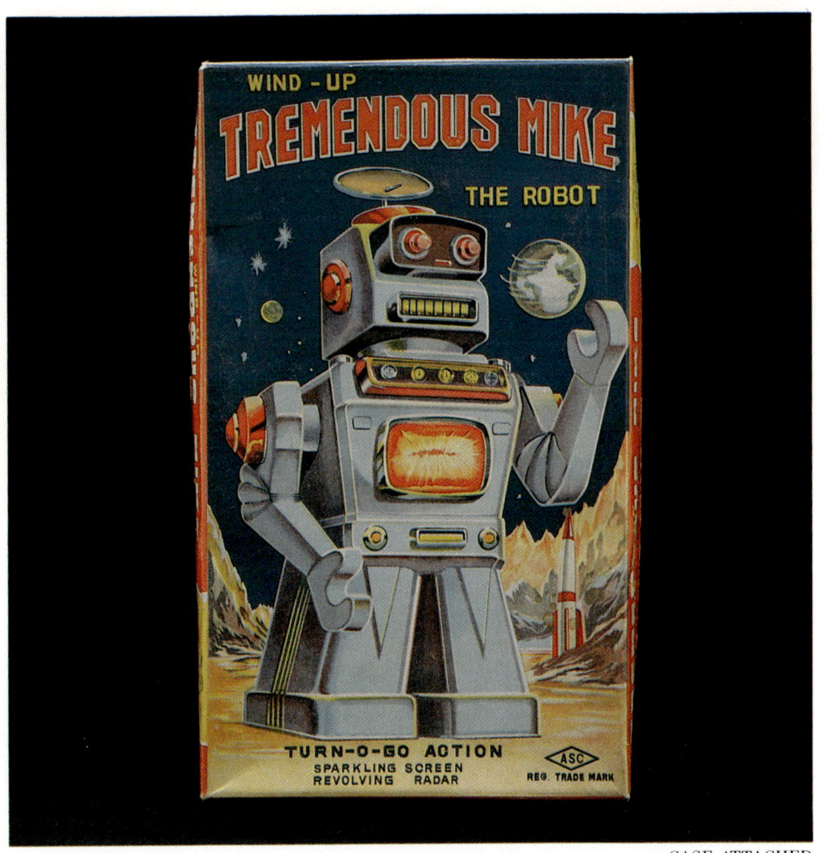

CASE ATTACHED

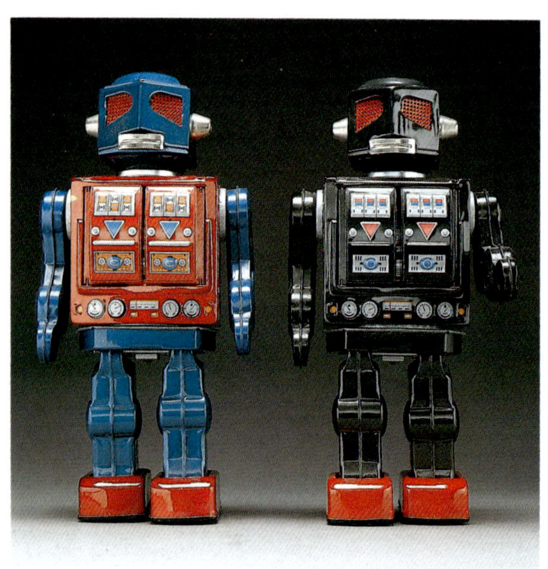

㊳㊴ 1960'S／ROBOT／HORIKAWA／100×140×290

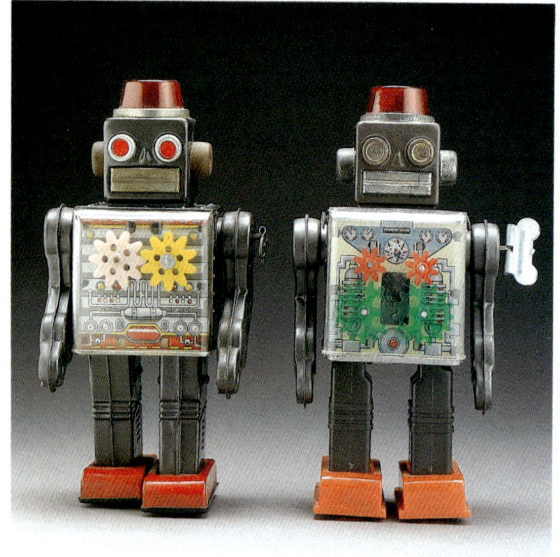

㊵㊶ 1960'S／GEAR ROBOT／HORIKAWA／65×115×210

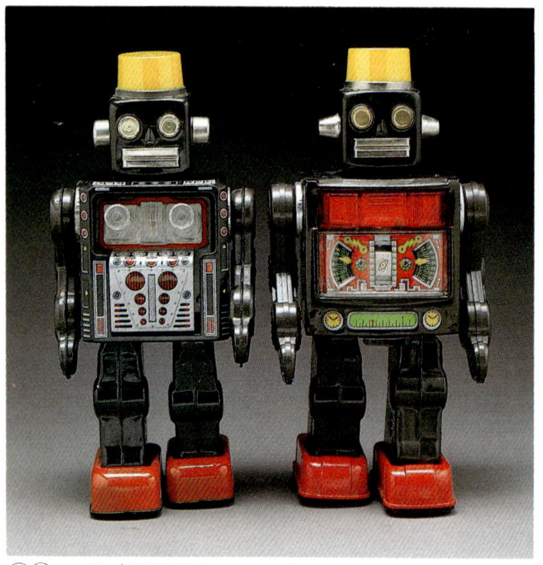

㊷㊸ 1960'S／THUNDER ROBOT／HORIKAWA／90×135×285, 85×135×285

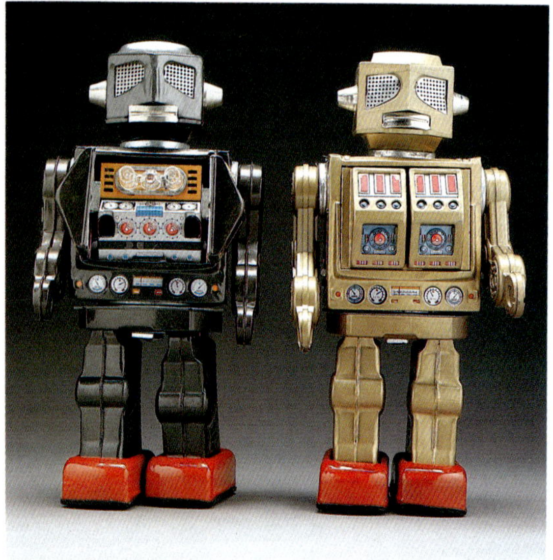

㊹㊺ 1960'S／ROBOT／HORIKAWA／105×140×290

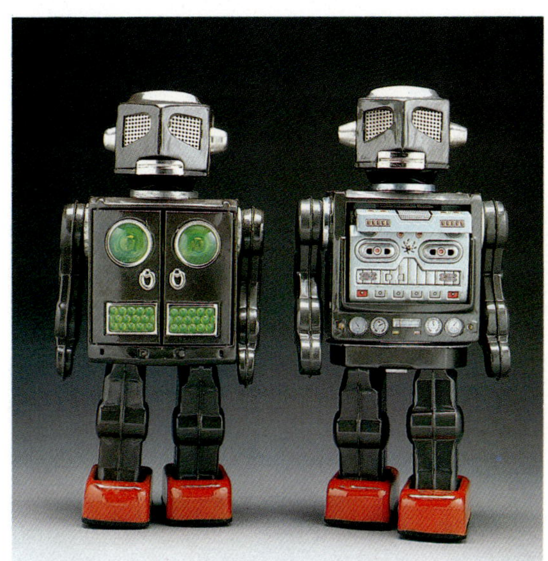
㊻㊼1960'S/ROBOT/HORIKAWA/87×135×280, 87×135×290

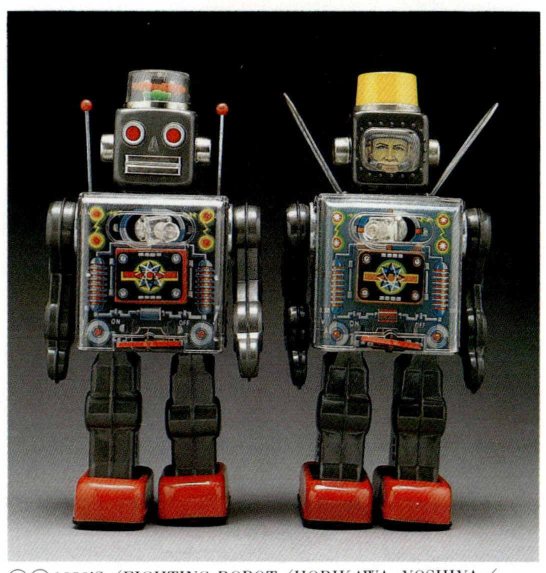
㊽㊾1950'S/FIGHTING ROBOT/HORIKAWA, YOSHIYA/90×135×285

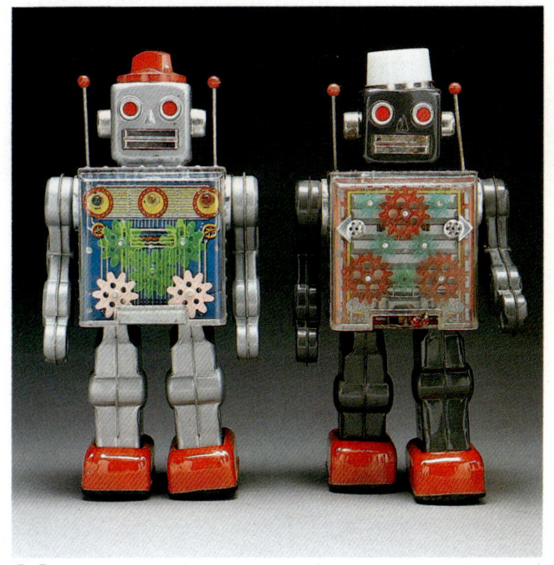
㊿51 1950'S, 1960'S/GEAR ROBOT/UNKNOWN, HORIKAWA/82×138×282

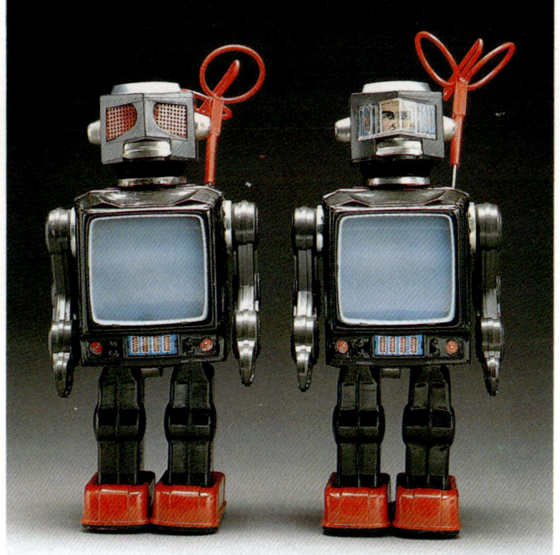
52 53 1960'S/TV ROBOT/HORIKAWA/110×136×325

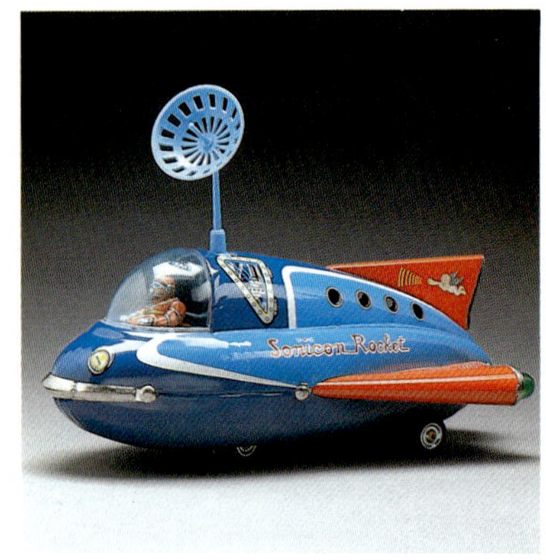

54 1950'S／SONICON ROCKET／MASUDAYA／340×170×230

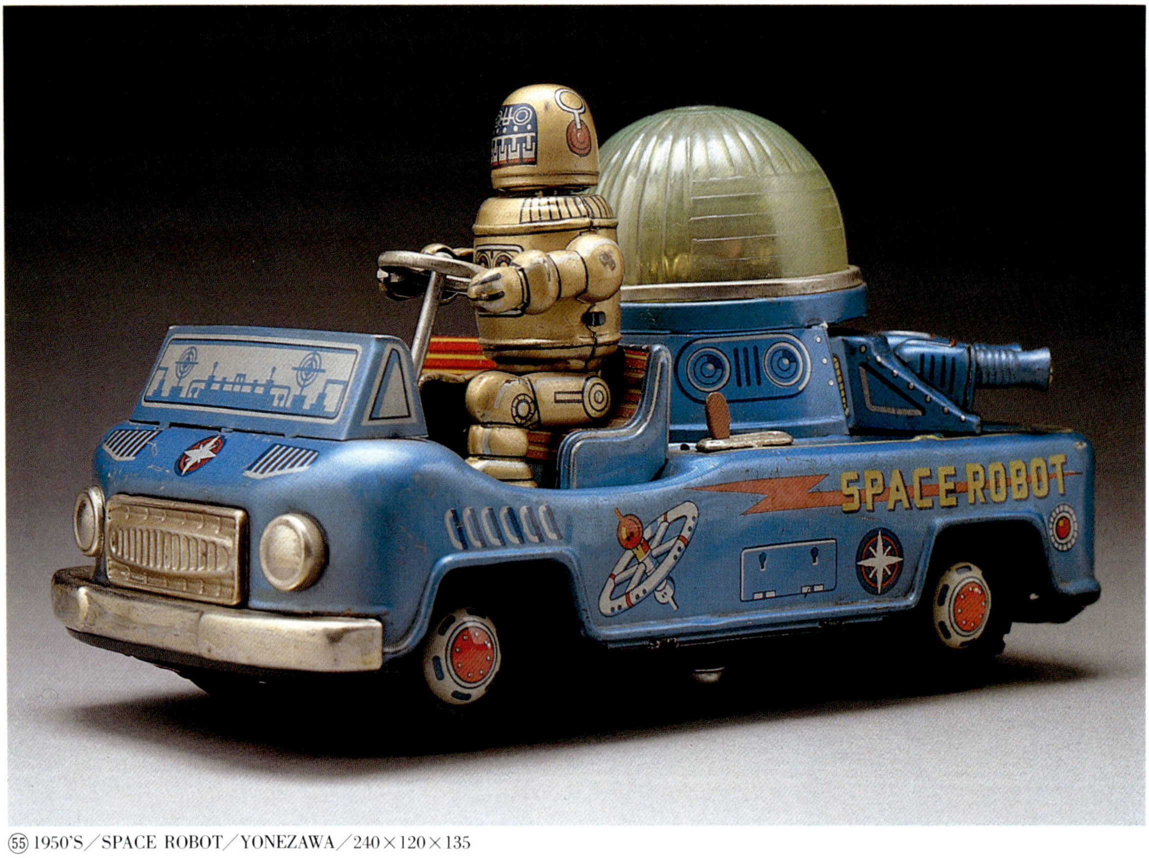

55 1950'S／SPACE ROBOT／YONEZAWA／240×120×135

56 1950'S／SONICON ROCKET／MASUDAYA ／340×170×230

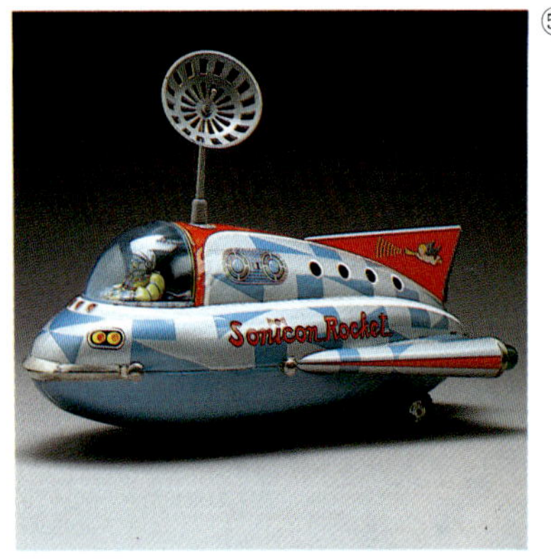

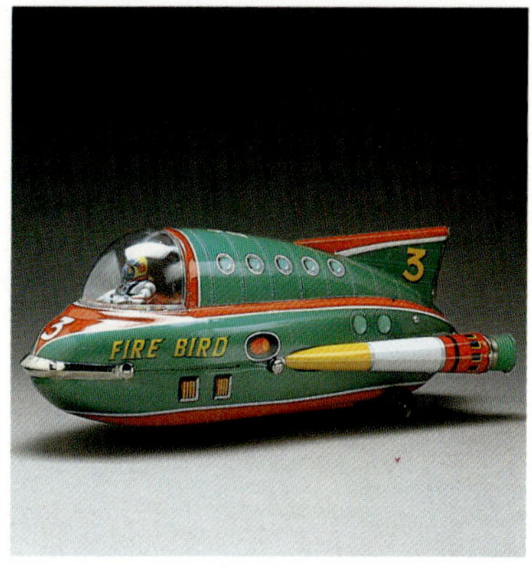

⑰ 1960'S／FIRE BIRD／MASUDAYA／340×170×130

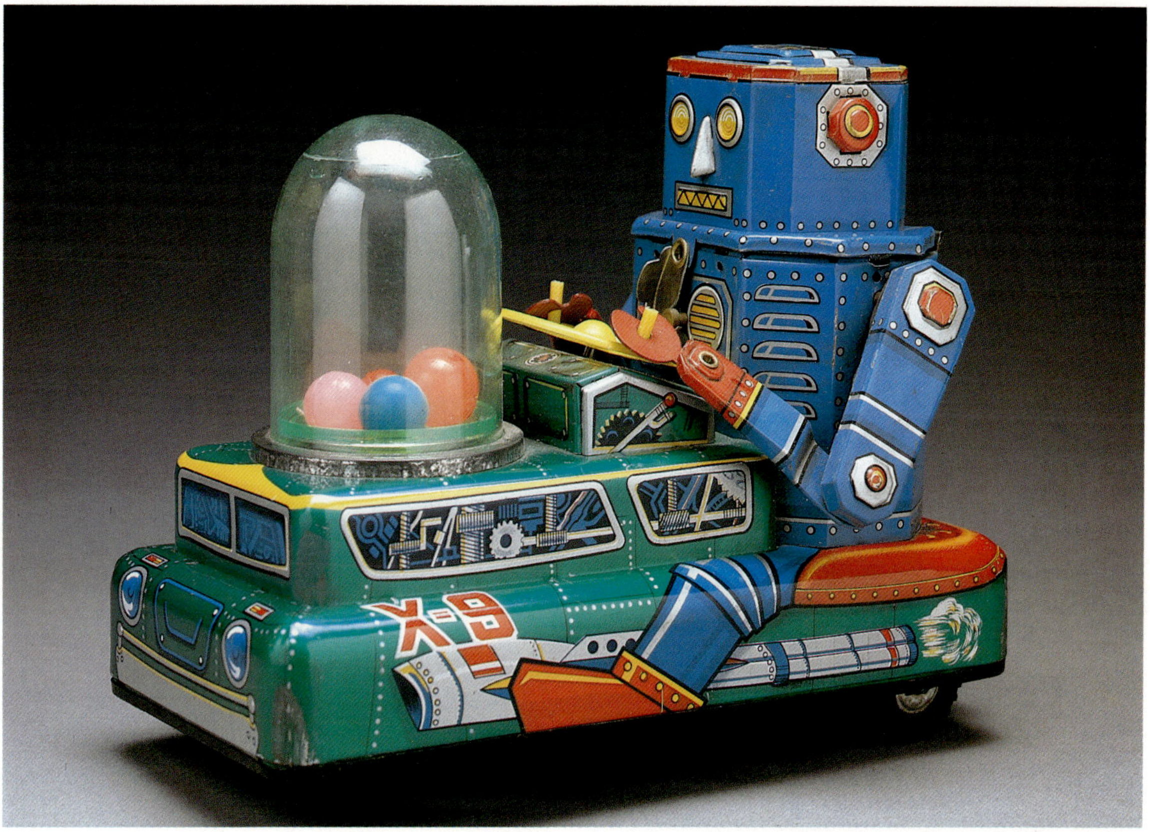

⑱ 1950'S／X-9 ROBOT／MASUDAYA／190×115×155

⑲ 1960'S／MOON EXPLORER／MASUDAYA／340×170×130

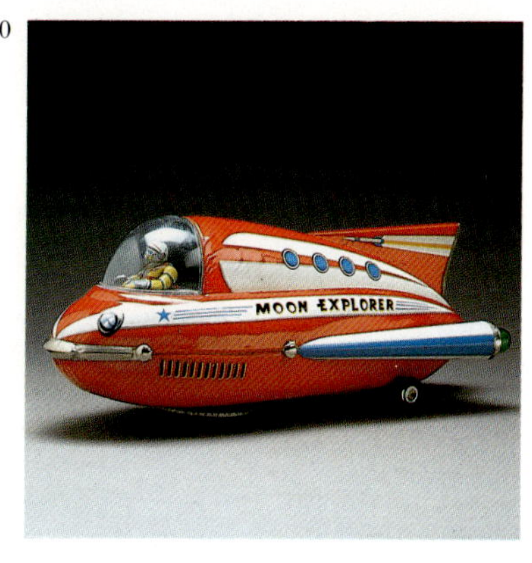

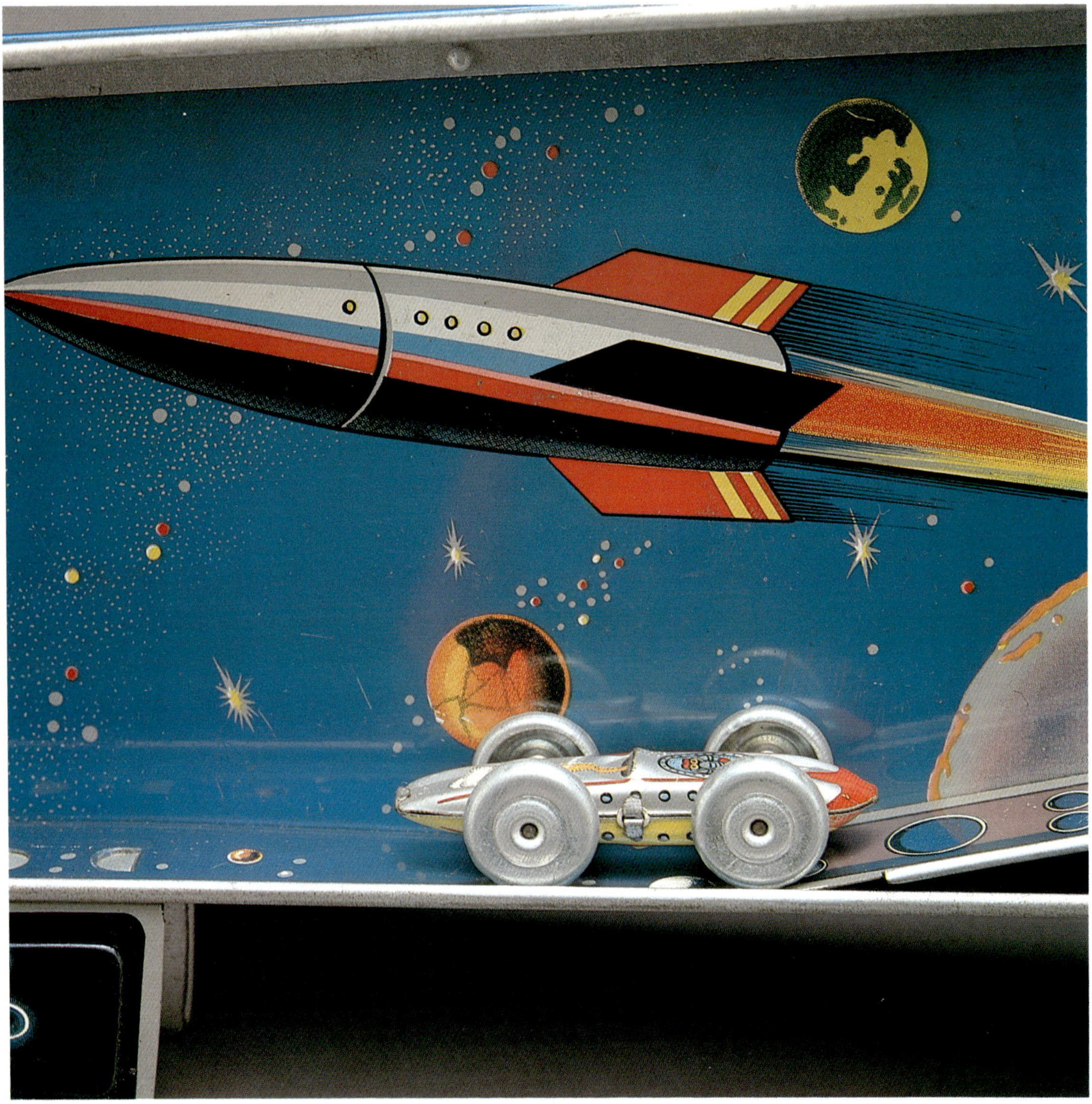

(60) 1960'S／SPACE RACE／MASUDAYA／50×490×200

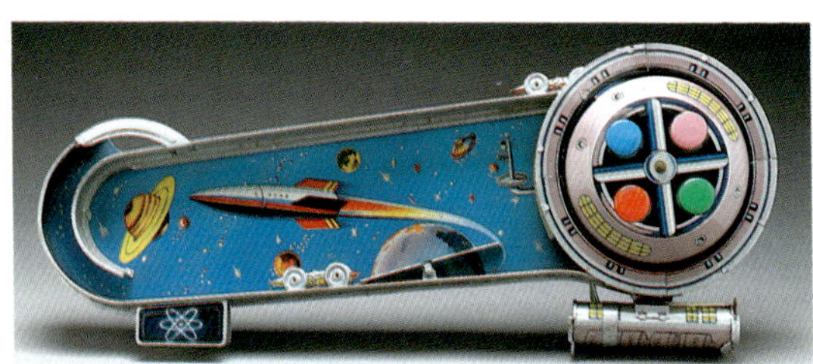

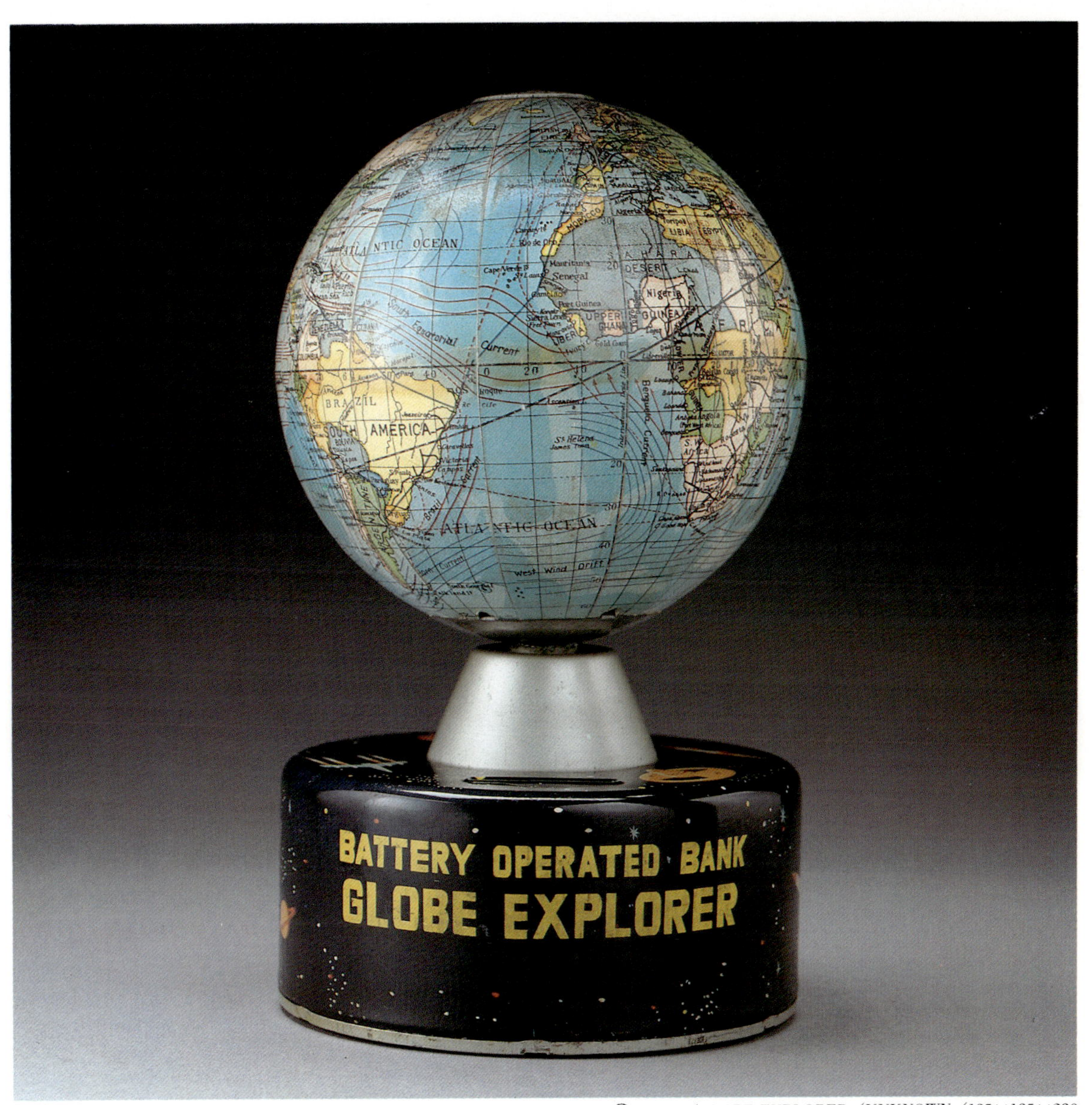

⑥① 1950'S／GLOBE EXPLORER／UNKNOWN／135×135×230

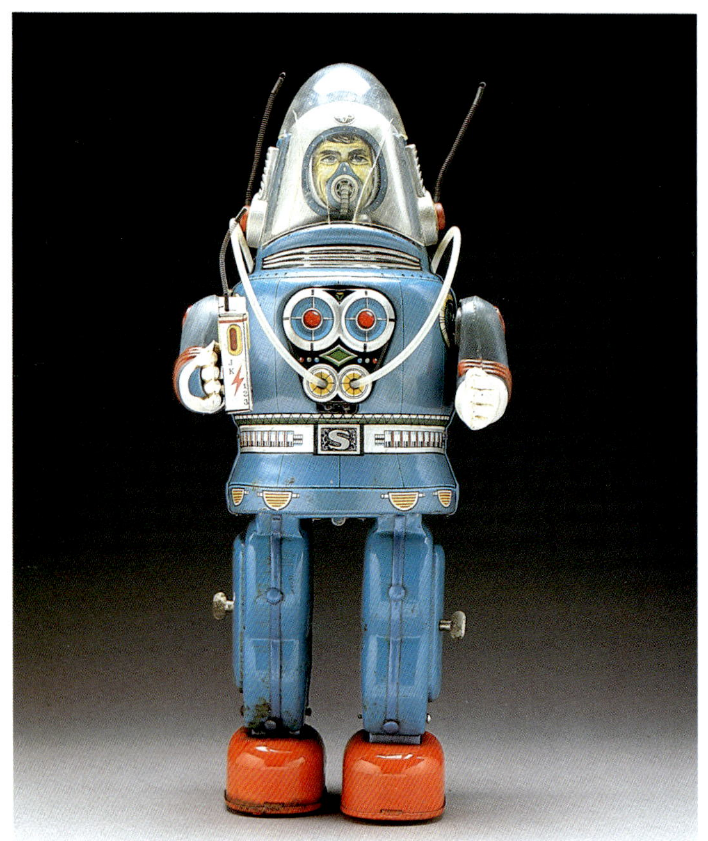

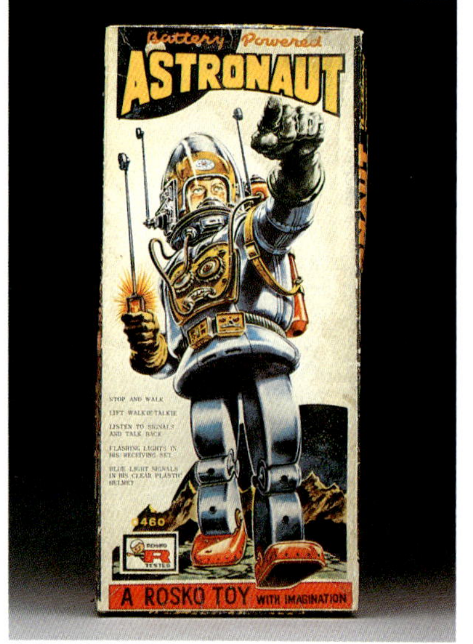

⑥② 1960'S／ASTRONAUT／ROSKO TOY／110×135×330

CASE ATTACHED

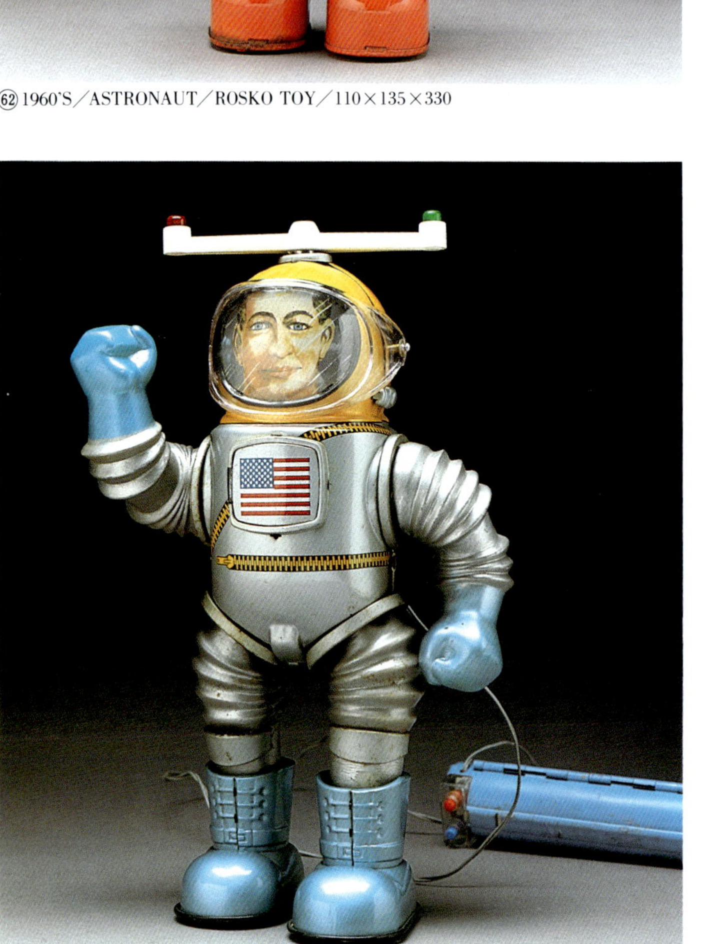

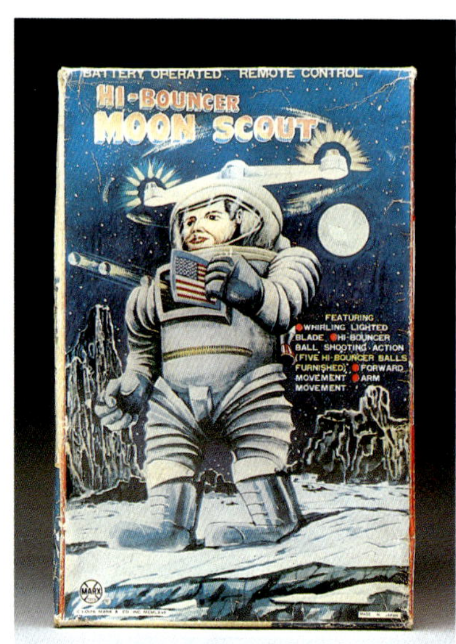

CASE ATTACHED

⑥③ 1960'S／MOON SCOUT／LOUIS MARX／90×160×290

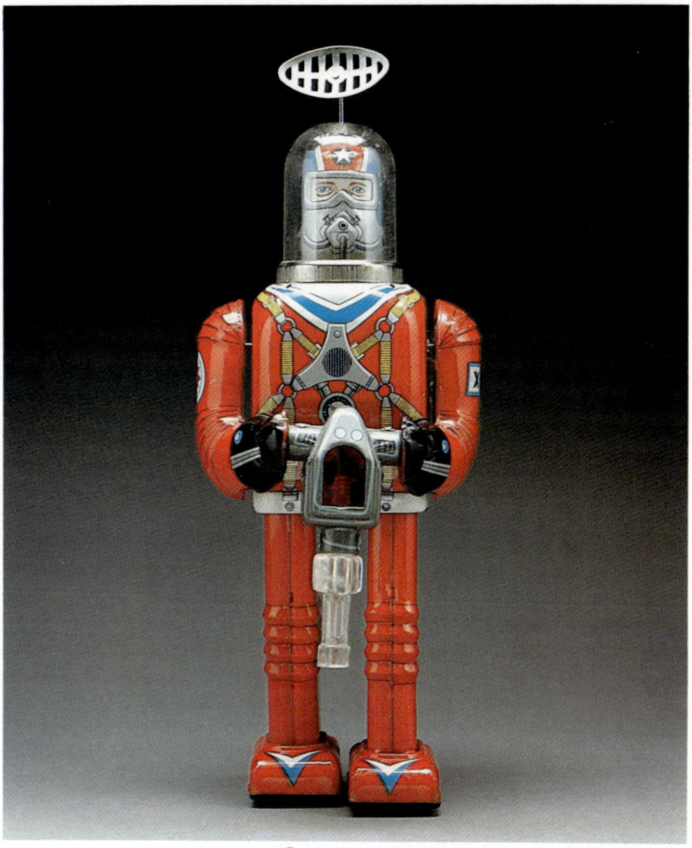

(64) 1950'S／ASTRONAUT／DAIYA／137×110×298

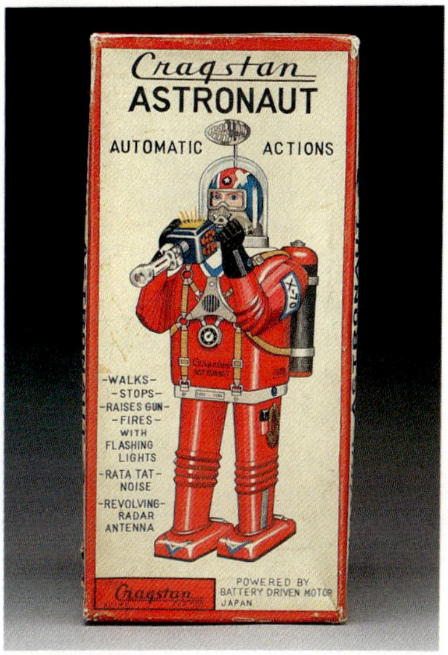

CASE ATTACHED

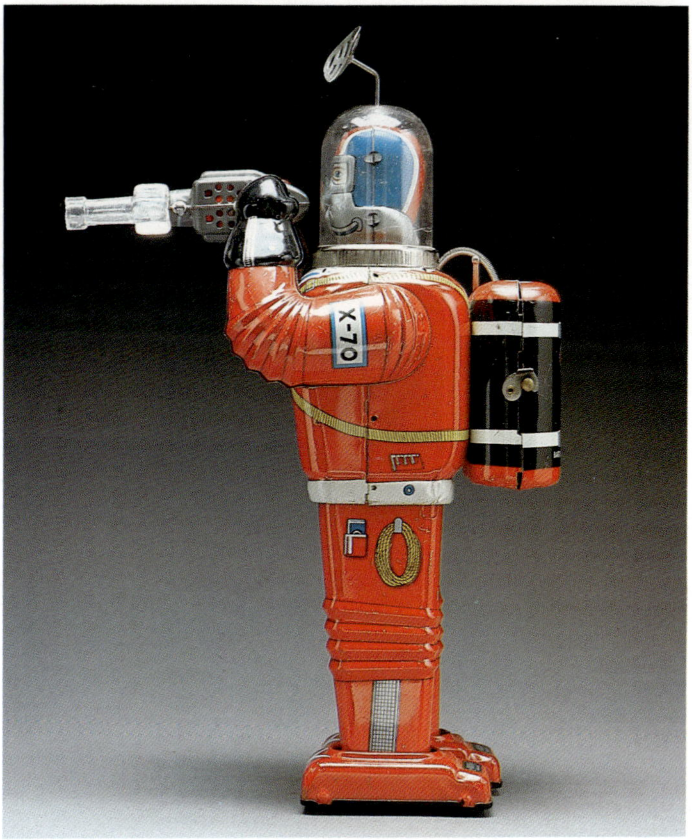

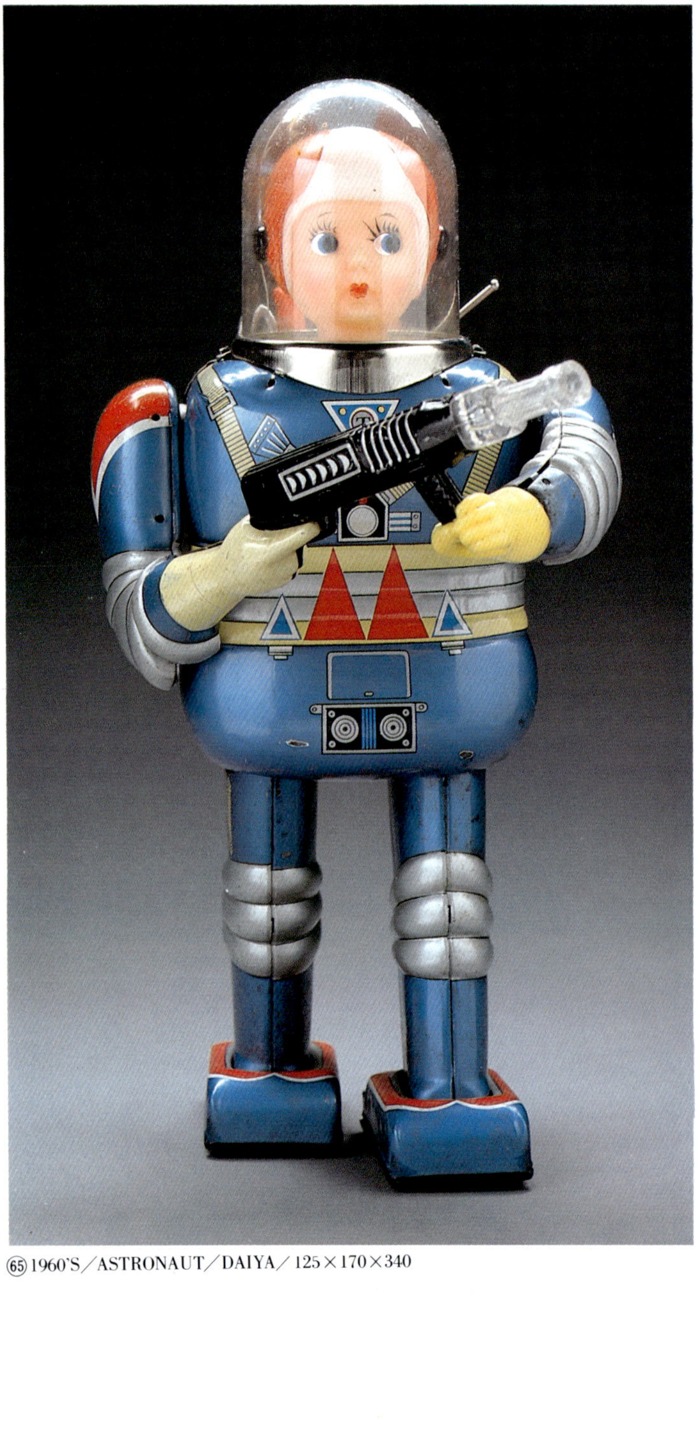

⑥⑤ 1960'S/ASTRONAUT/DAIYA/125×170×340

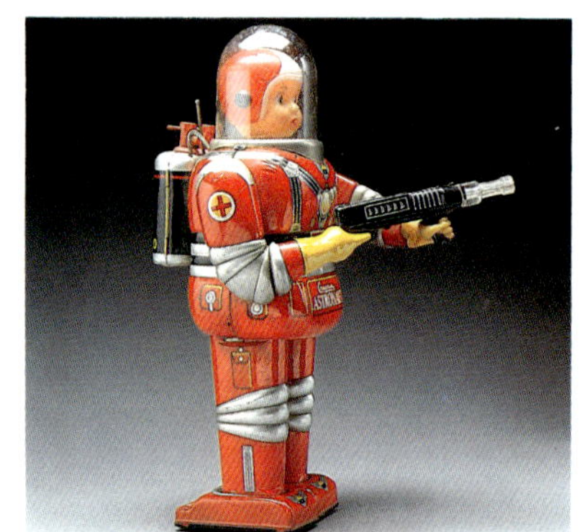

⑥⑥ 1960'S/ASTRONAUT/DAIYA/125×170×340

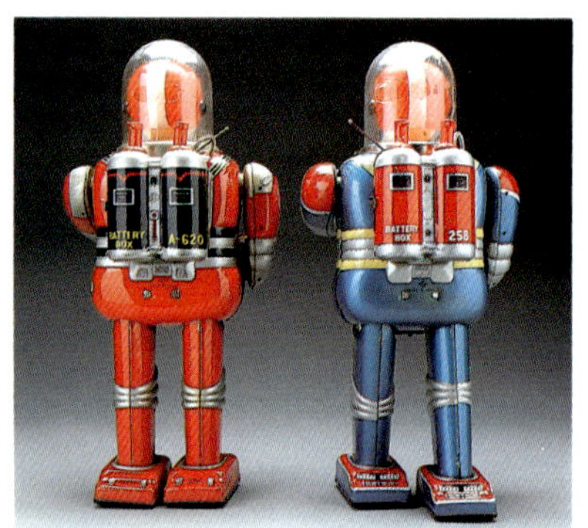

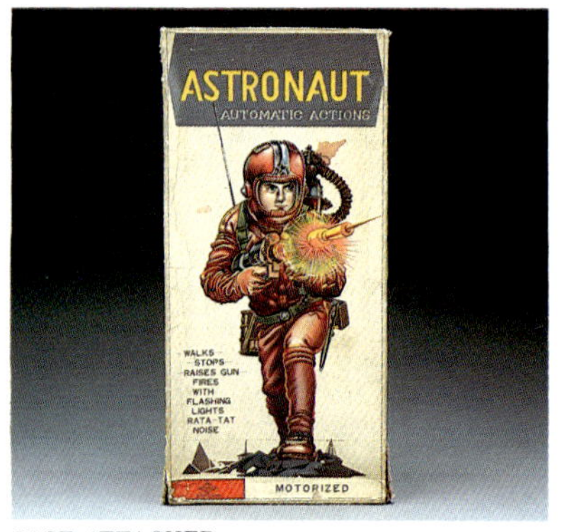

CASE ATTACHED

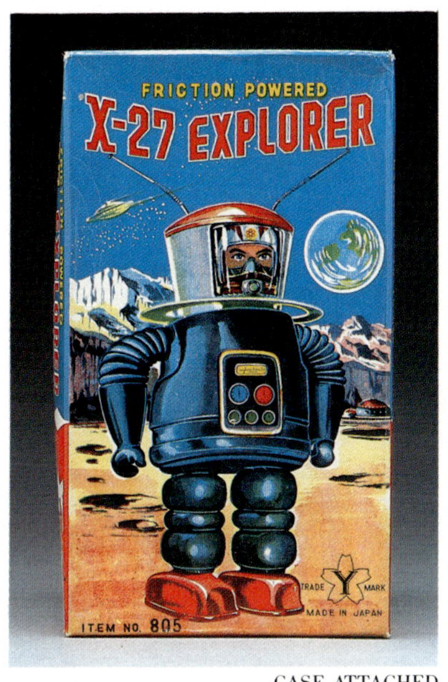

CASE ATTACHED

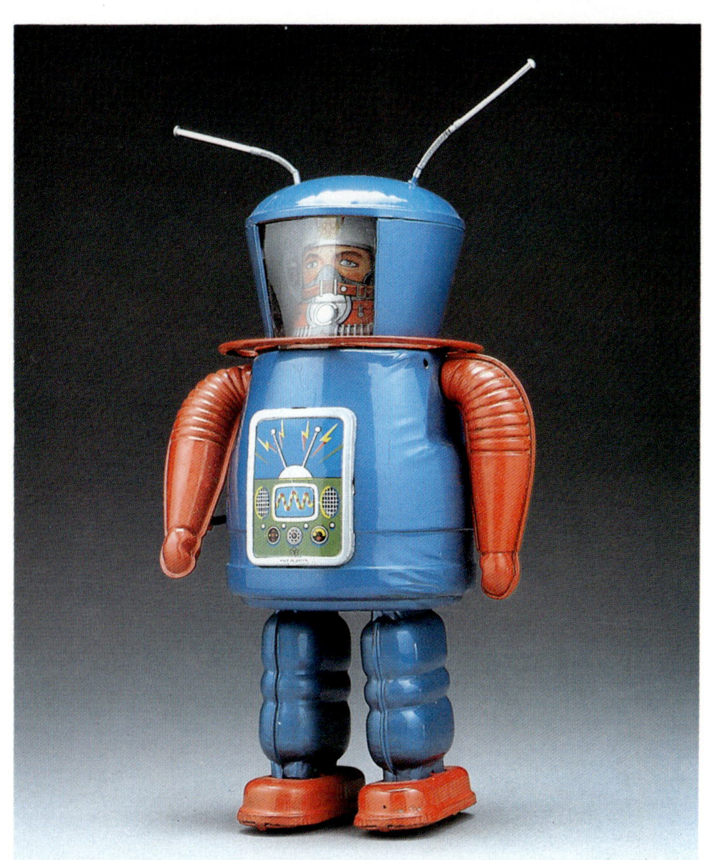

⑥⑦ 1950'S／X-27 EXPLORER／YONEZAWA／85×125×213

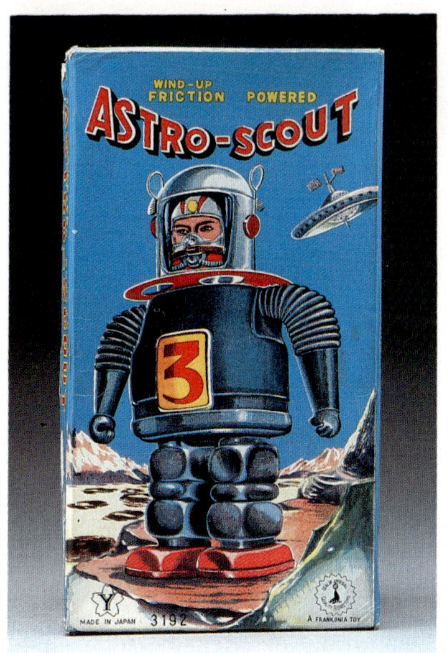

CASE ATTACHED

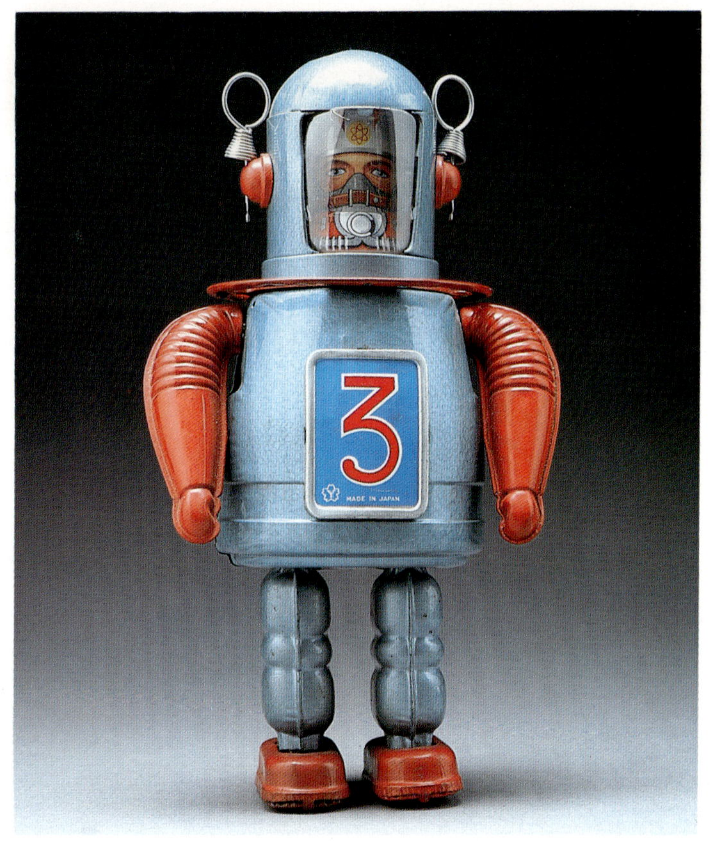

⑥⑧ 1950'S／ASTRO SCOUT／YONEZAWA／85×130×230

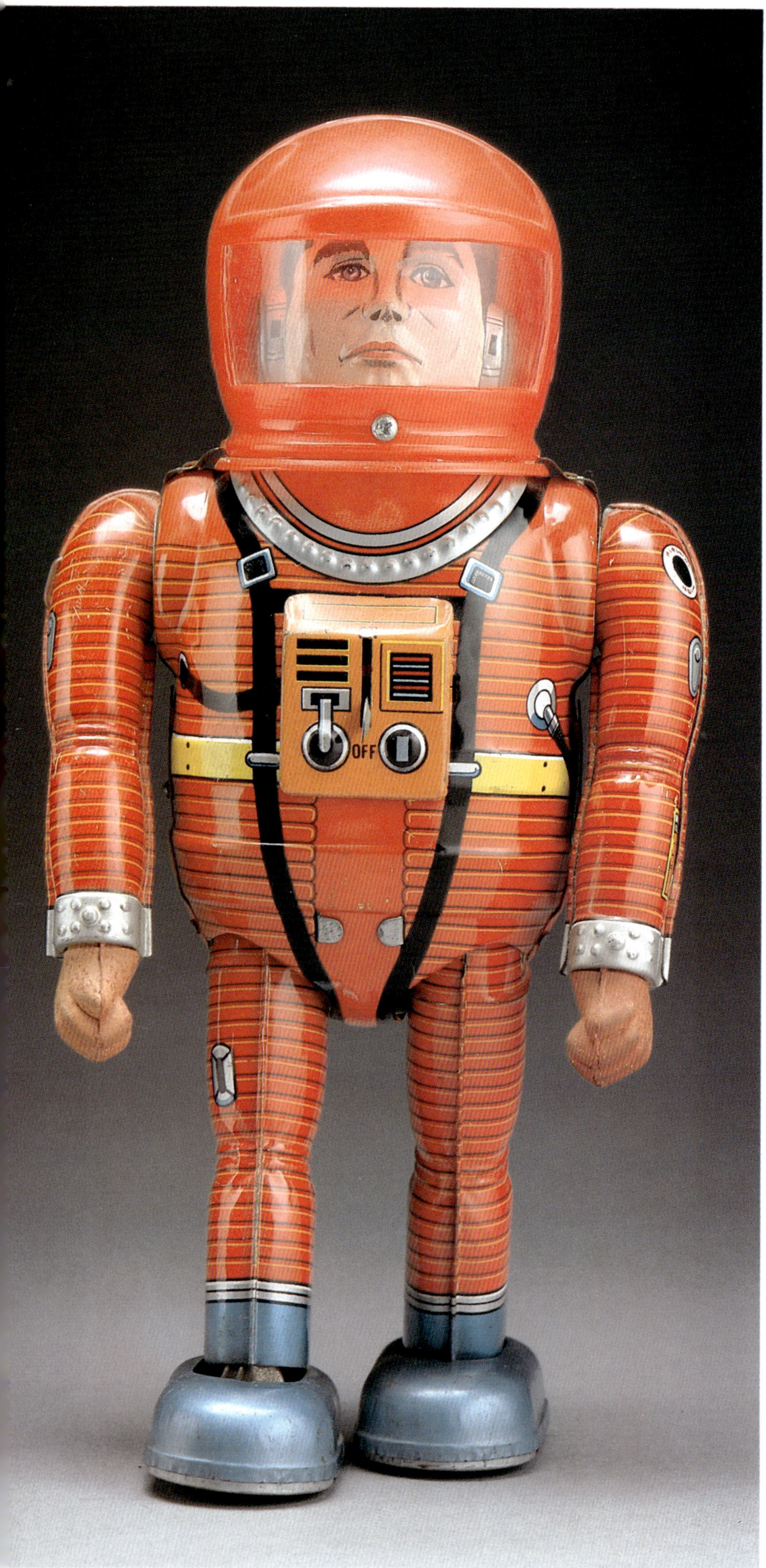

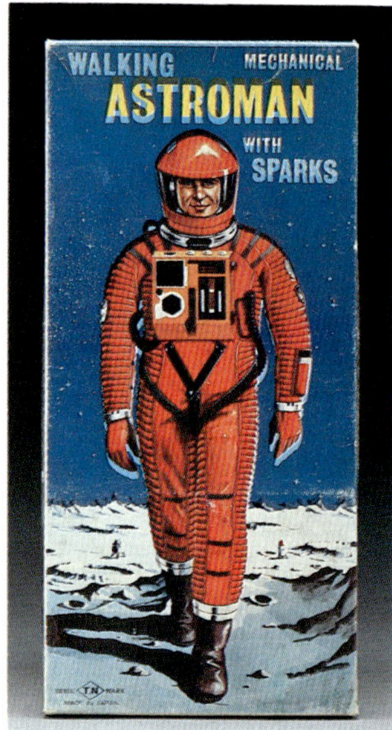

CASE ATTACHED

(69) 1960'S／ASTRO MAN／NOMURA／90×135×260

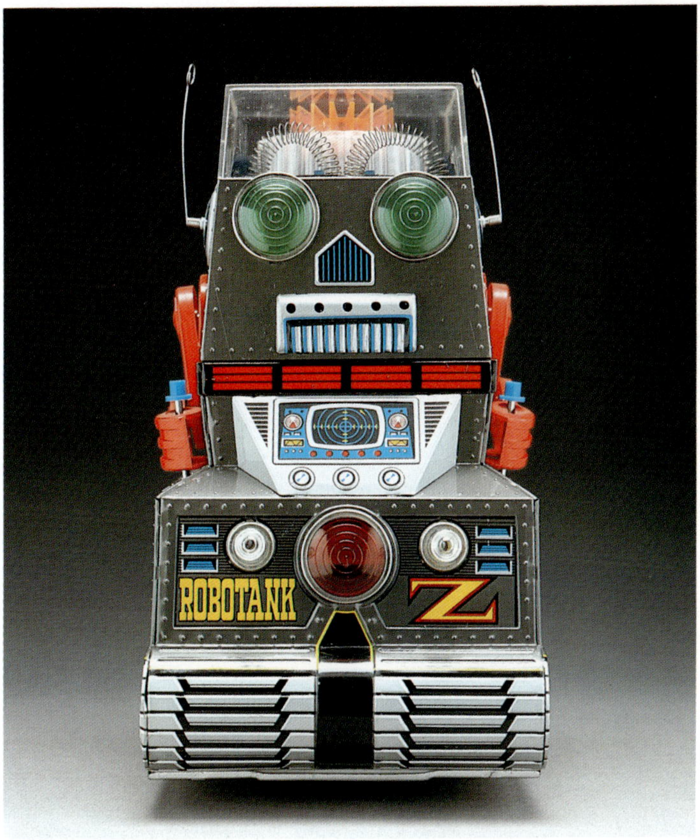

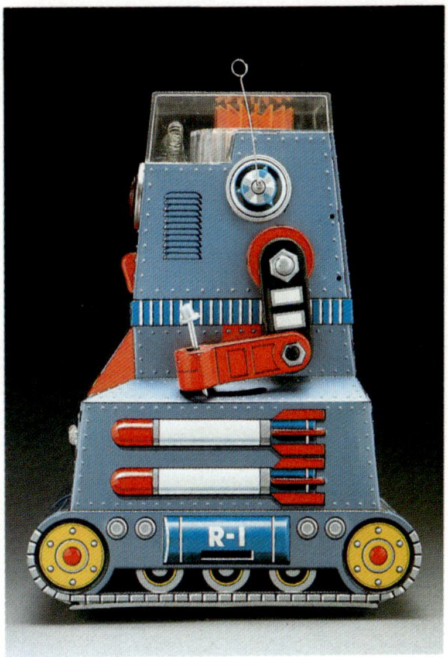

(70) 1960'S／ROBOTANK-Z／NOMURA／195×140×260

(71) 1960'S／ROBOTANK R-1／NOMURA／195×140×260

CASE ATTACHED

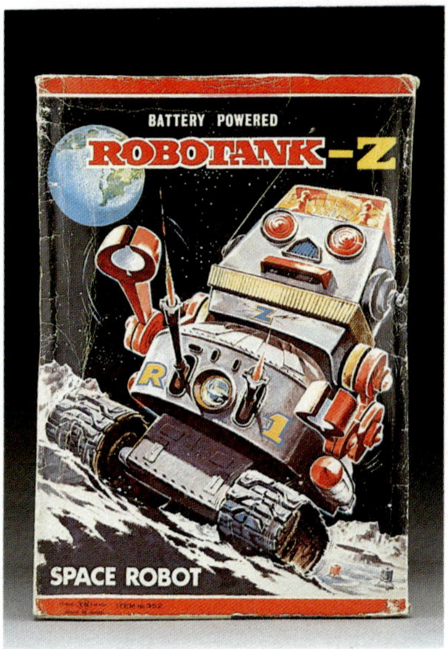

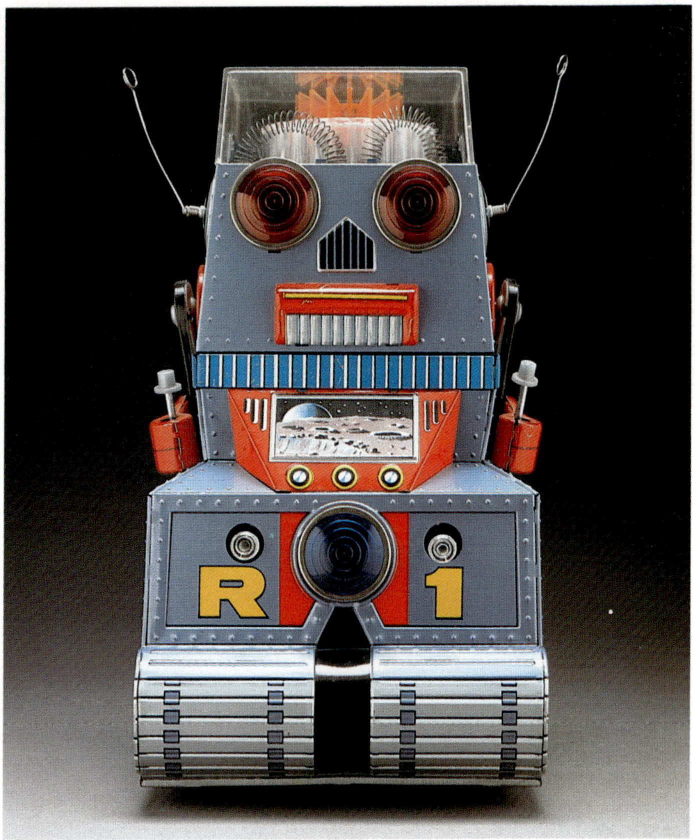

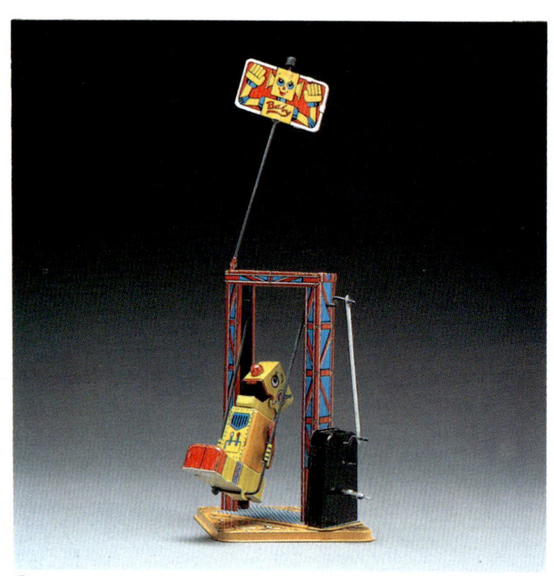

(72) 1960'S／ROBOT ON SWING／YONEZAWA／135×135×160

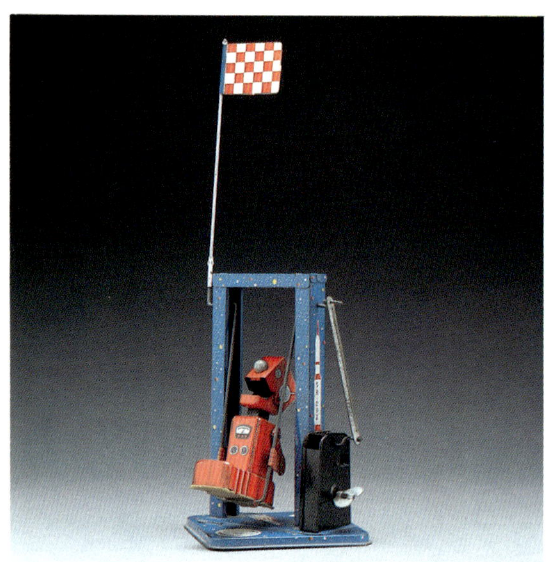

(73) 1960'S／ROBOT ON SWING／YONEZAWA／135×135×160

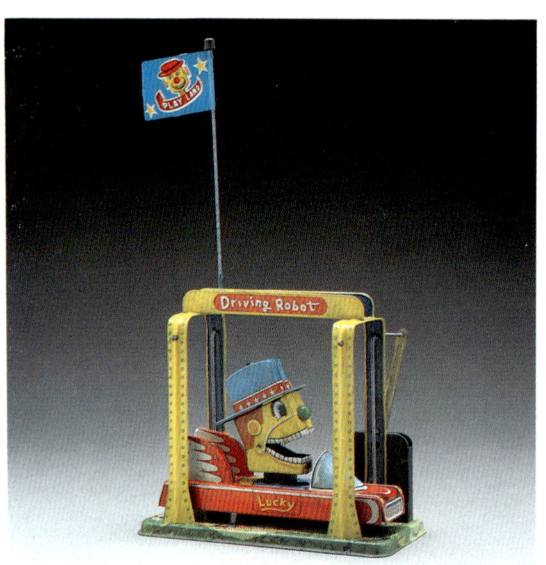

(74) 1950'S／DRIVING ROBOT／SY TOYS／155×80×138

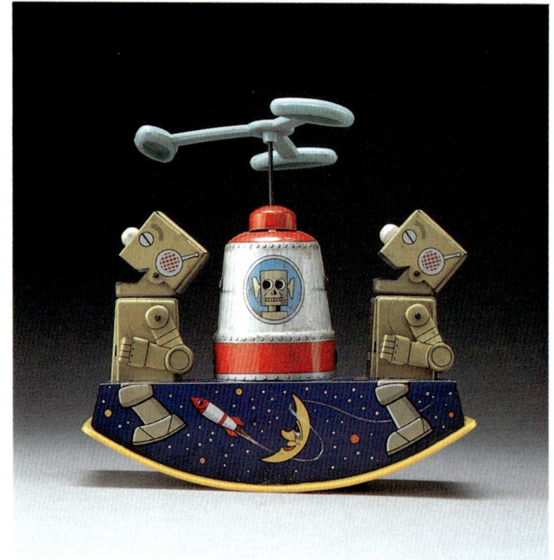

(75) 1960'S／SEESAW ROBOT／YONEZAWA／160×65×150

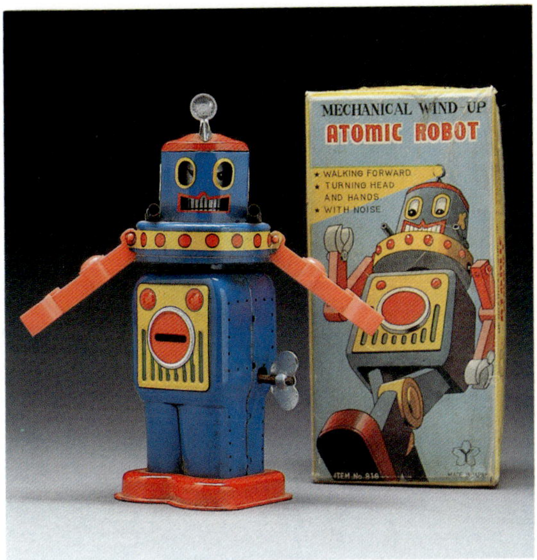

(76) 1960'S/ATOMIC ROBOT AND CASE/YONEZAWA/55×140×160

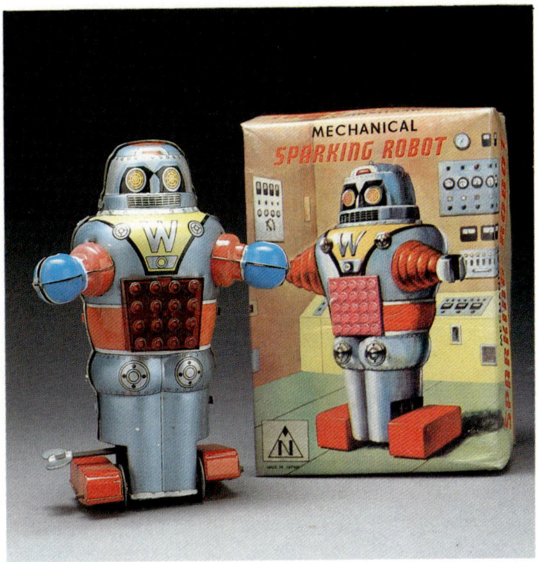

(77) 1950'S/SPARKING ROBOT AND CASE/UNKNOWN/75×115×160

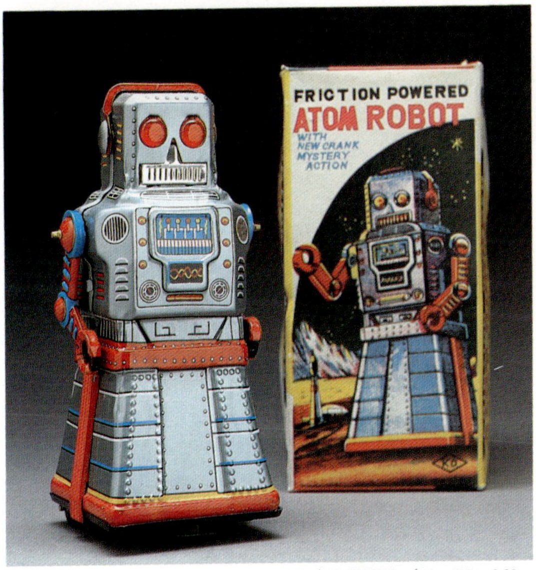

(78) 1960'S/ATOM ROBOT AND CASE/YOSHIYA/80×70×160

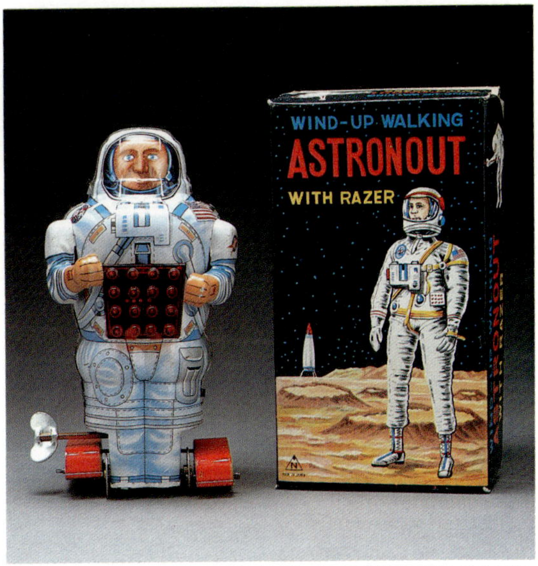

(79) 1970'S/ASTRONAUT AND CASE/UNKNOWN/85×95×155

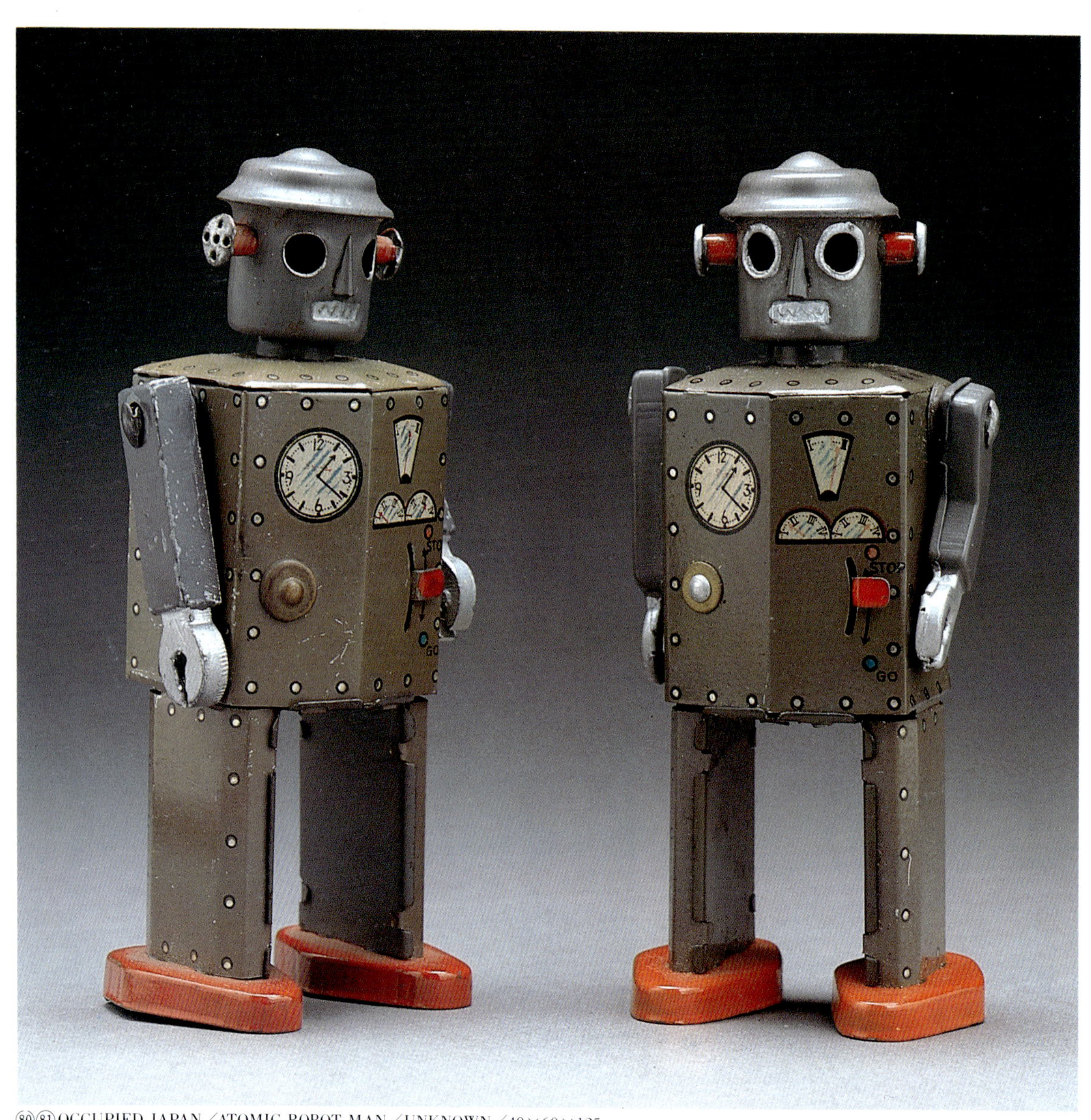

(80)(81) OCCUPIED JAPAN／ATOMIC ROBOT MAN／UNKNOWN／40×60×125

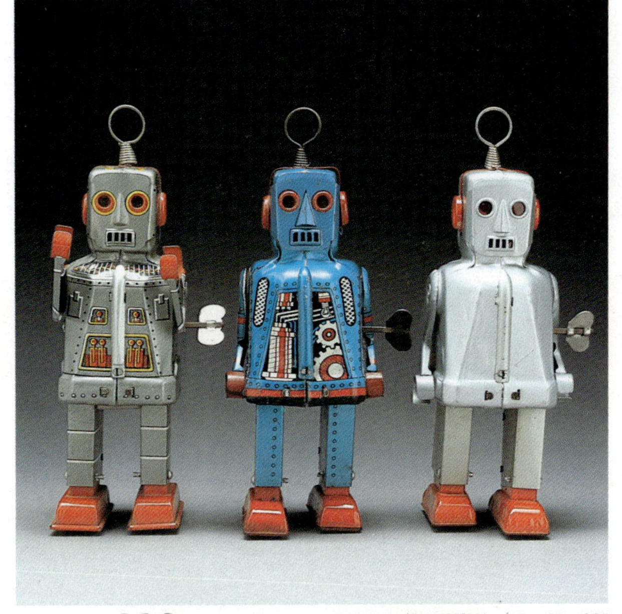

(82)(83)(84) 1950'S／SPARKY ROBOT／YOSHIYA／70×90×195

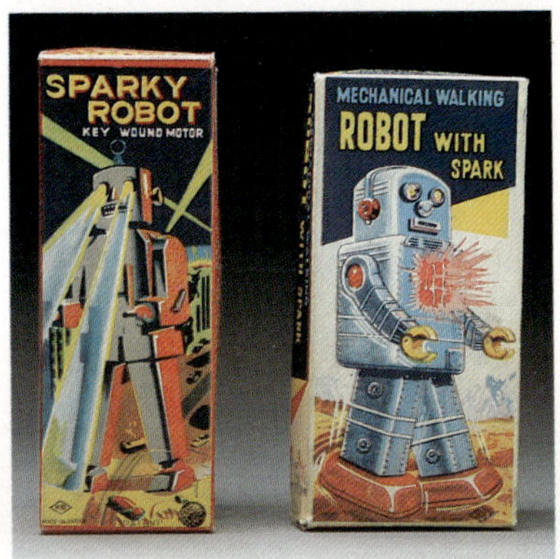

CASE ATTACHED

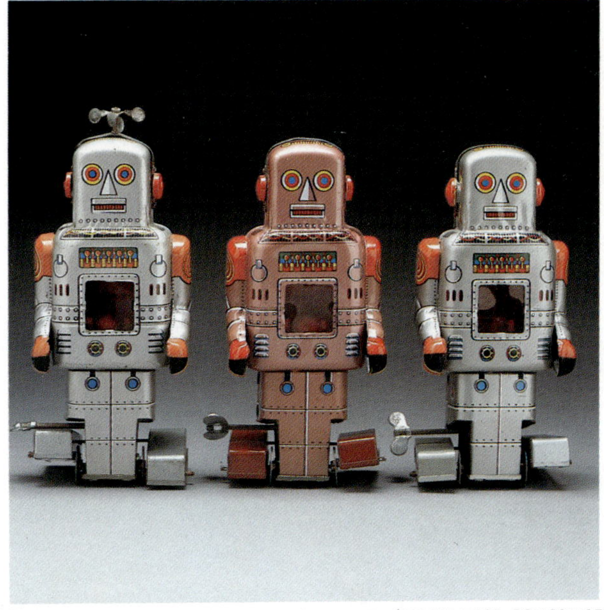

(85)(86)(87) 1950'S／ROBOT WITH SPARK／SY TOYS／56×80×190, 56×80×175, 56×80×175

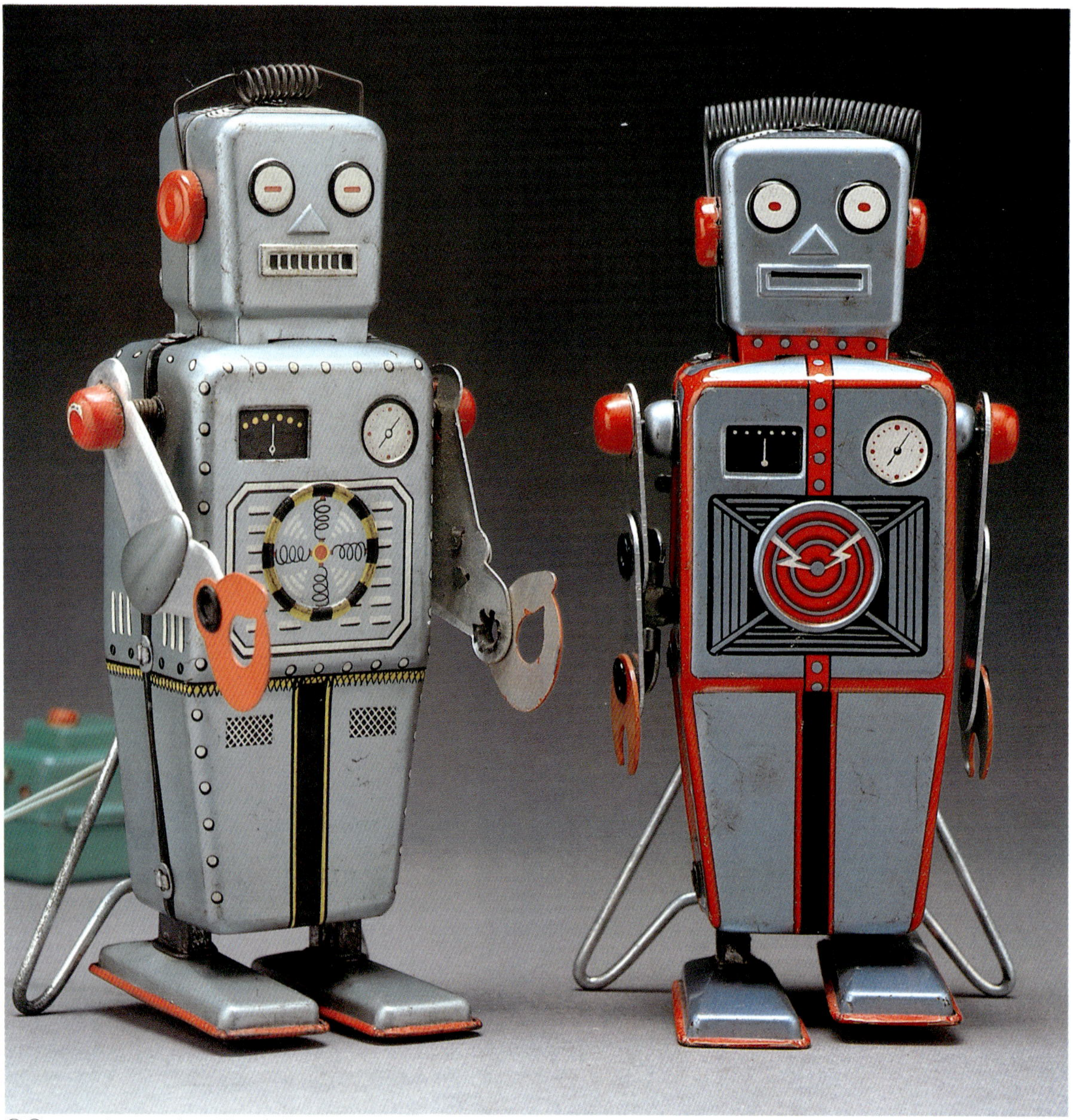

⑧⑧⑧⑨ 1950'S／ROBOT／YONEZAWA／52×70×150

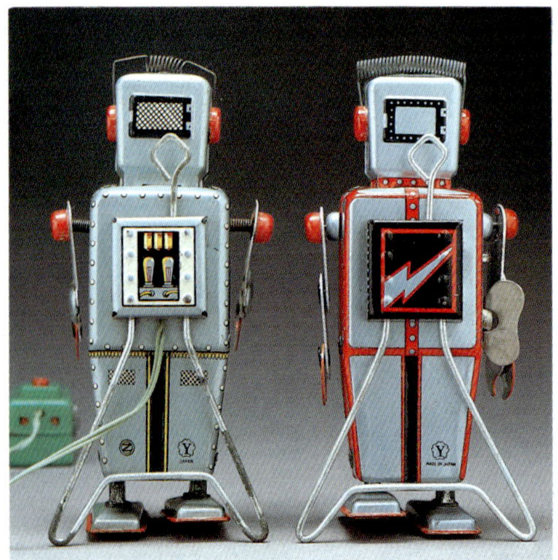

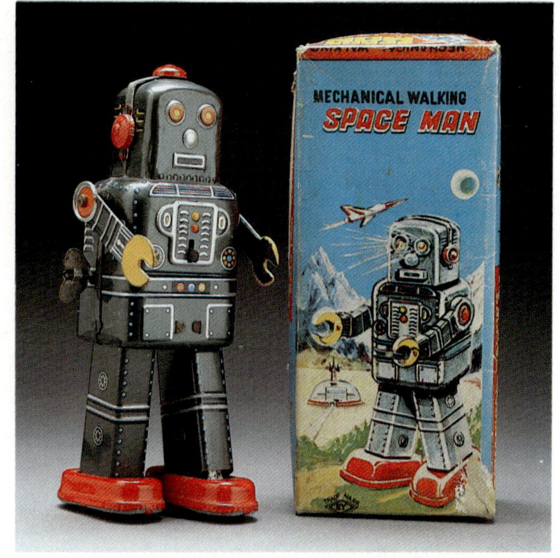

⑨⓪ 1950'S／SPACE MAN AND CASE／SY TOYS／64×80×195

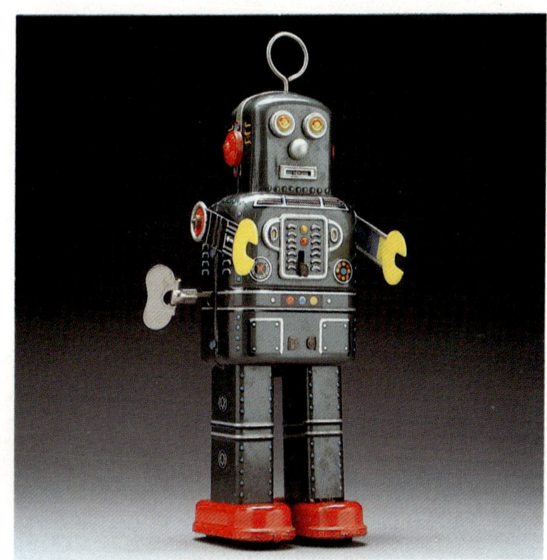

⑨① 1950'S／SPACE MAN／YOSHIYA／65×75×215

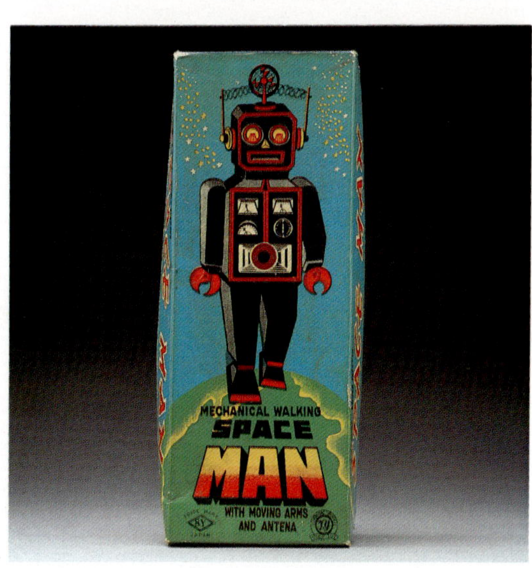

CASE ATTACHED

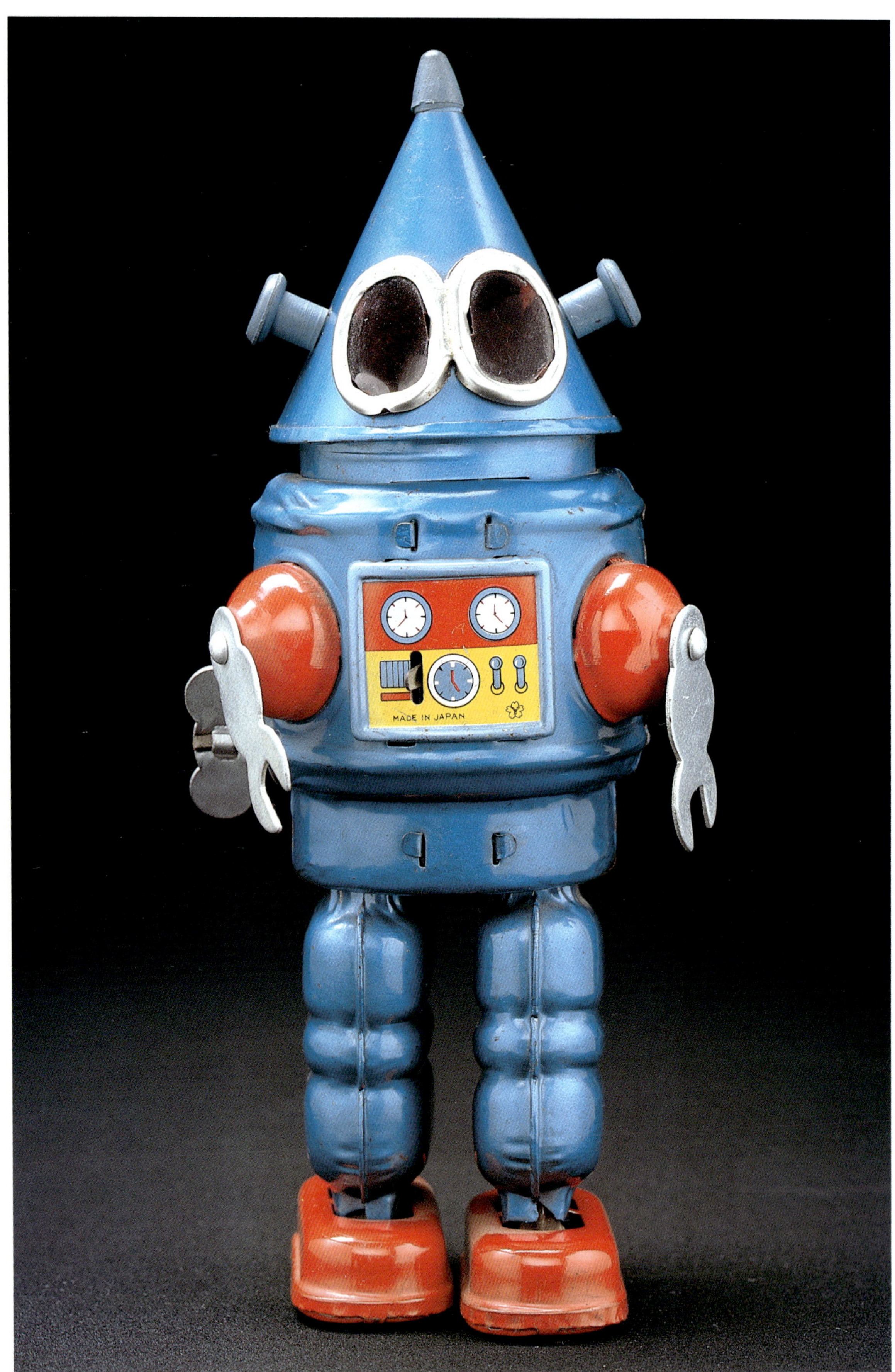

(92) 1950'S／ROBOT／YONEZAWA／70×85×215

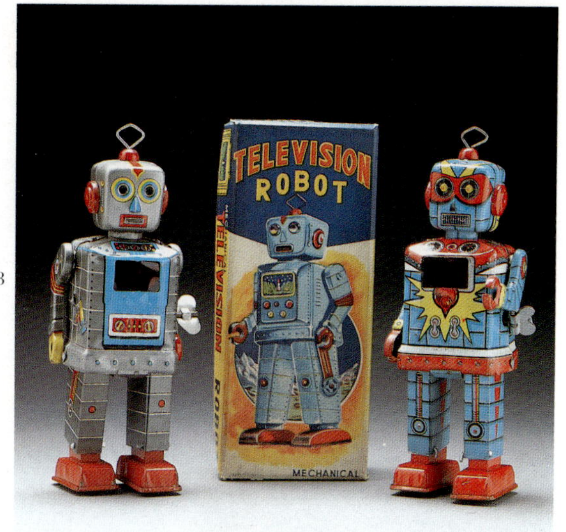

⑨③⑨④ 1950'S/TELEVISION ROBOT AND CASE/SANKEI/65×80×198

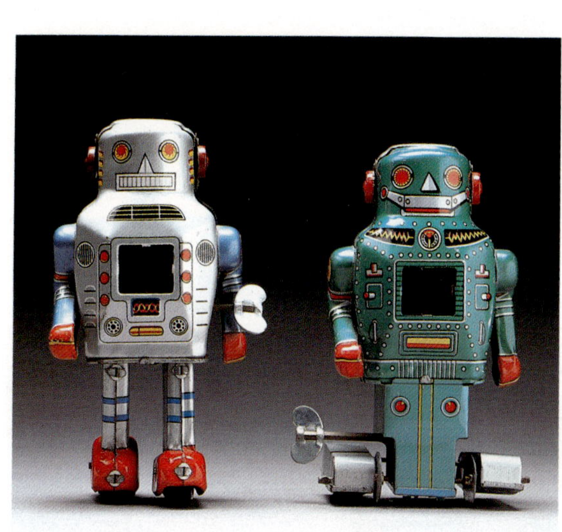

⑨⑤⑨⑥ 1950'S/SPARKY ROBOT/SY TOYS, UNKNOWN/50×83×143, 57×90×138

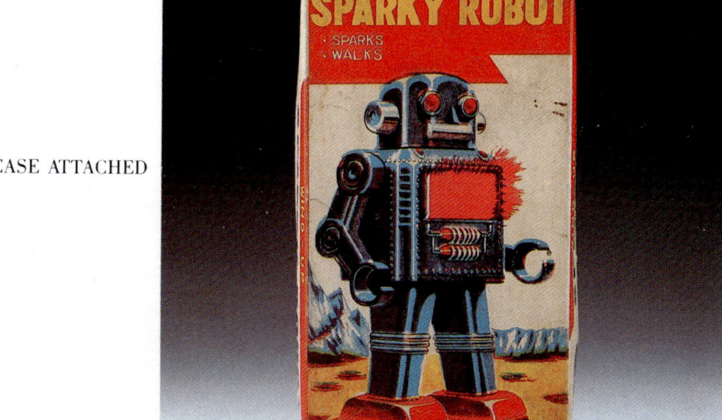

CASE ATTACHED

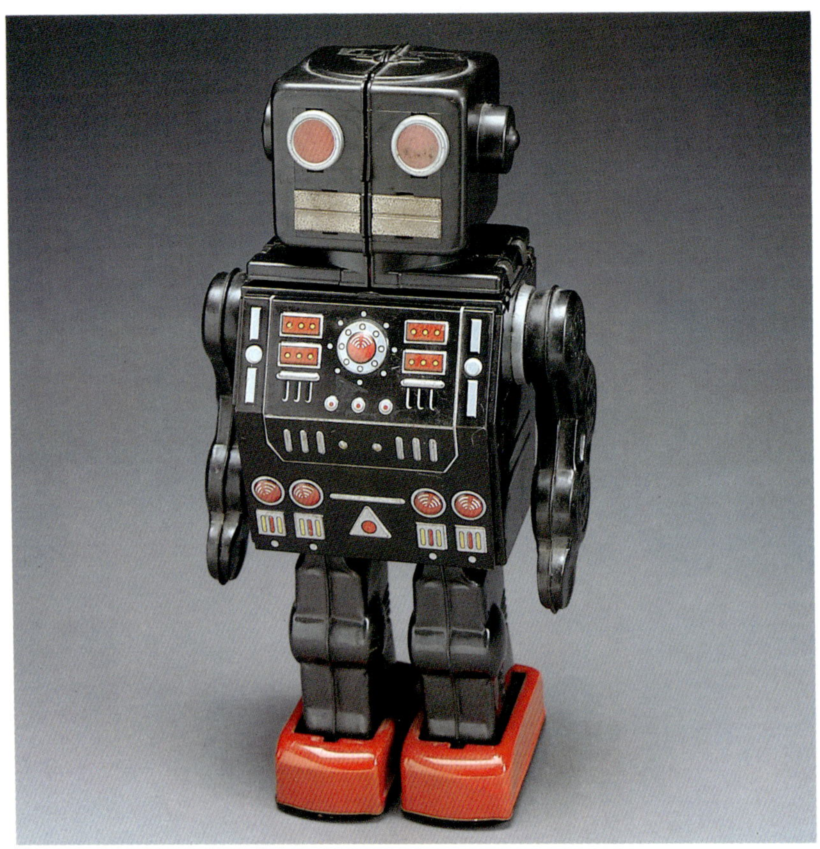

⑨⑦ 1960'S／CHANGE ROBOT／HORIKAWA／98×140×283

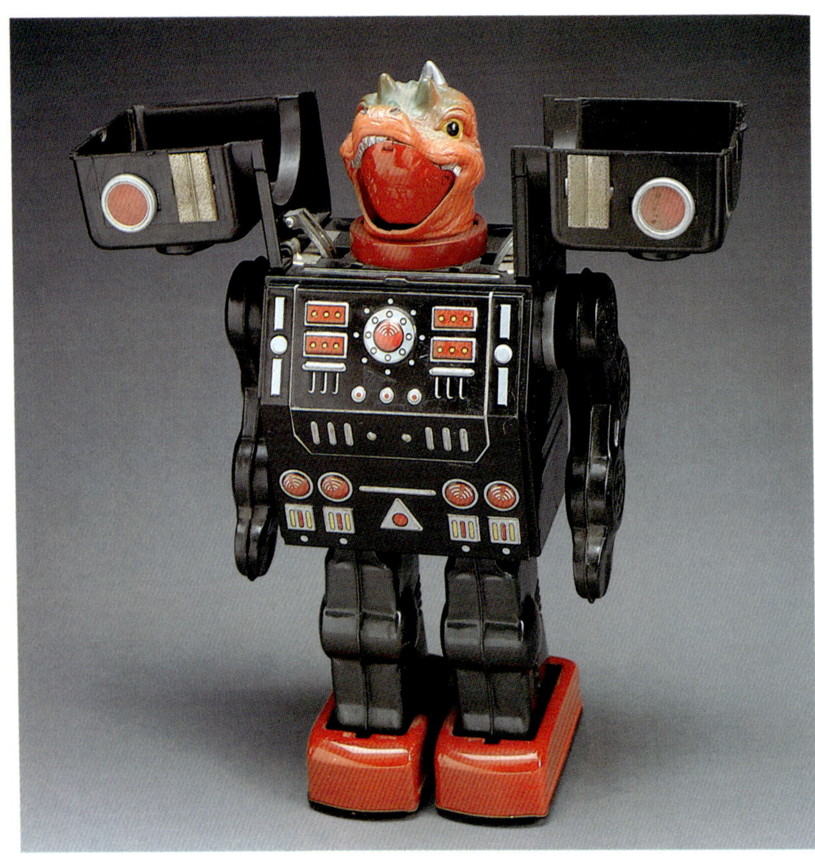

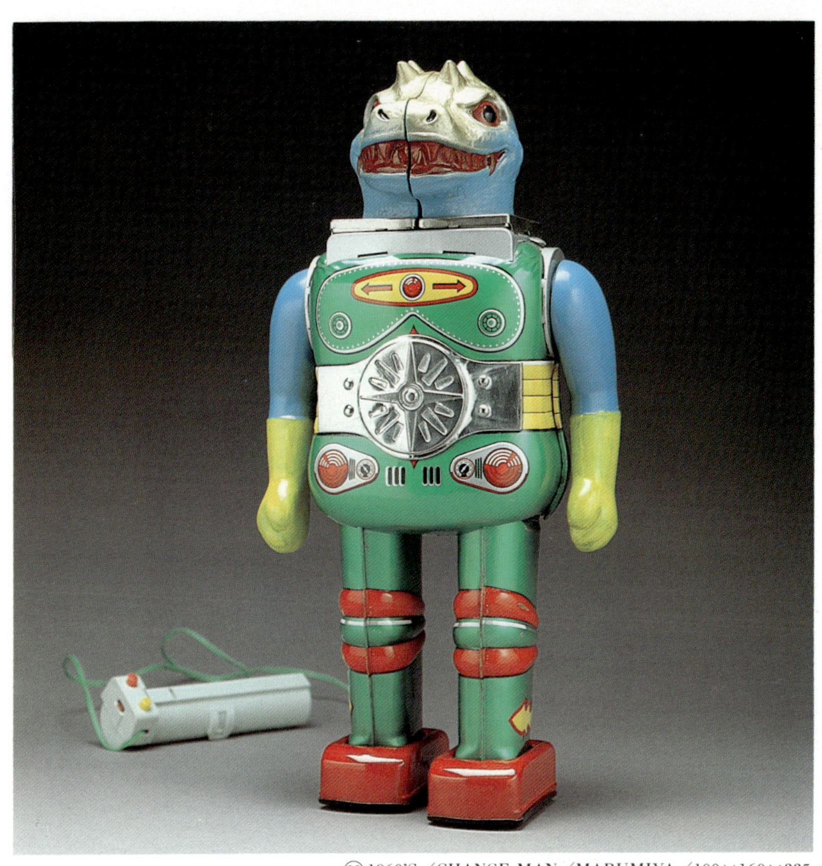

⑱ 1960'S／CHANGE MAN／MARUMIYA／100×160×335

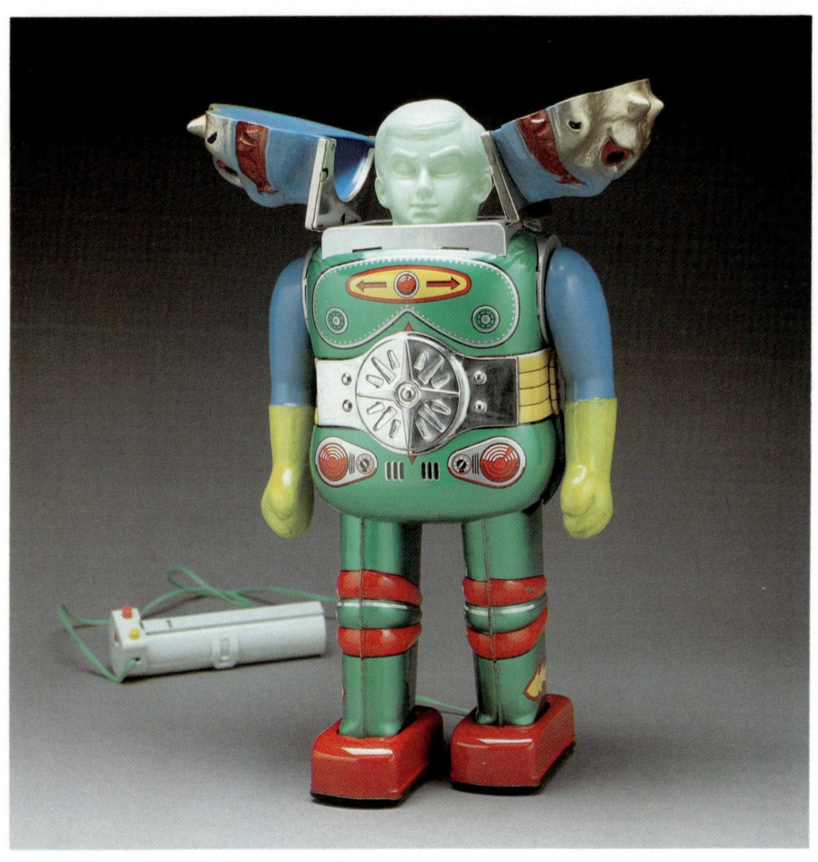

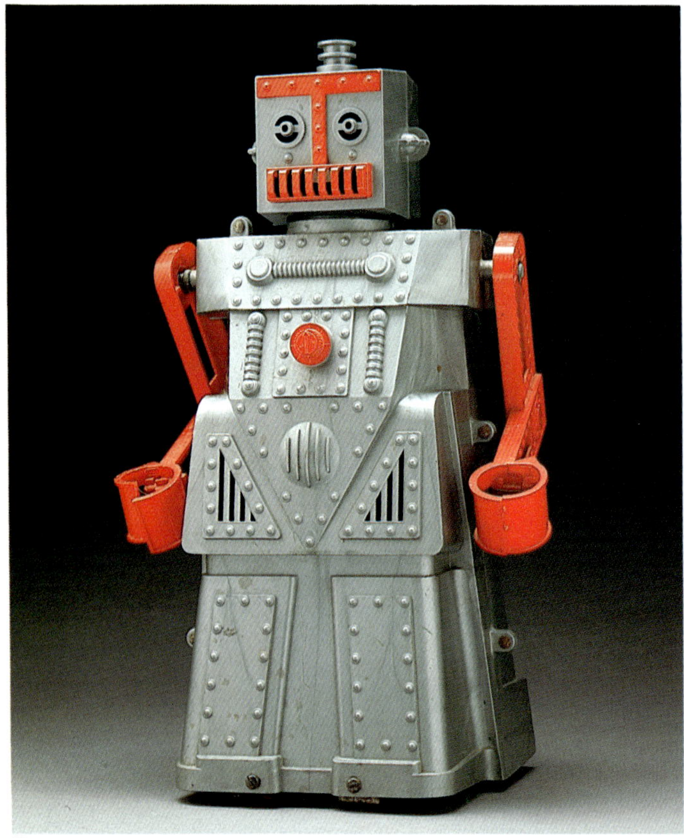

(99) 1950'S／ROBERT ROBOT／UNKNOWN／160×180×345

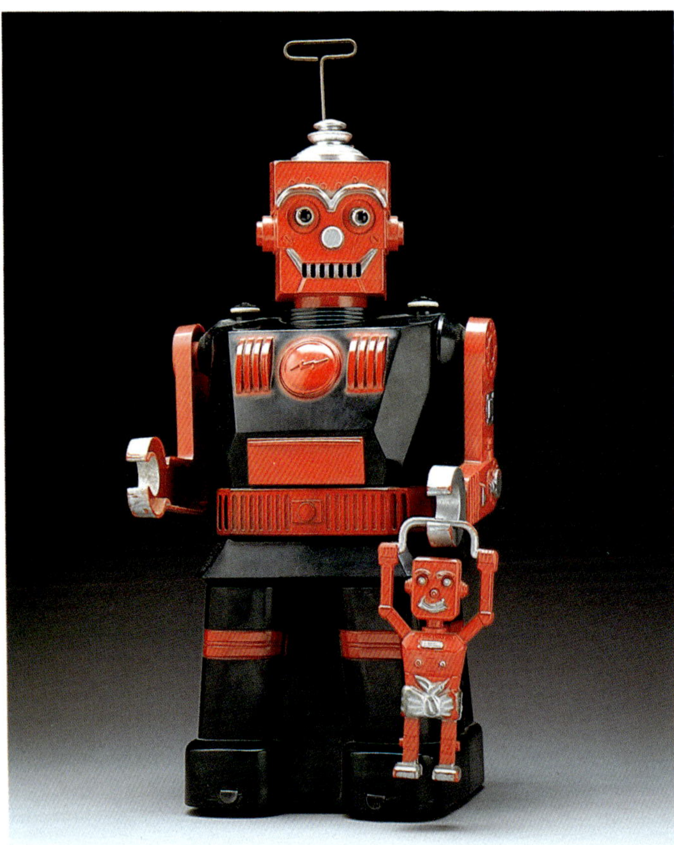

(100) 1950'S／ROBOT AND SON／LOUIS MARX／150×185×365

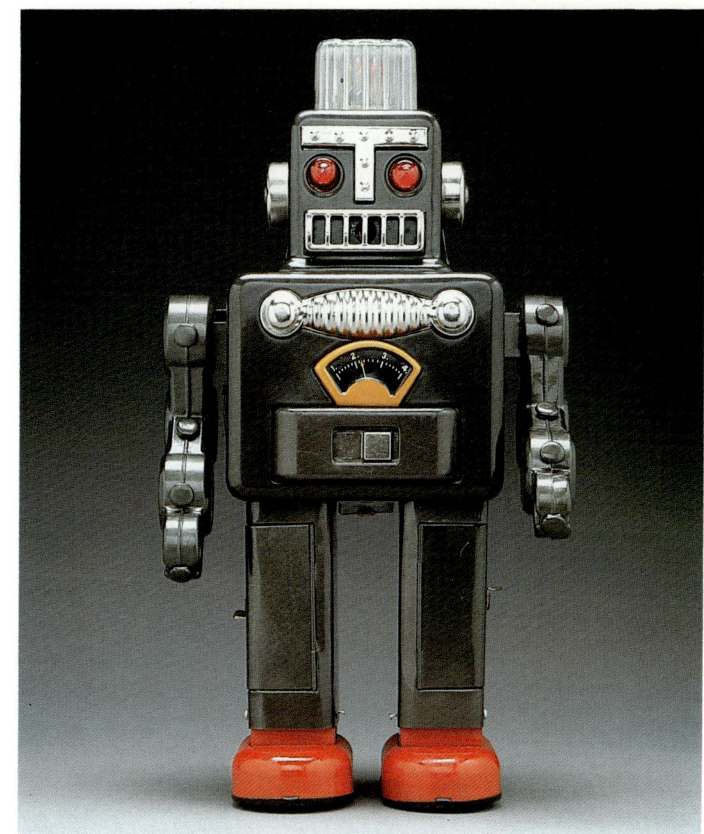

⑩① 1950'S／SMOKING ROBOT／YONEZAWA／105×160×300

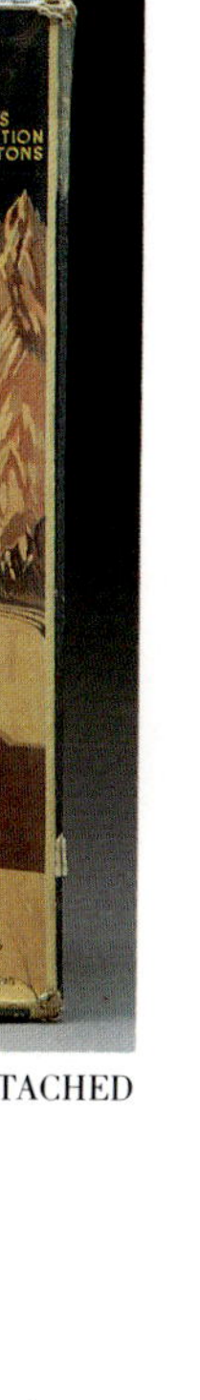

CASE ATTACHED

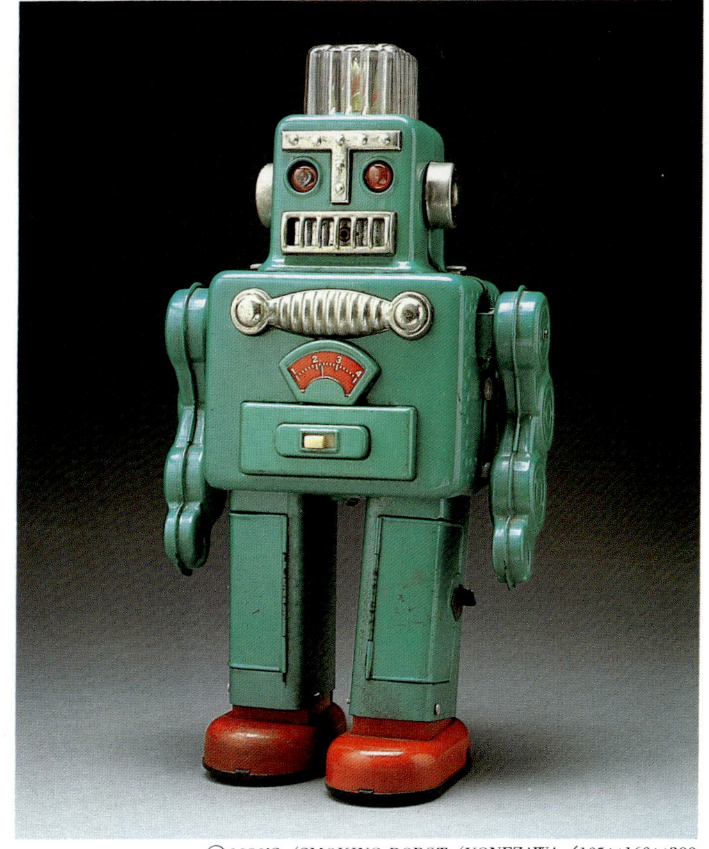

⑩② 1950'S／SMOKING ROBOT／YONEZAWA／105×160×300

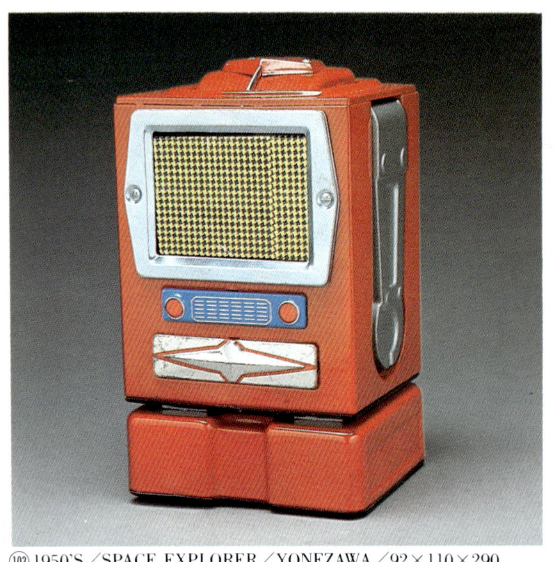

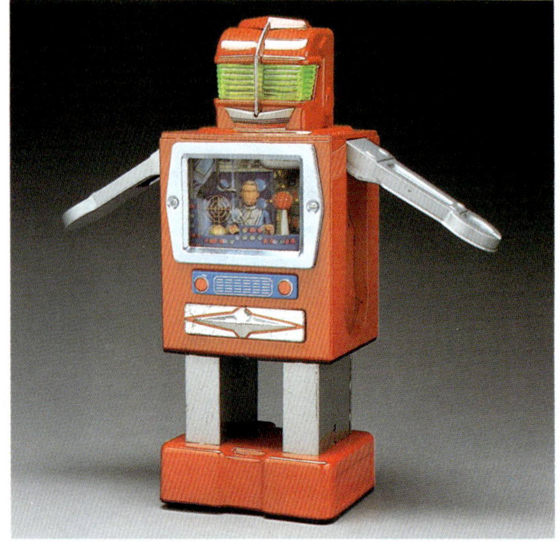

⑩③ 1950'S／SPACE EXPLORER／YONEZAWA／92×110×290

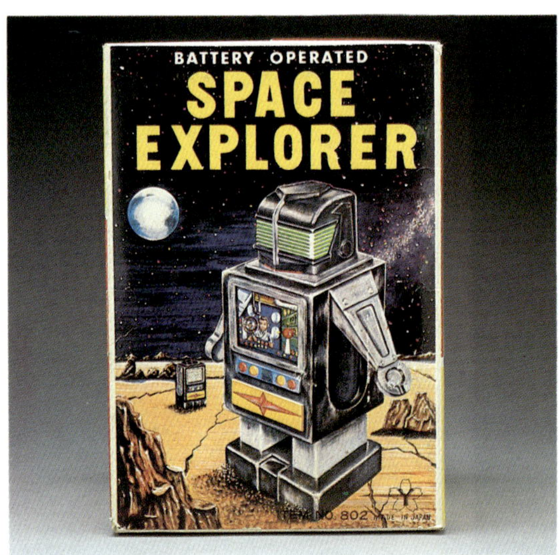

CASE ATTACHED

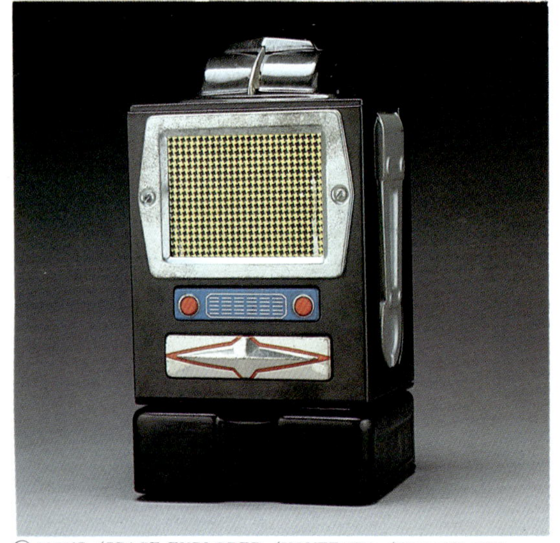

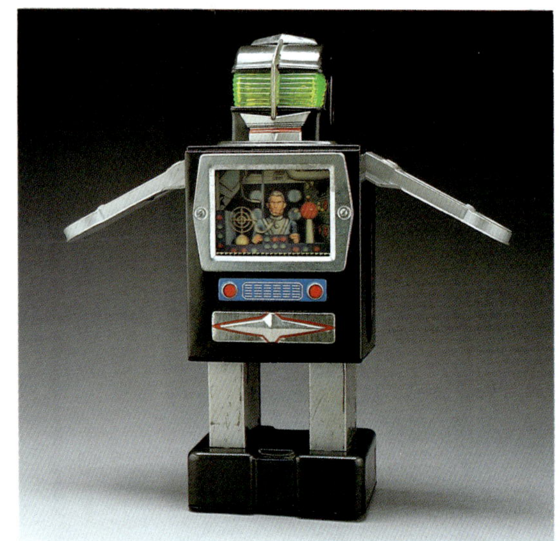

⑩④ 1950'S／SPACE EXPLORER／YONEZAWA／92×110×290

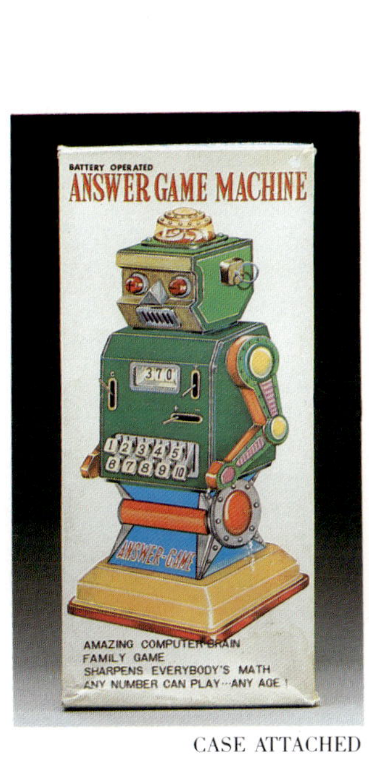

CASE ATTACHED

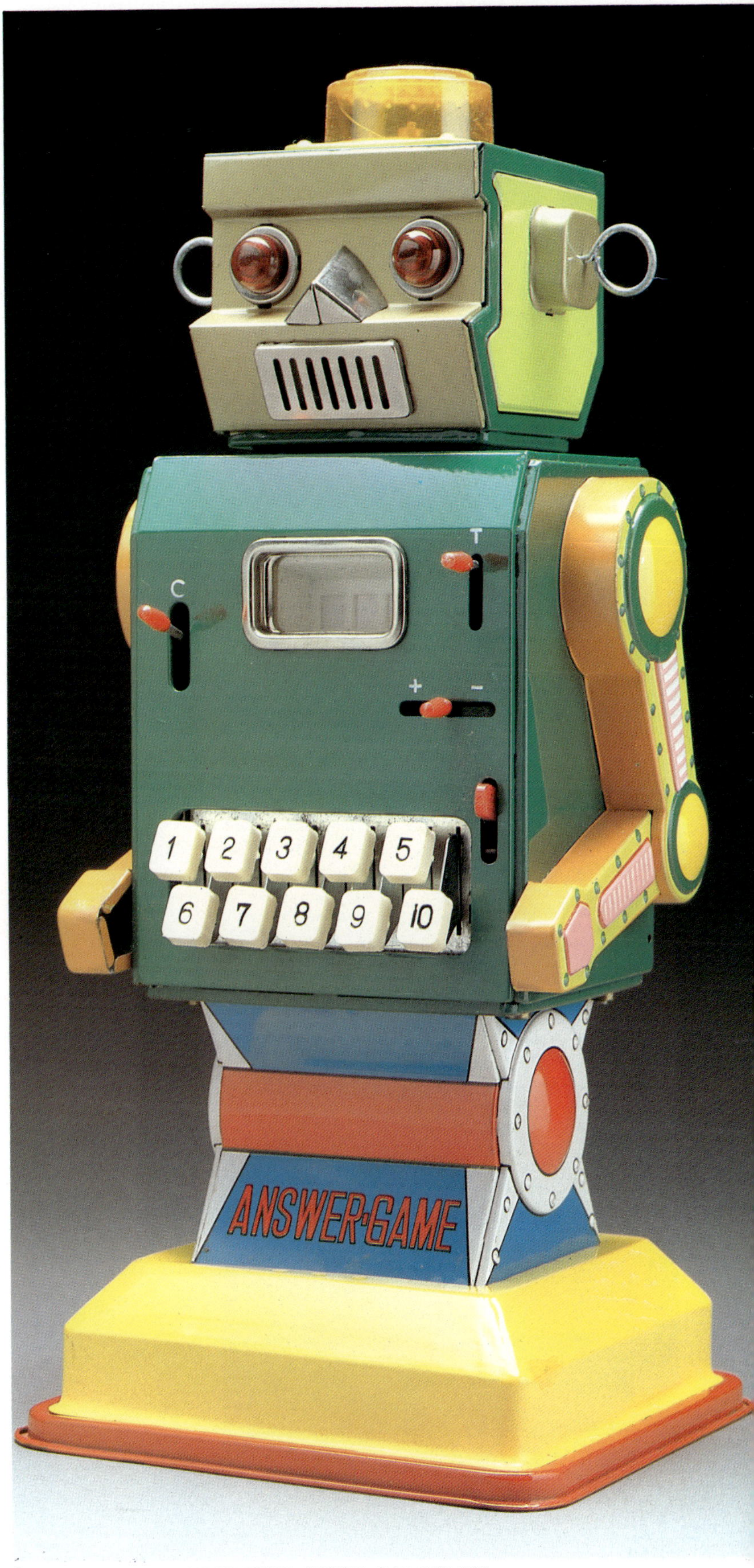

(105) 1960'S／ANSWER GAME MACHINE／ICHIDA／165×165×365

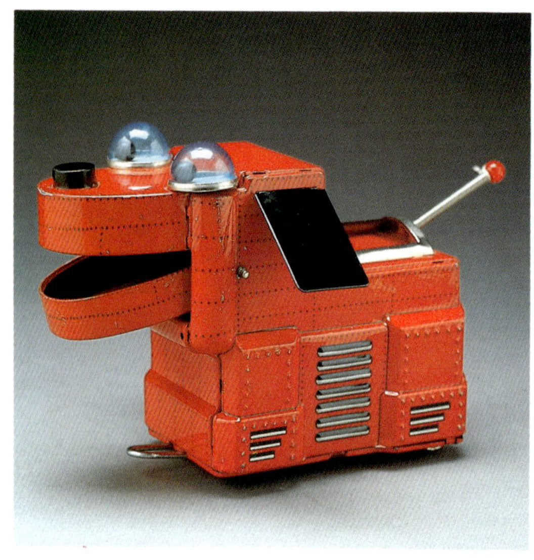

⑯ 1950'S／SPACE DOG／YOSHIYA／185×75×115

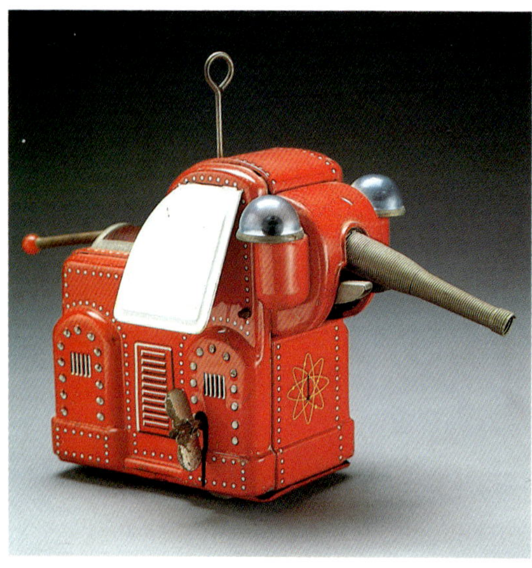

⑰ 1950'S／ELEPHANT ROBOT／YOSHIYA／130×90×120

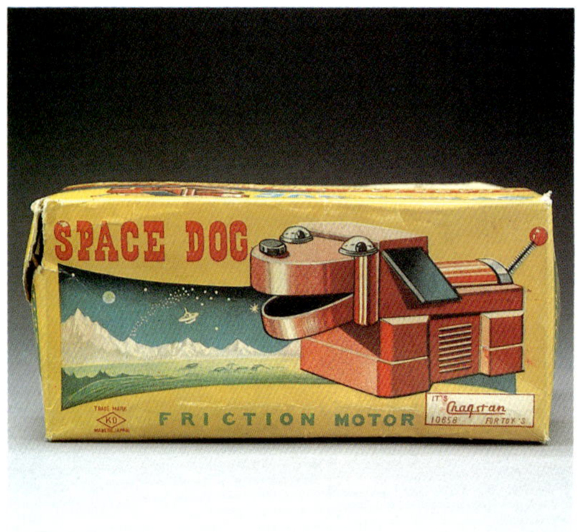

CASE ATTACHED

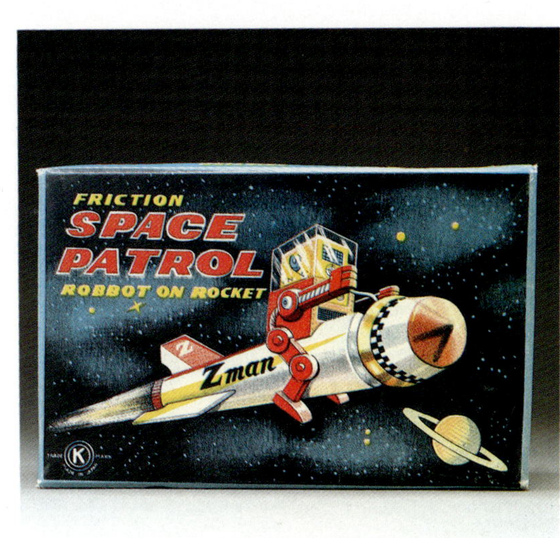

CASE ATTACHED

108 1950'S／SPACE PATROL／OHTA／180×63×110

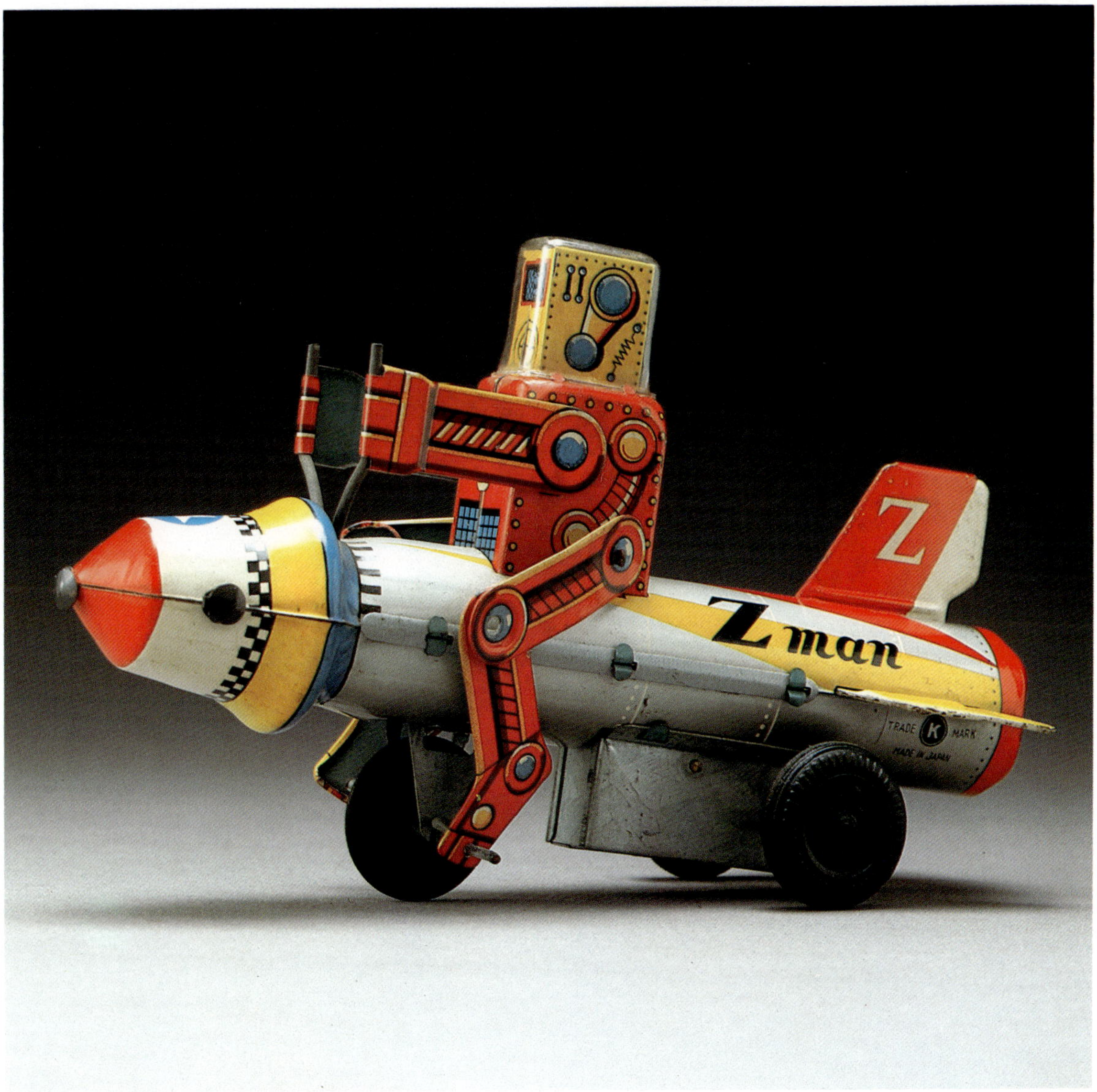

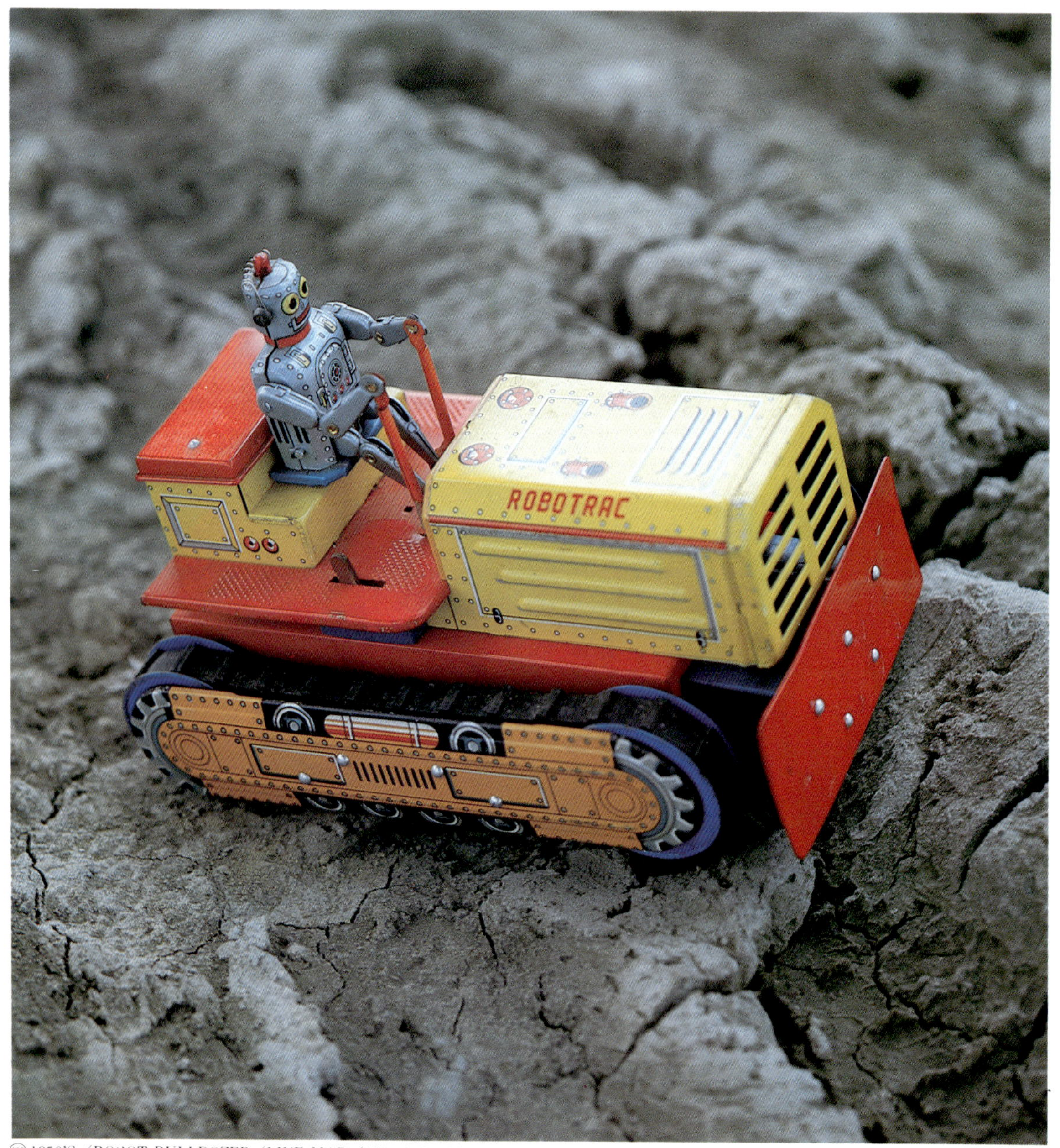

⑩⑨ 1950'S／ROBOT BULLDOZER／LINE MAR／235×145×165

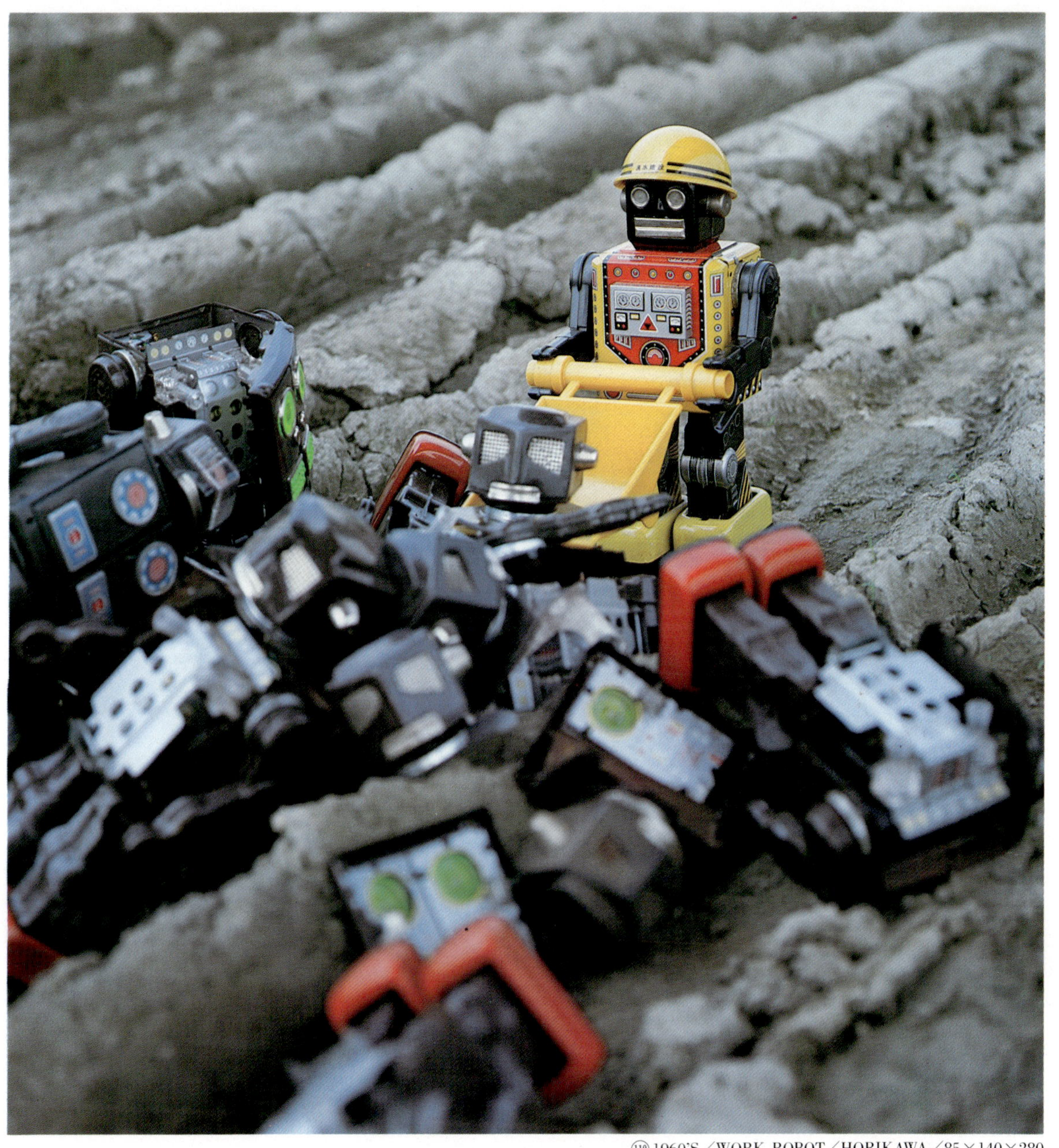

(110) 1960'S／WORK ROBOT／HORIKAWA／85×140×280

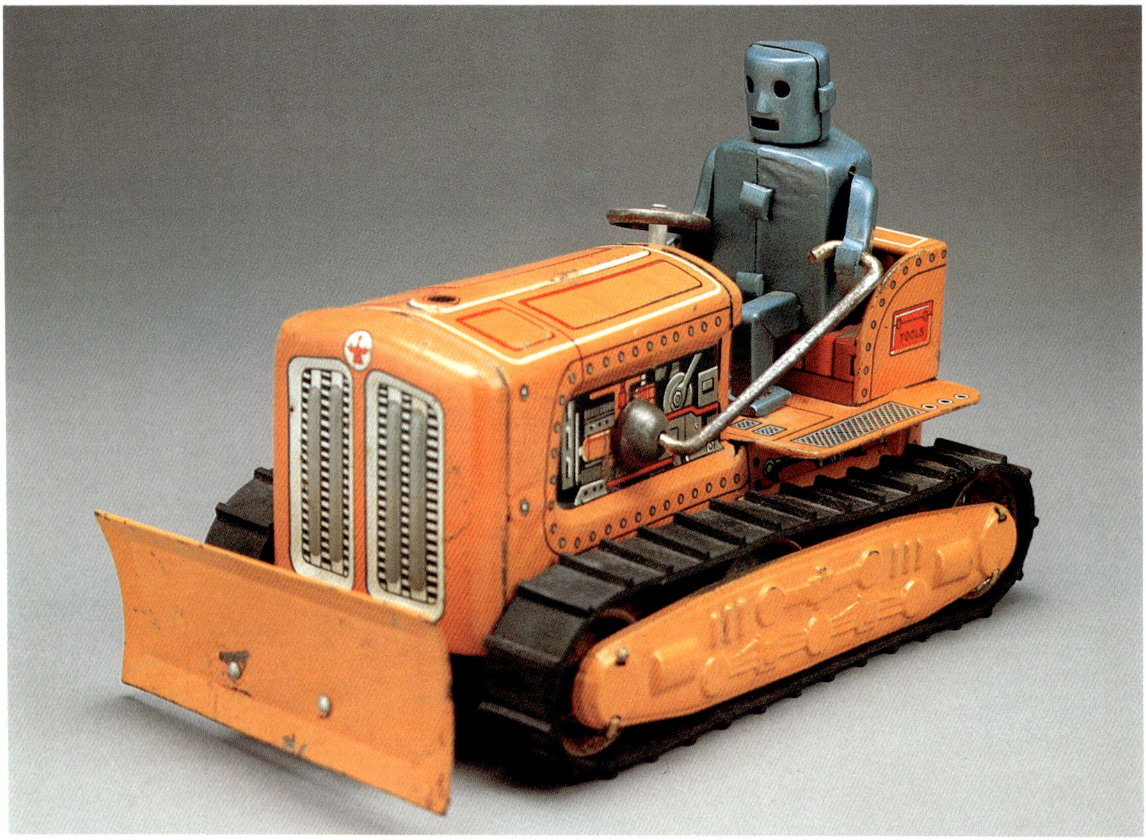

⑪ 1950'S／ROBOT BULLDOZER／YOSHIYA／180×97×120

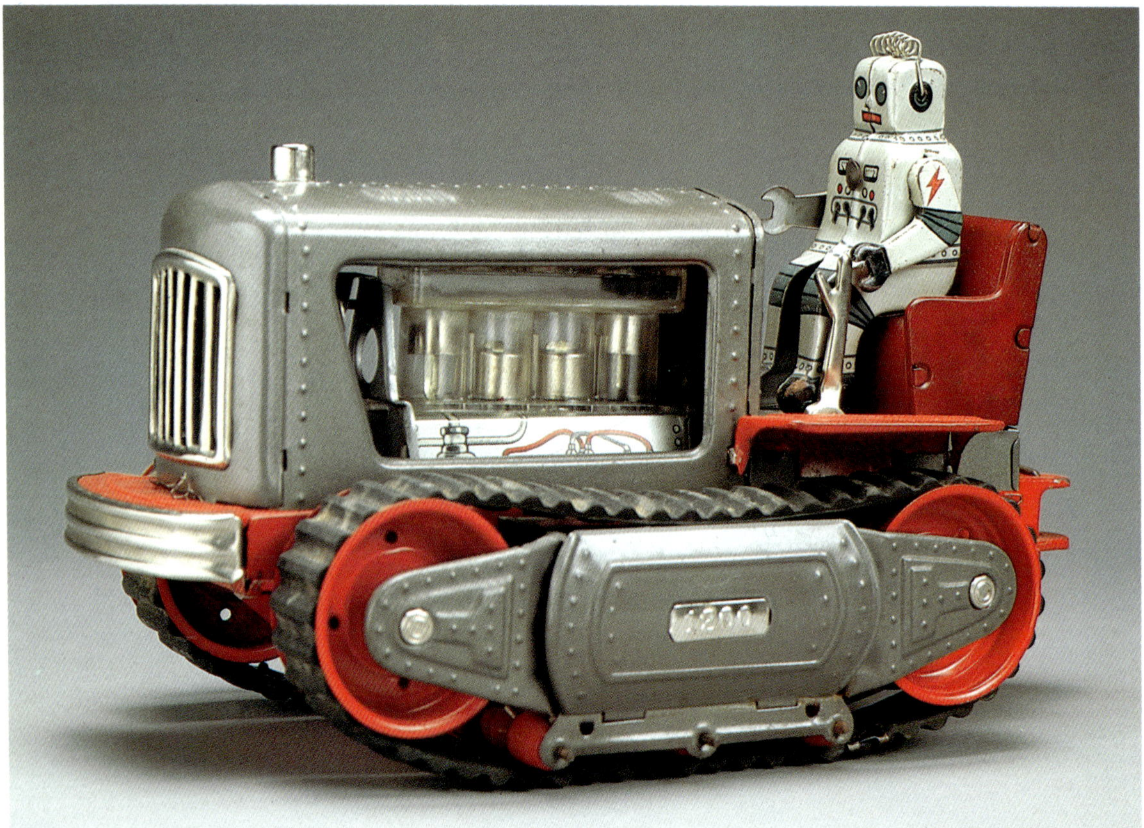

⑫ 1950'S／ROBOT TRACTOR／SHOWA／250×125×150

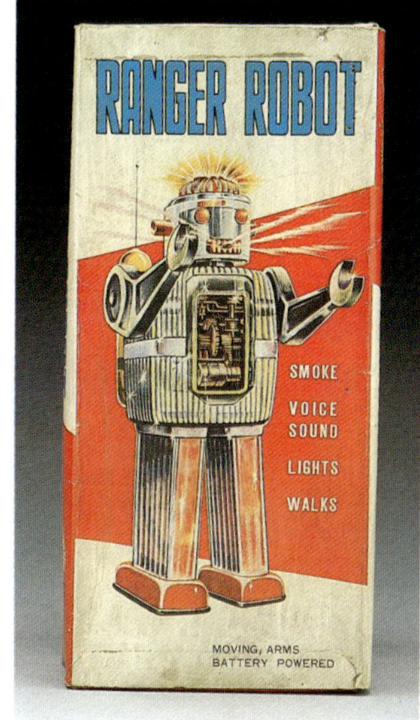

CASE ATTACHED

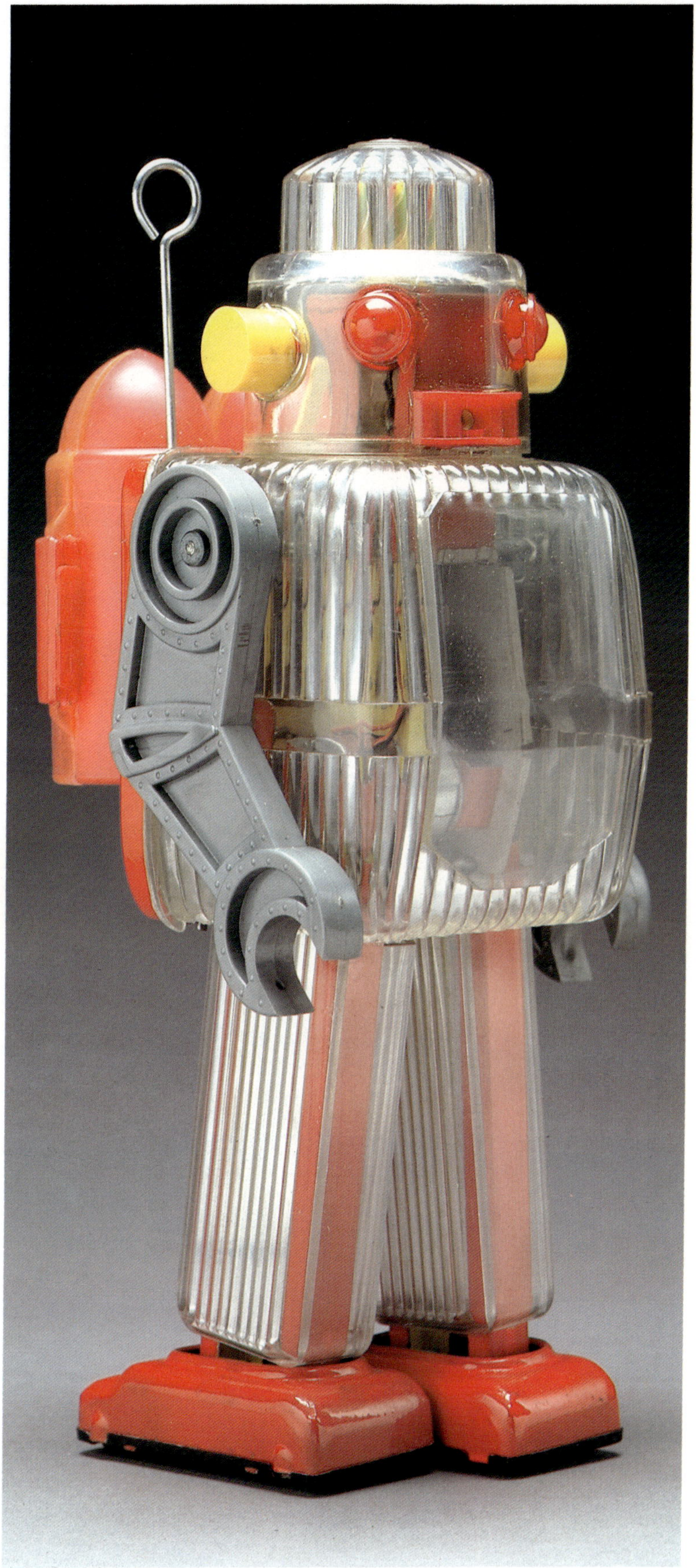

(113) 1950'S／RANGER ROBOT／DAIYA／115×110×265

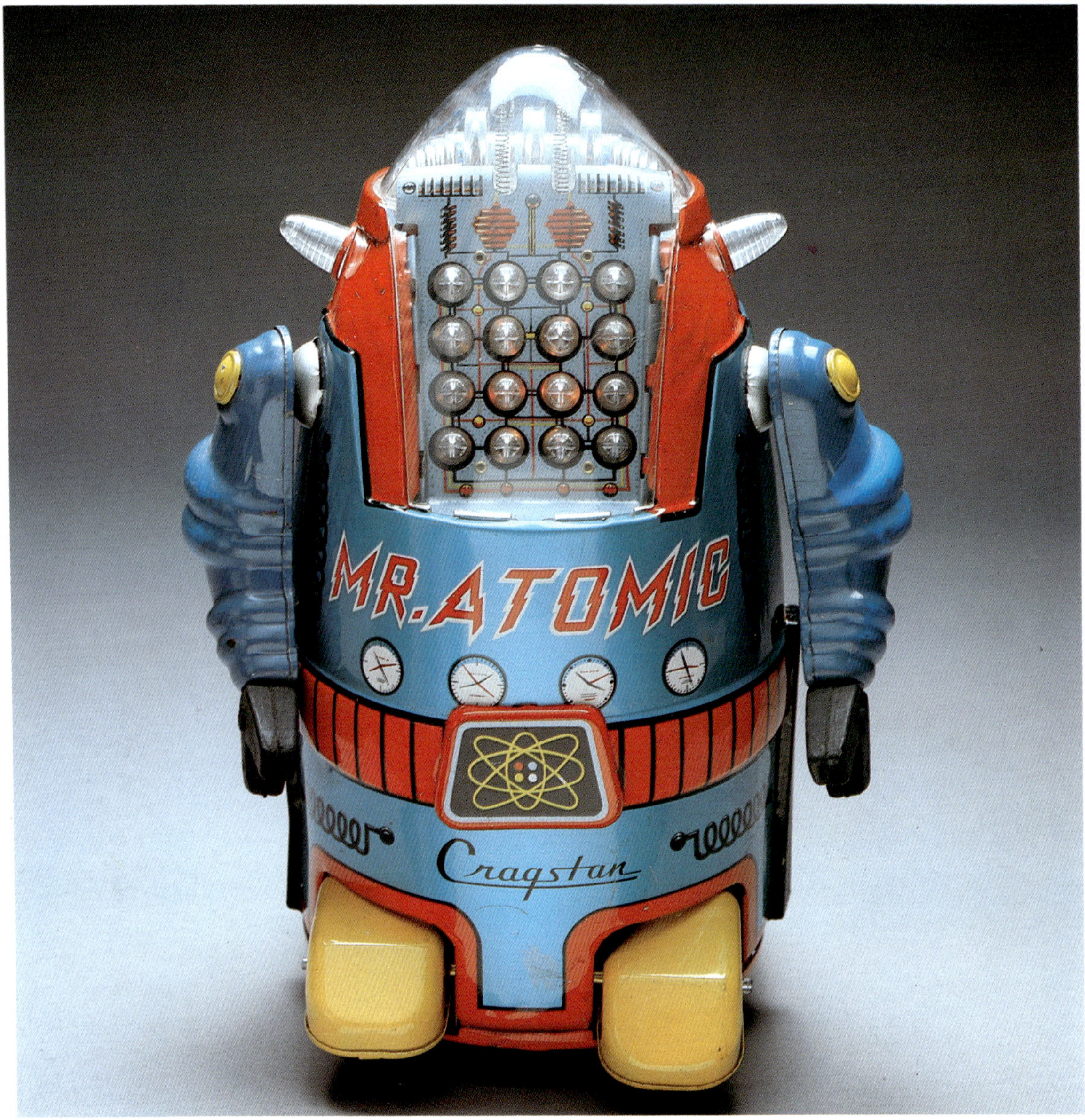

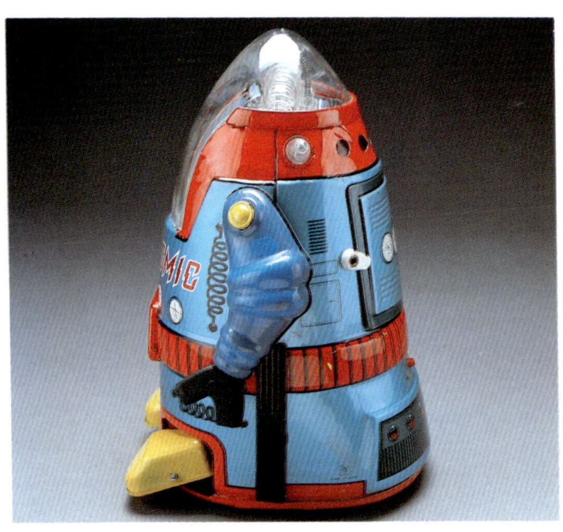

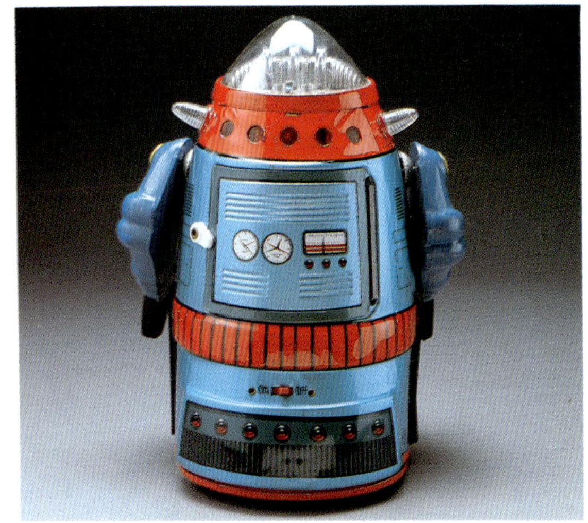

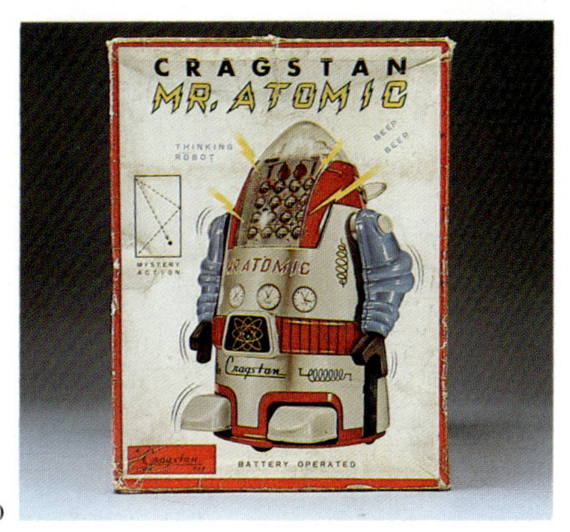

CASE ATTACHED

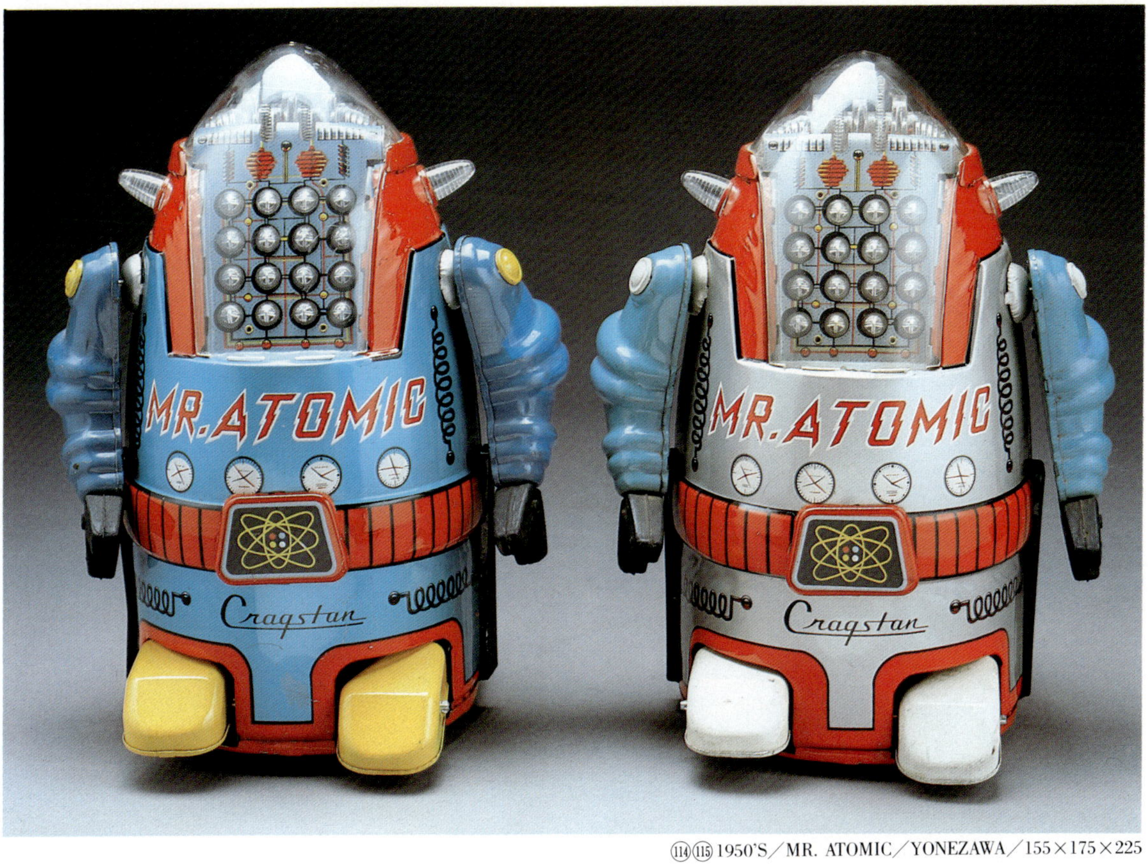

114 115 1950'S／MR. ATOMIC／YONEZAWA／155×175×225

CASE ATTACHED

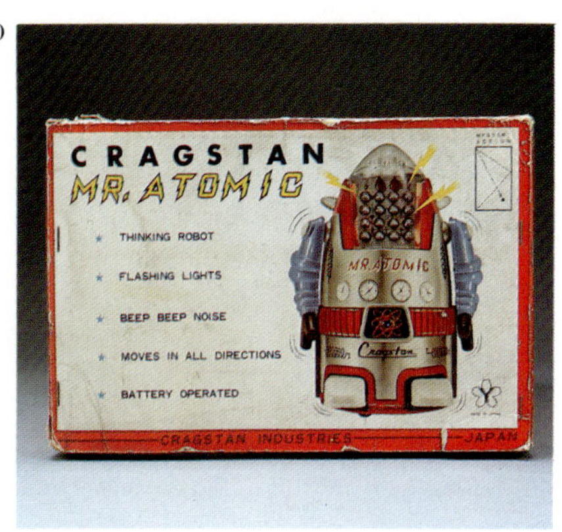

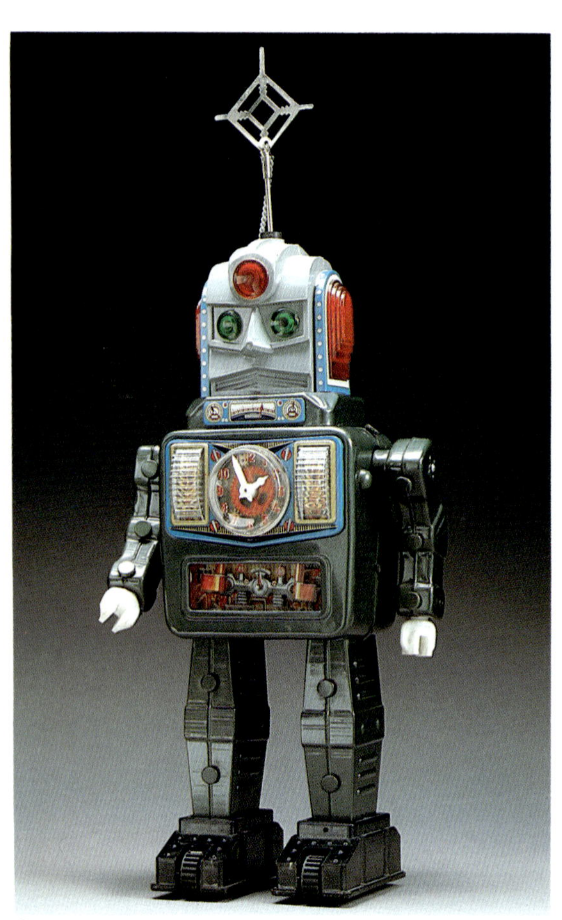

⑯ 1960'S／MOON EXPLORER／BANDAI／107×165×452

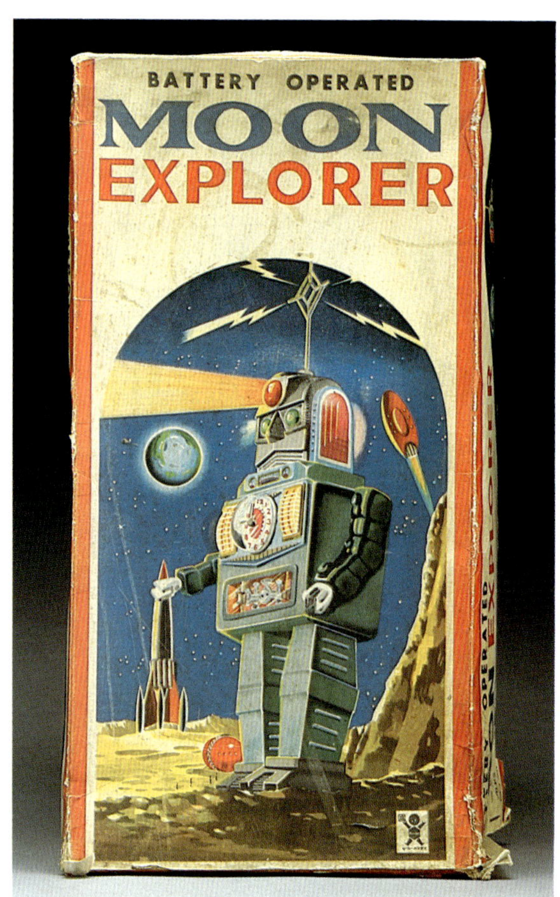

CASE ATTACHED

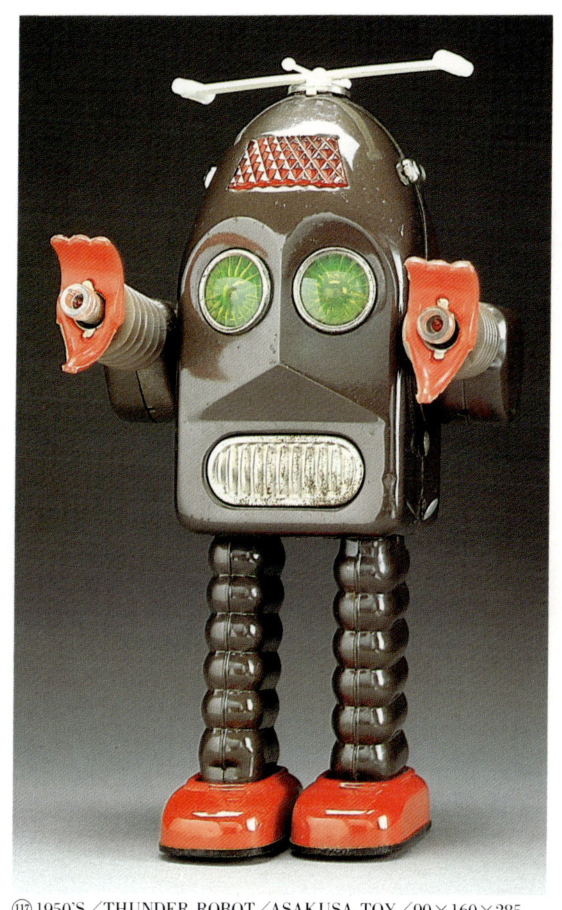

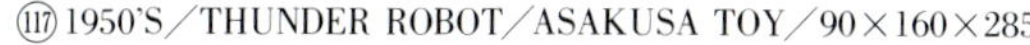

(117) 1950'S／THUNDER ROBOT／ASAKUSA TOY／90×160×285

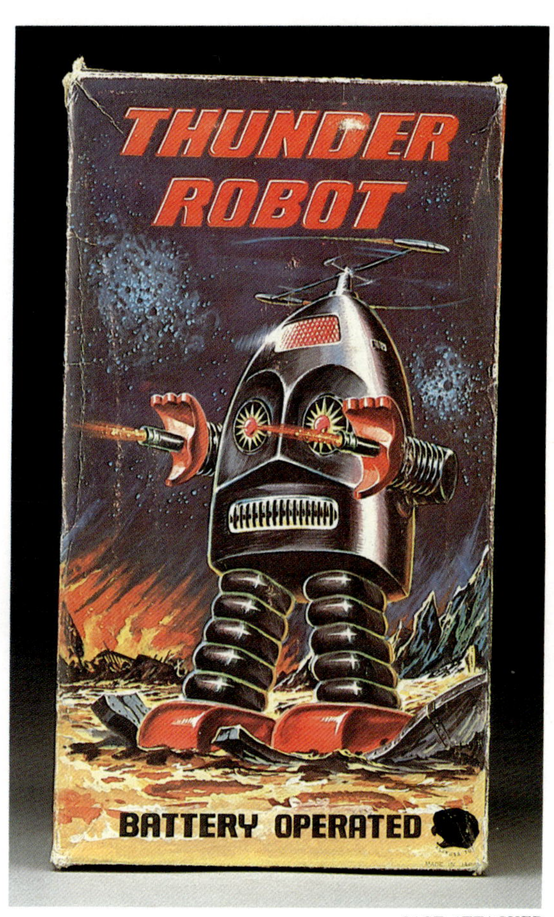

CASE ATTACHED

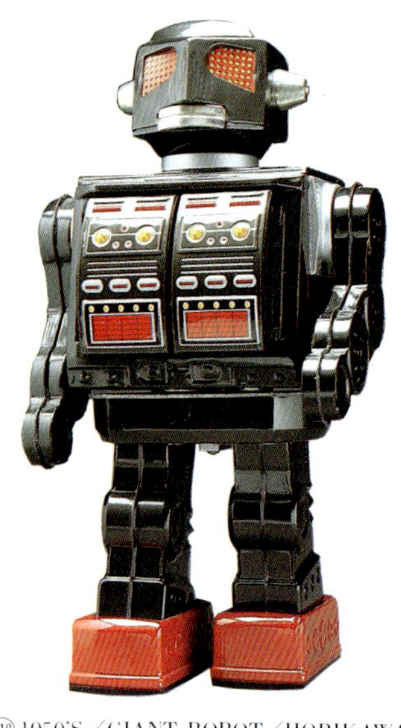

(118) 1950'S／GIANT ROBOT／HORIKAWA／148×220×400

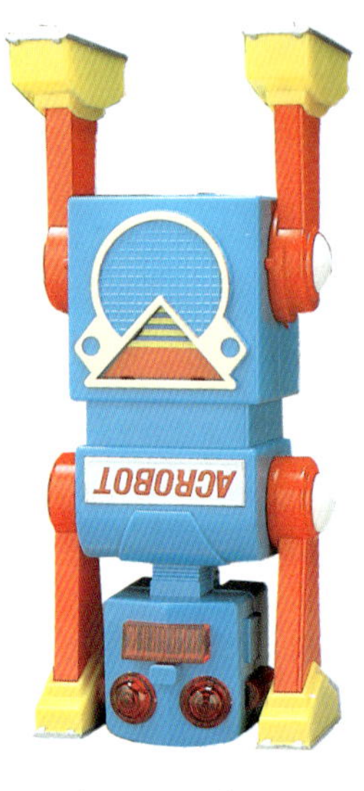

(119) 1960'S／ACROBOT／YONEZAWA／70×100×245

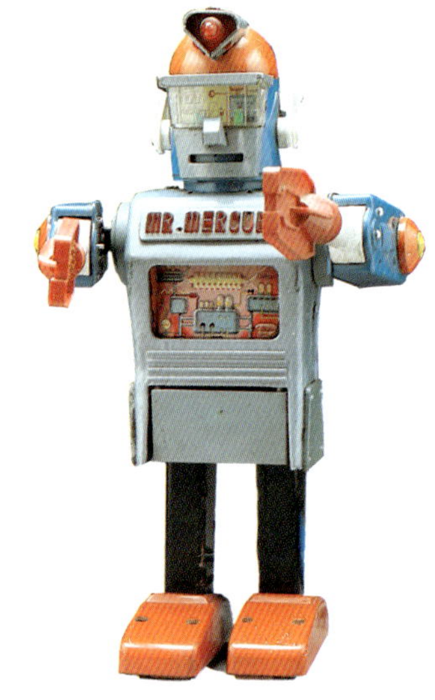

(120) 1950'S／MR. MERCURY／YONEZAWA／120×210×330

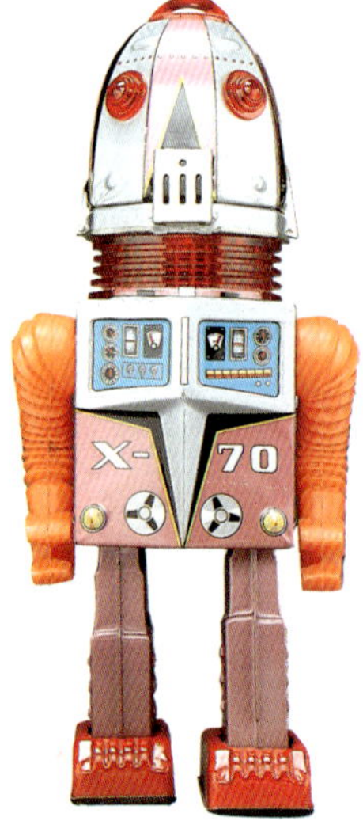

(121) 1960'S／X-70 ROBOT／UNKNOWN／90×130×305

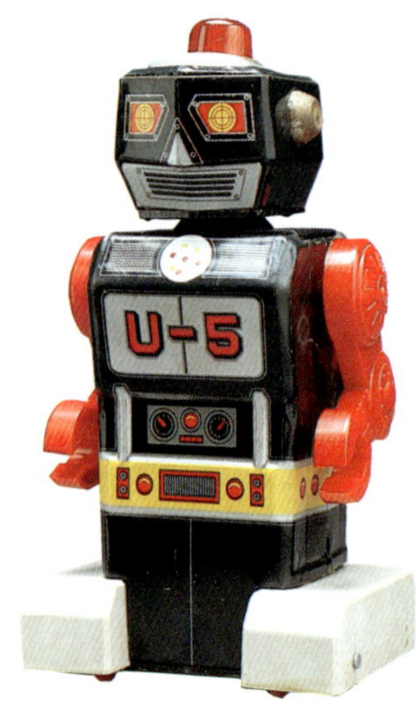

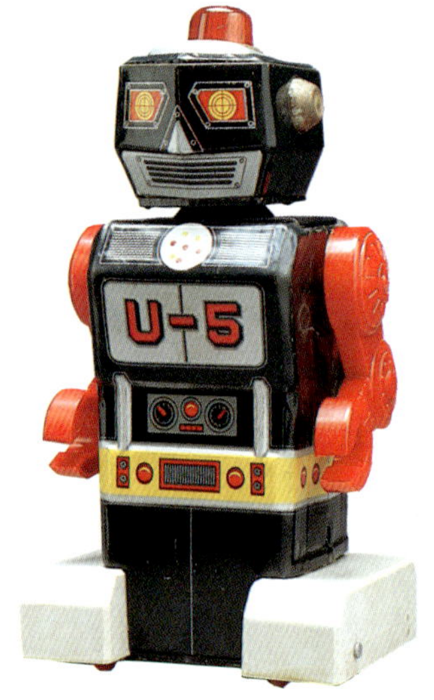

(122) 1960'S／U-5 ROBOT／DAIYA／83×105×193

(123) 1960'S／R ROBOT／BANDAI／155×180×340

(124) 1960'S／K-ROBO／CRAGSTAN／100×105×195

(125) 1960'S／RT-8 ROBOT／NOMURA／95×73×120

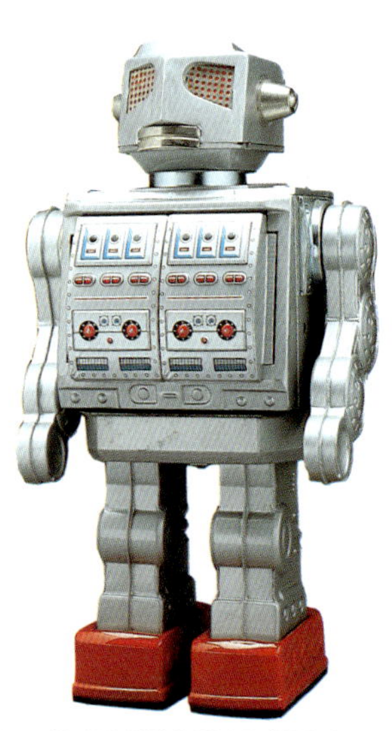

(126) 1950'S／GIANT ROBOT／HORIKAWA／148×220×400

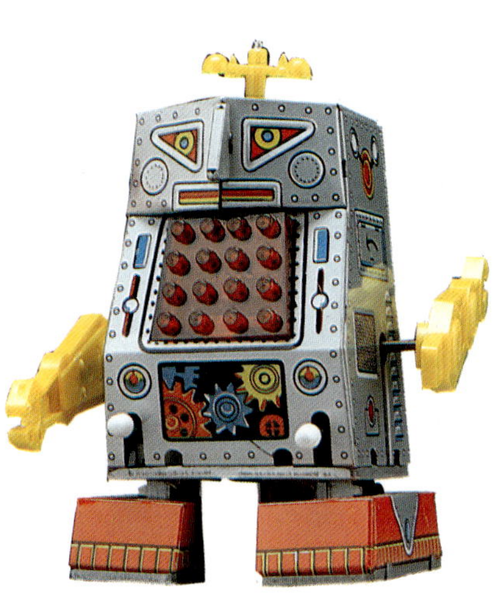

⑫⑦ 1960'S／ROBOT／UNKNOWN／80×95×135

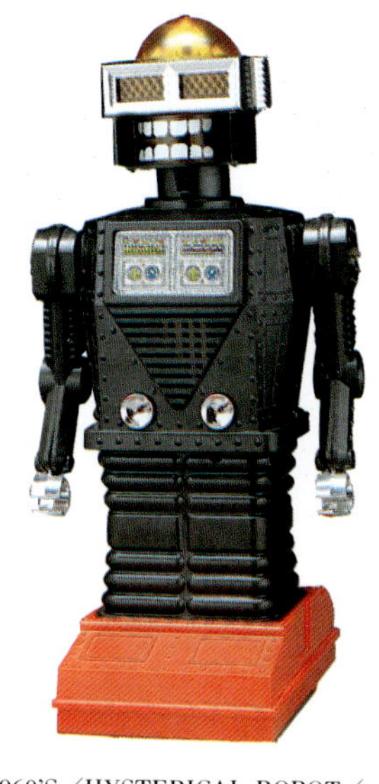

⑫⑧ 1960'S／HYSTERICAL ROBOT／UNKNOWN／165×160×340

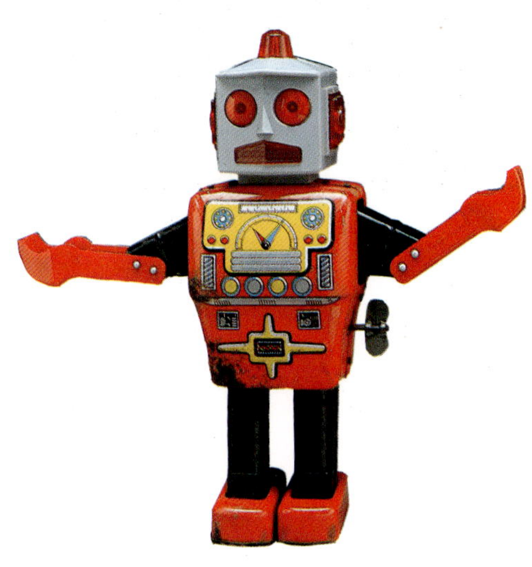

⑫⑨ 1960'S／ROBOT／YONEZAWA／70×150×260

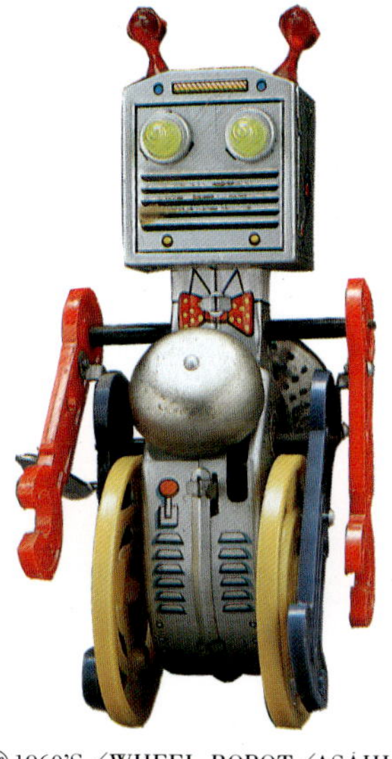

⑬⓪ 1960'S／WHEEL ROBOT／ASAHI／120×95×170

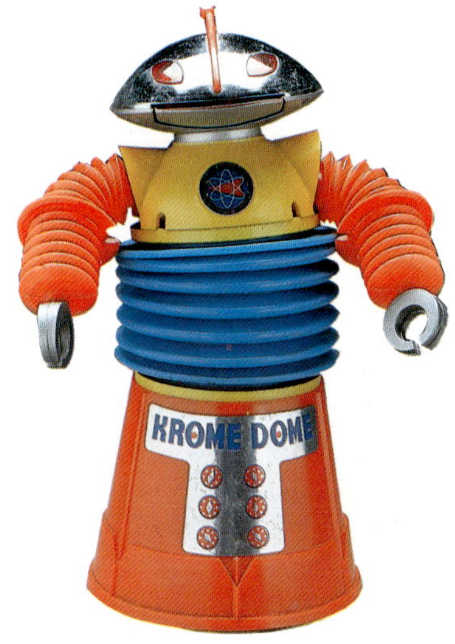

⑬① 1960'S／KROME DOME／YONEZAWA／130×130×260

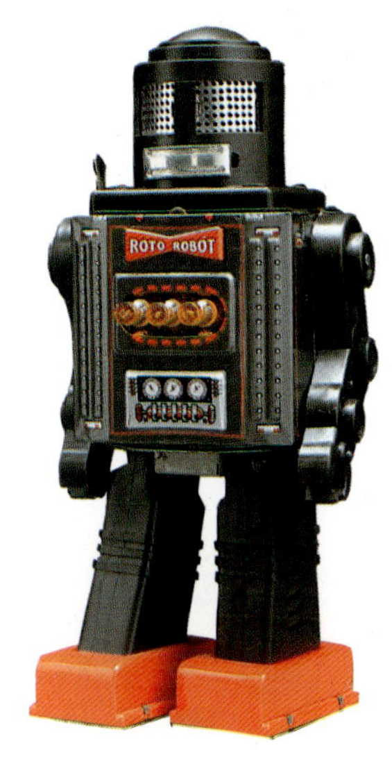

⑬② 1960'S／ROTO ROBOT／HORIKAWA／73×105×220

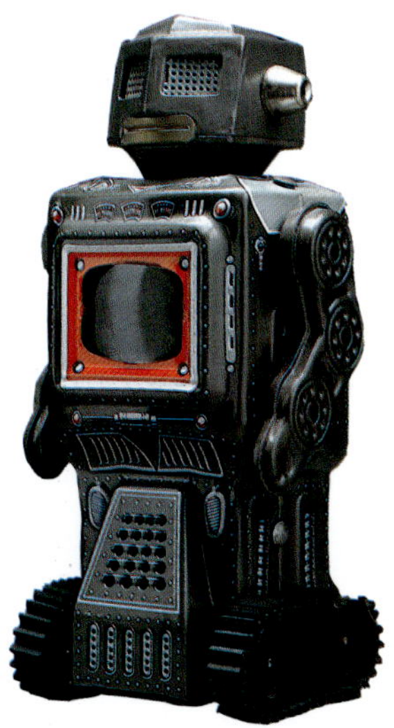

⑬③ 1960'S／TANK ROBOT／HORIKAWA／100×115×240

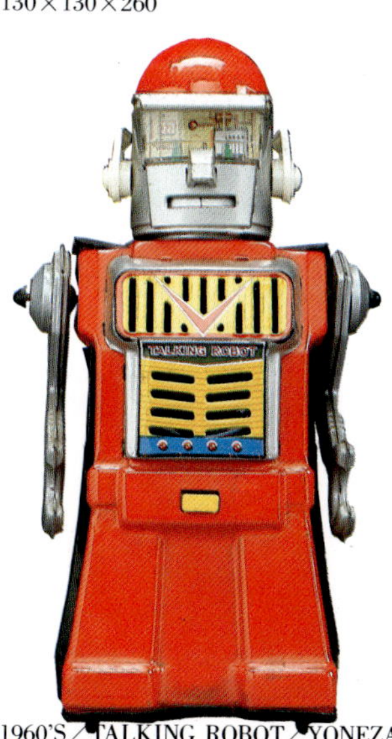

⑬④ 1960'S／TALKING ROBOT／YONEZAWA／112×150×275

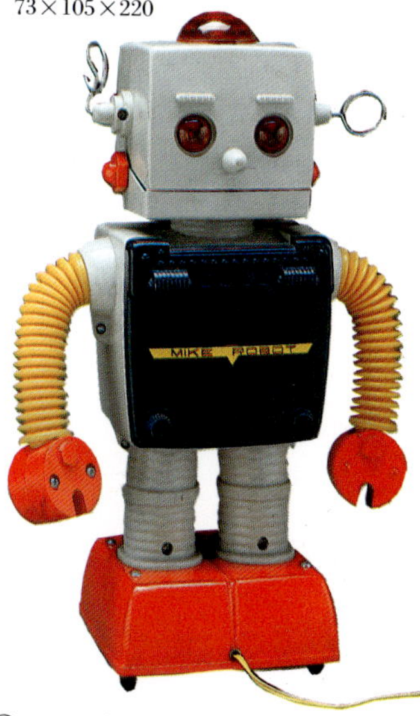

⑬⑤ 1960'S／MIKE ROBOT／TOMY／110×190×305

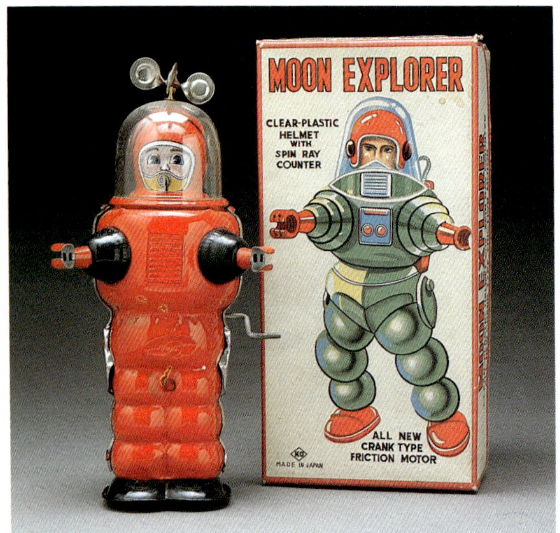

(136) 1950'S／MOON EXPLORER AND CASE／YOSHIYA／57×90×175

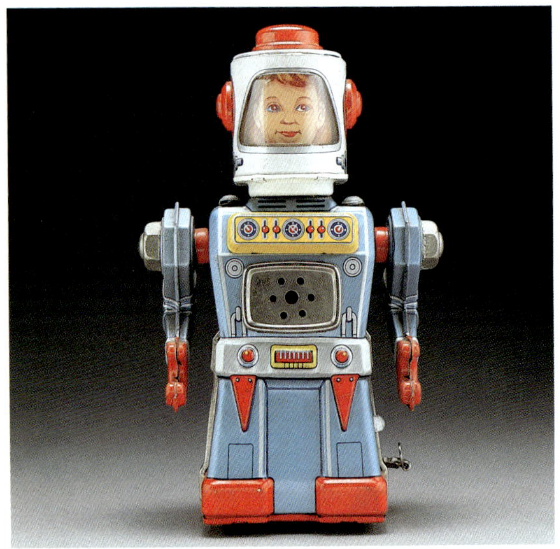

(137) 1950'S／CHIME TROOPER／AOSHIN／90×150×237

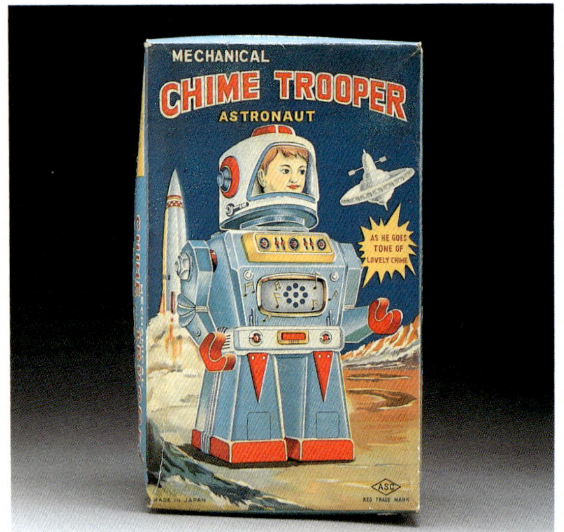

CASE ATTACHED

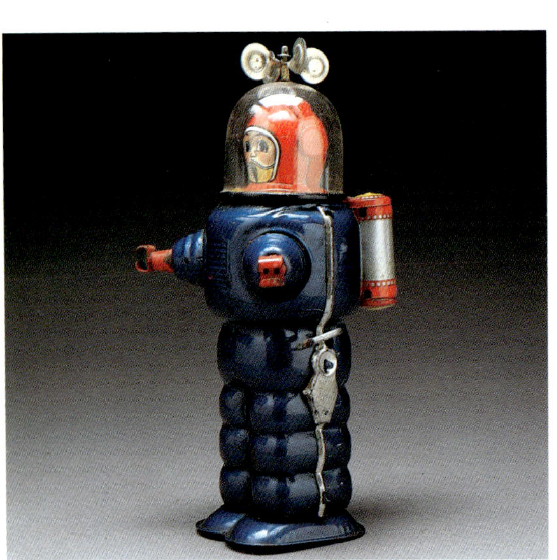

(138) 1950'S／MOON EXPLORER／YOSHIYA／57×90×175

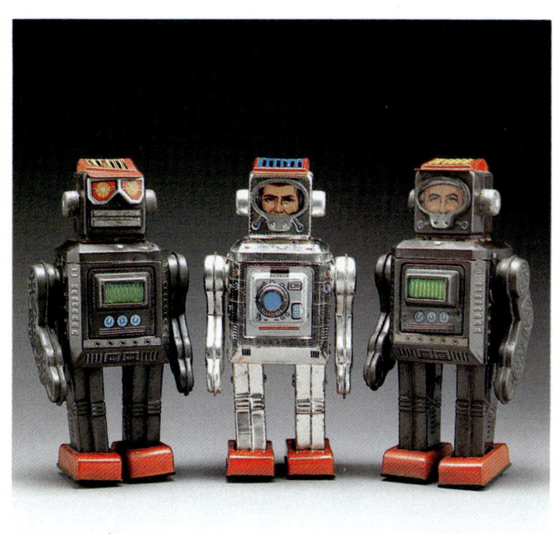

⑬⑭⑭ 1960'S／ROBOT／UNKNOWN／82×105×220

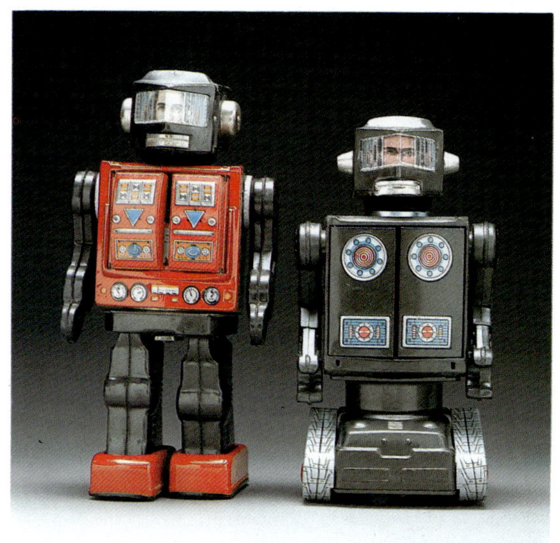

⑭⑭ 1960'S／SPACE MAN, SPACE COMMANDER／HORIKAWA／95×140×280, 120×140×260

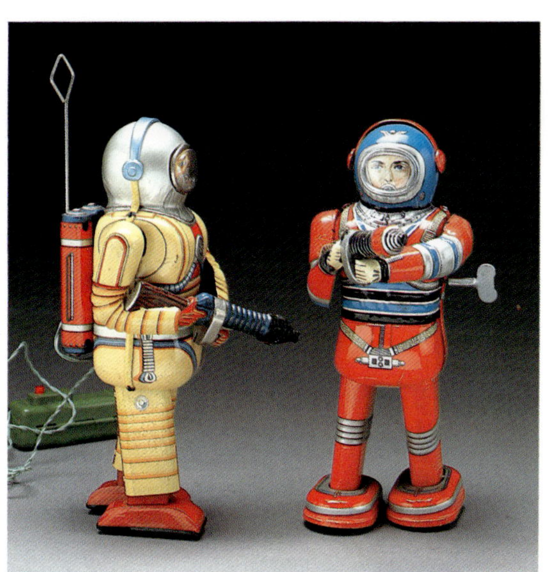

⑭⑭ 1950'S／ASTRONAUT／NOMURA, DAIYA／75×95×230

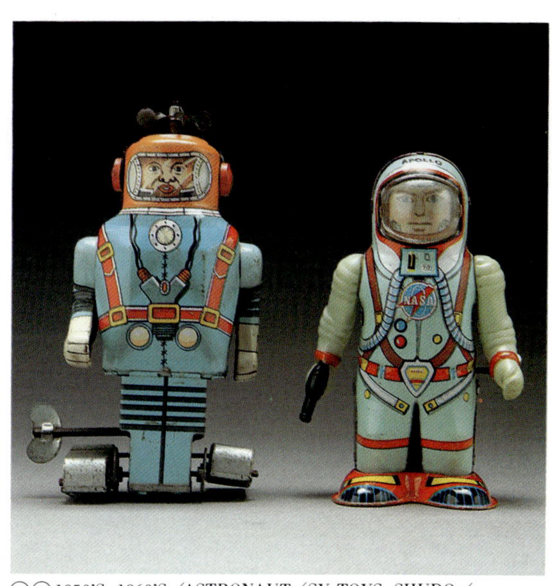

⑭⑭ 1950'S, 1960'S／ASTRONAUT／SY TOYS, SHUDO／50×90×145, 45×85×128

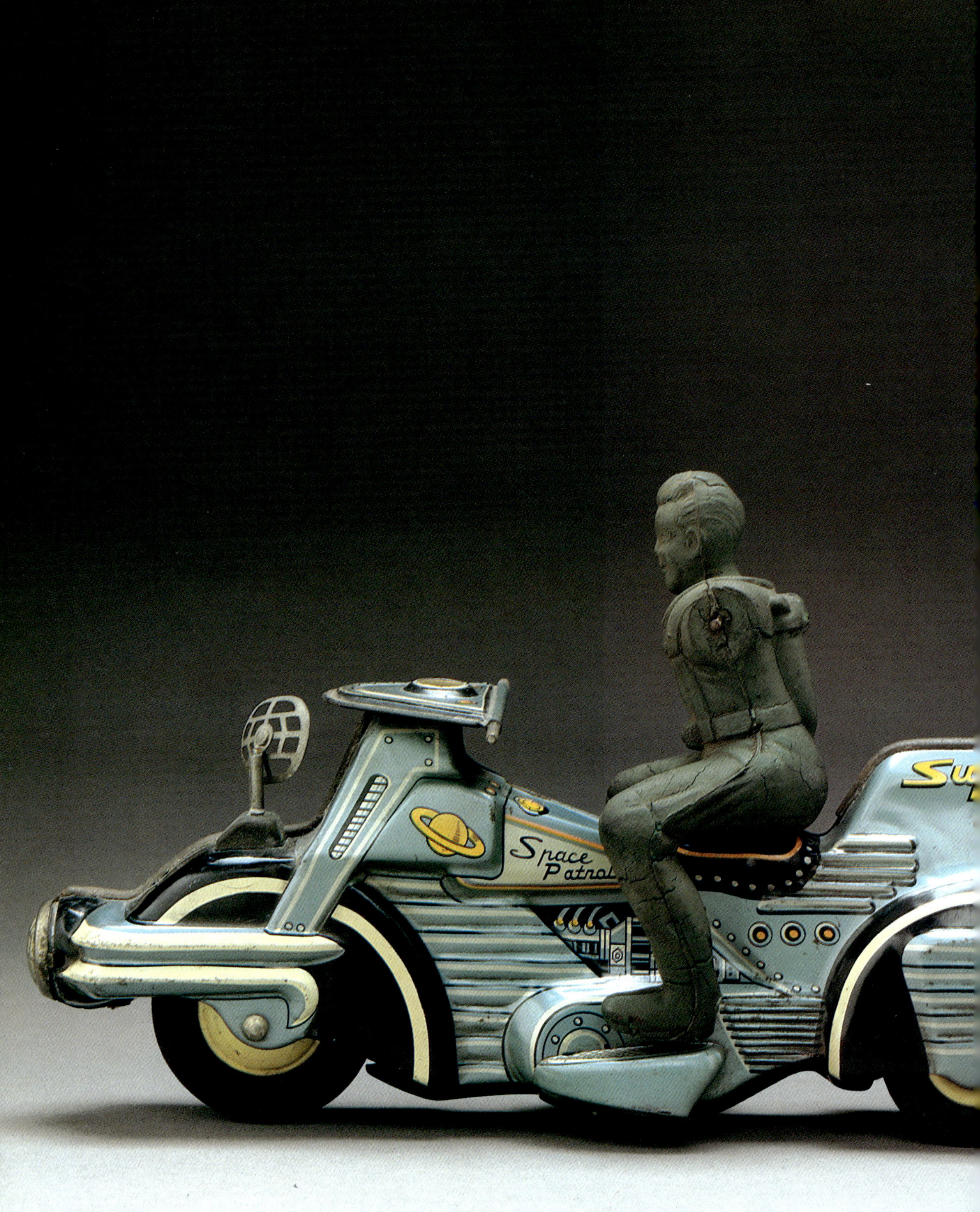
Space Patrol

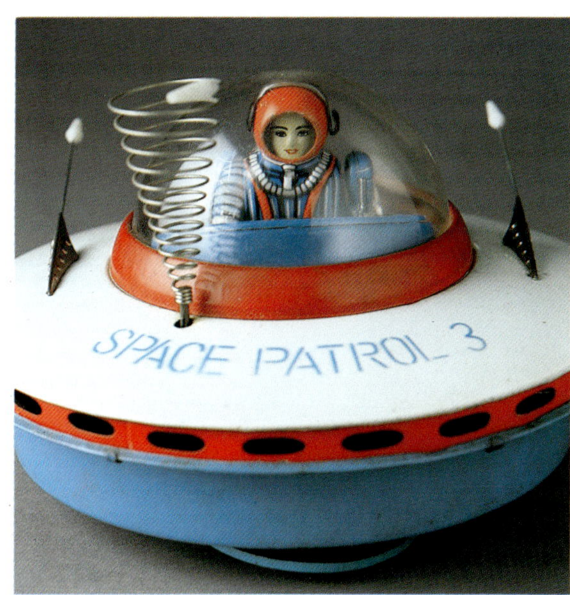

⑭⑨ 1960'S／SPACE PATROL／YOSHIYA／190×190×120

⑮⓪ 1960'S／ SPACE PATROL／YOSHIYA／190×190×120

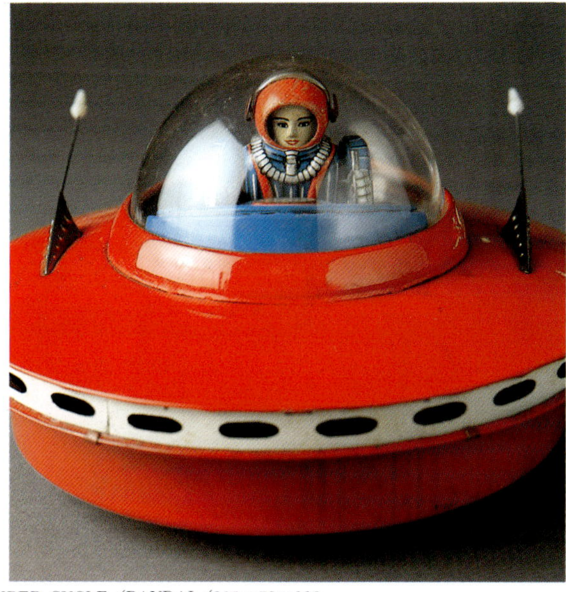

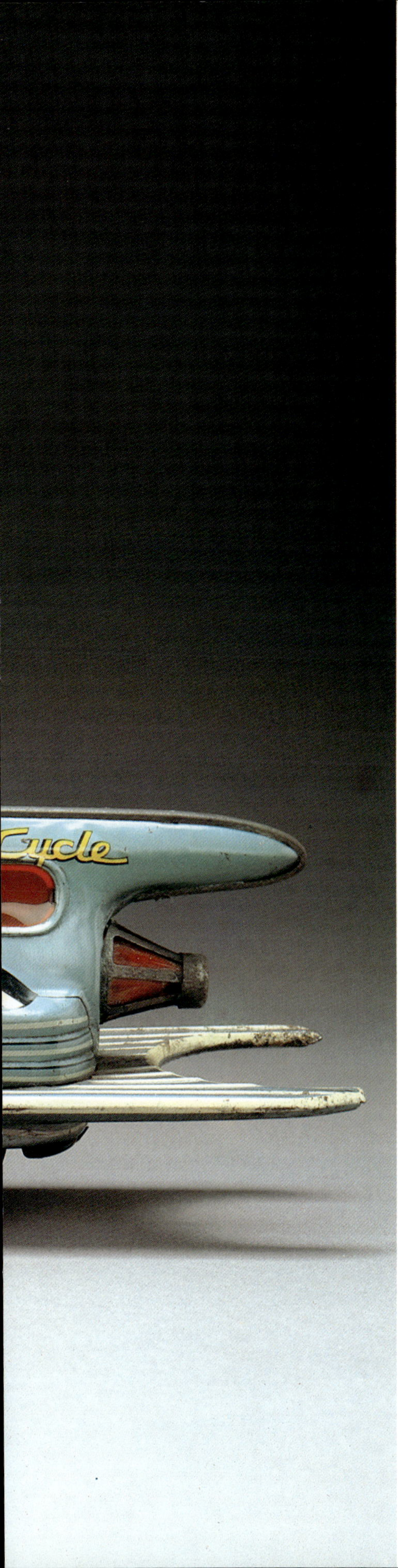

⑭⑧ 1950'S／SUPER CYCLE／BANDAI／305×70×138

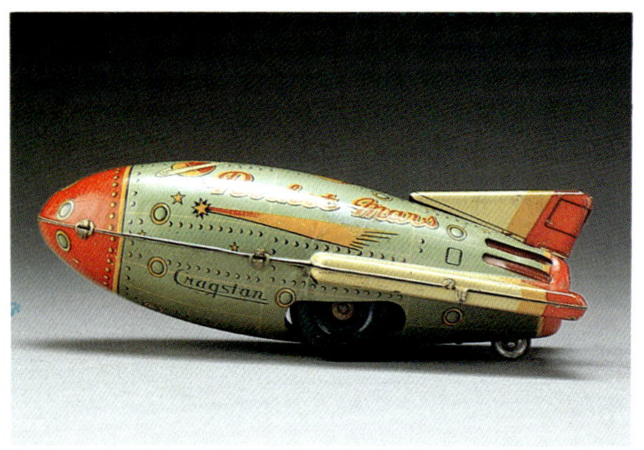

⑮1 1950'S／ROCKET MARS／CRAGSTAN／140×62×47

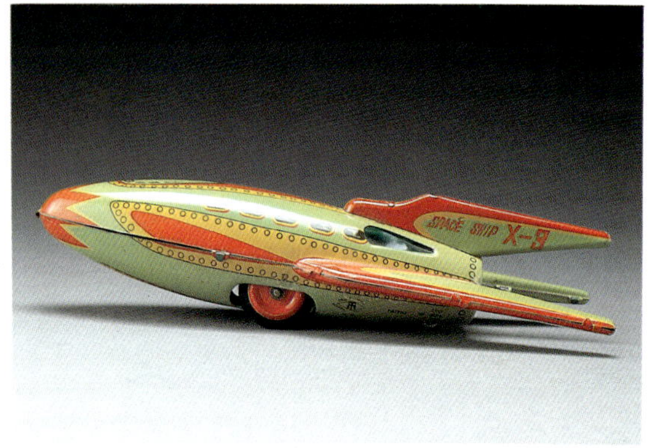

⑮2 1950'S／SPACE SHIP X-3／MASUDAYA／205×62×47

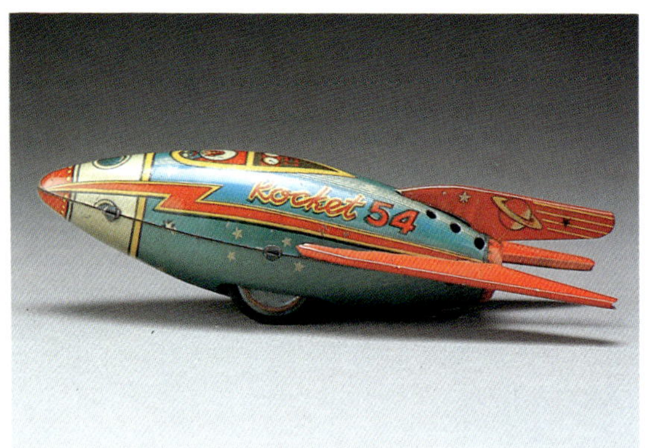

⑮3 1950'S／ROCKET 54／UNKNOWN／168×58×45

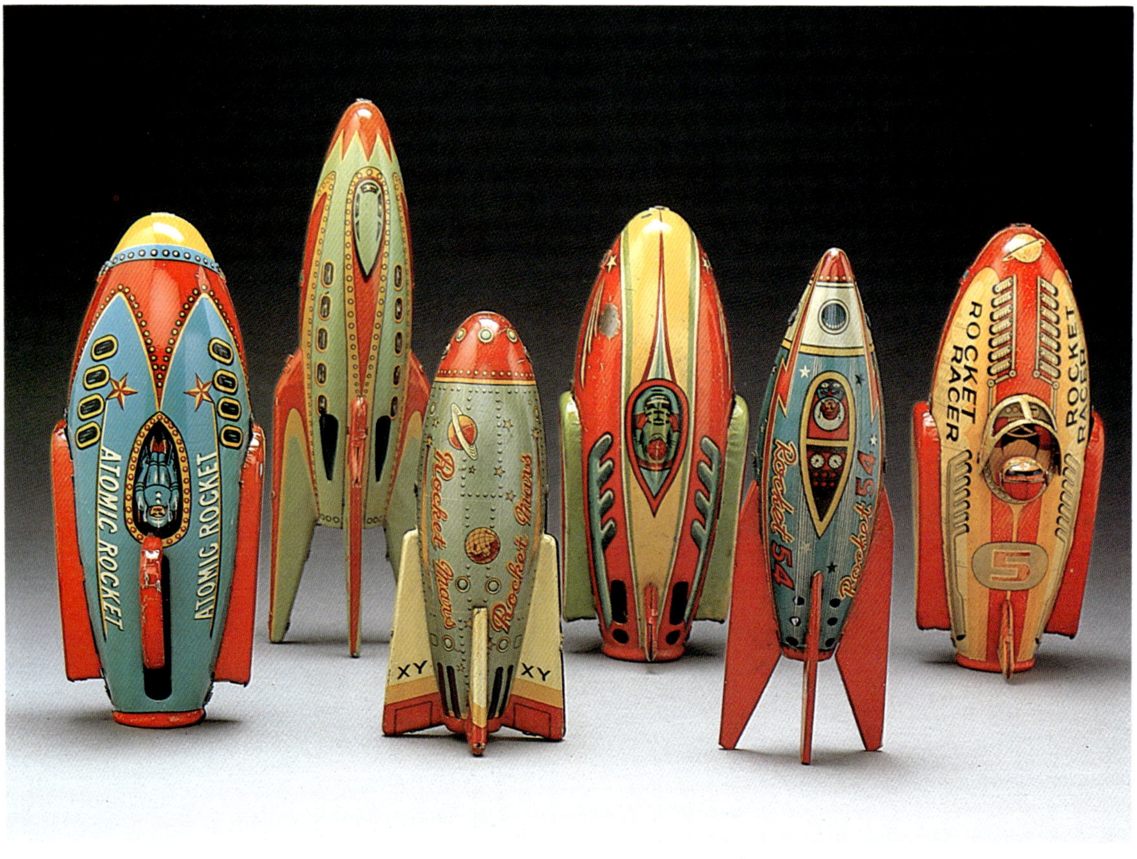

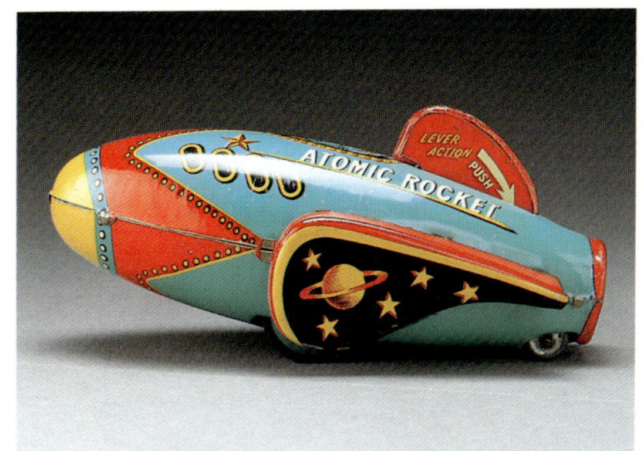

⑮④ 1950'S／ATOMIC ROCKET／MASUDAYA／170×70×72

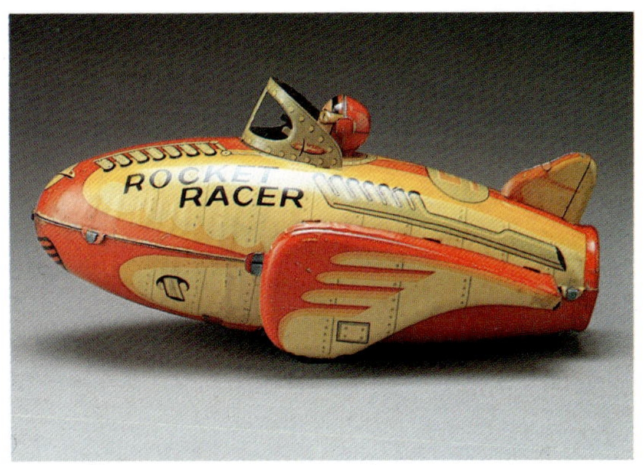

⑮⑤ 1950'S／ROCKET RACER／MASUDAYA／165×70×75

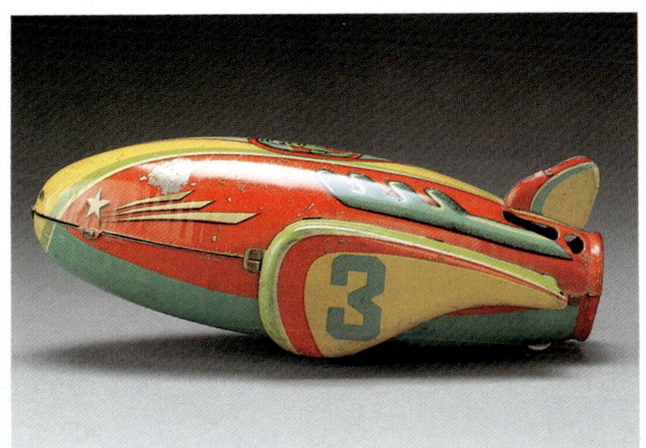

⑮⑥ 1950'S／ROCKET NO.3／MASUDAYA／165×70×60

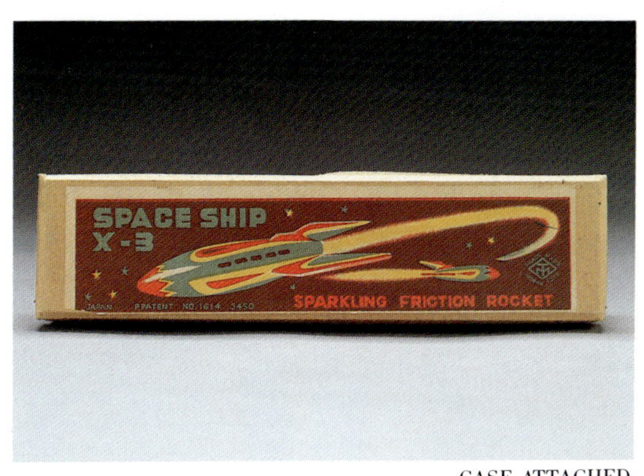

CASE ATTACHED

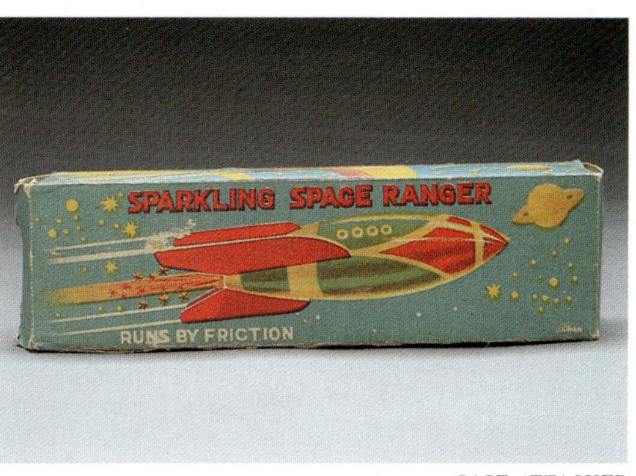

CASE ATTACHED

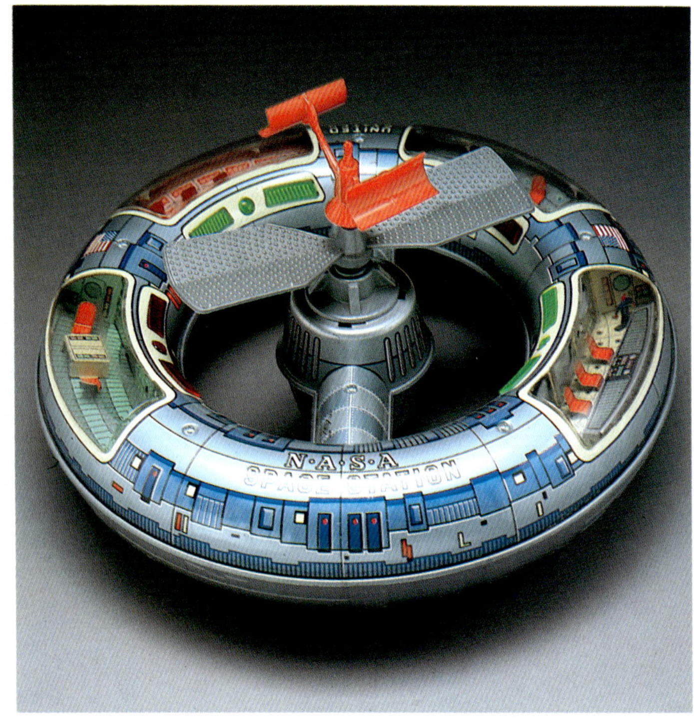

⑮⑺ 1960'S／SPACE STATION／HORIKAWA／295×295×165

CASE ATTACHED

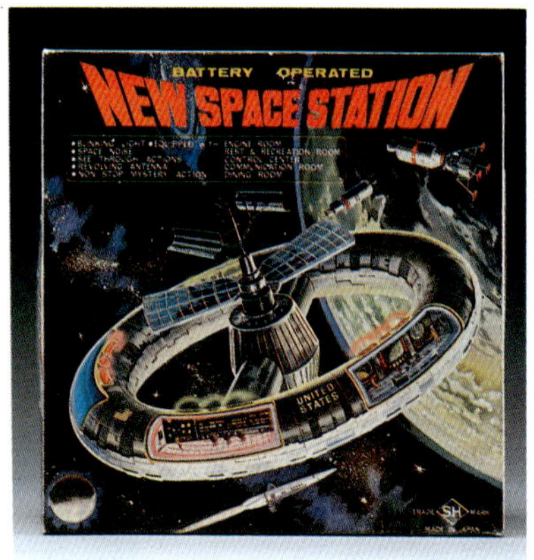

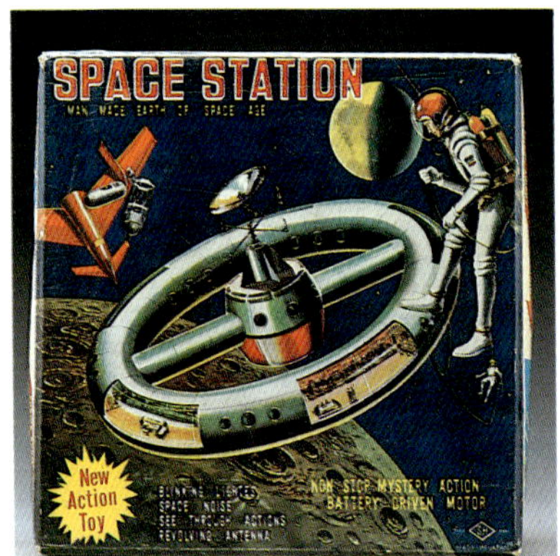

CASE ATTACHED

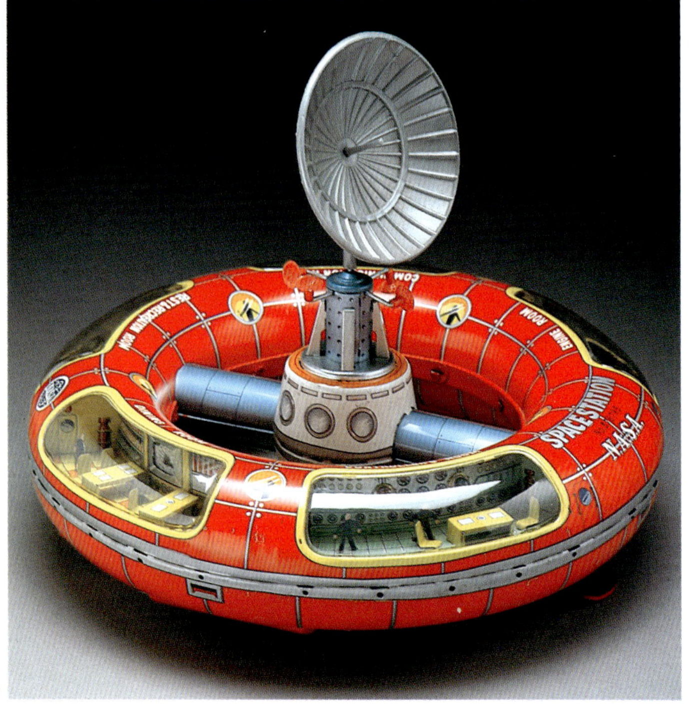

⑮⑻ 1950'S／SPACE STATION／HORIKAWA／300×300×230

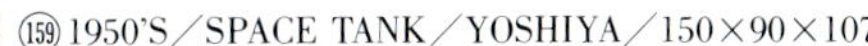
(159) 1950'S／SPACE TANK／YOSHIYA／150×90×107

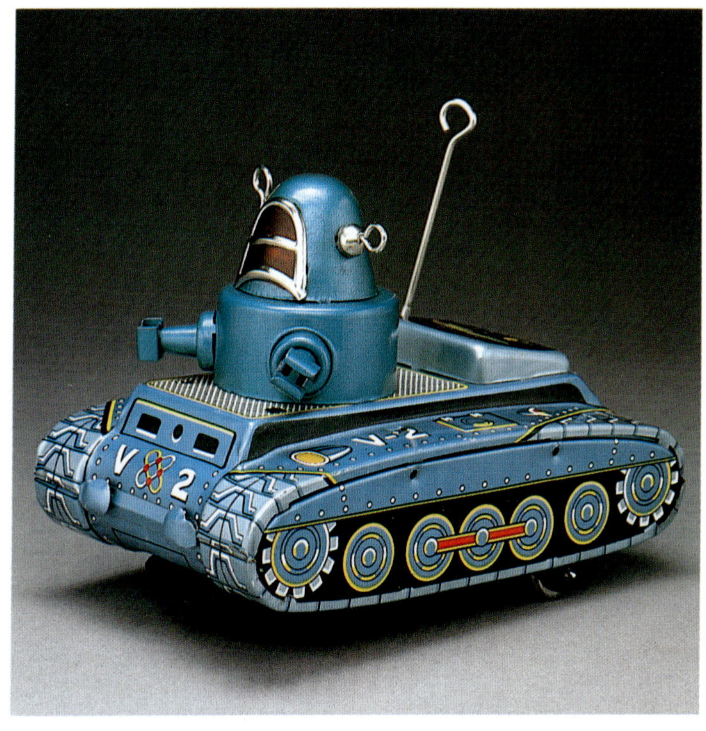

CASE ATTACHED

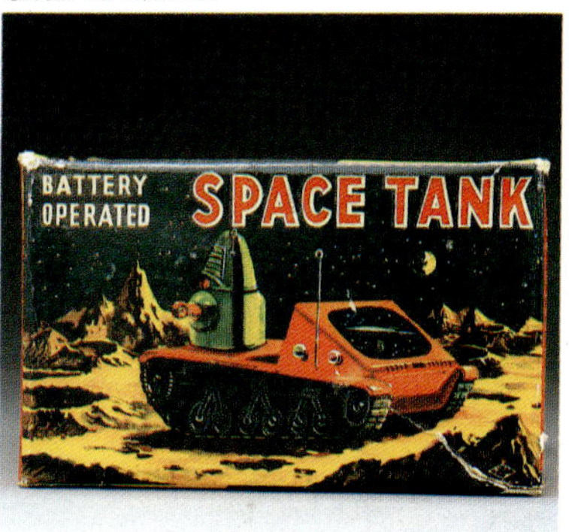

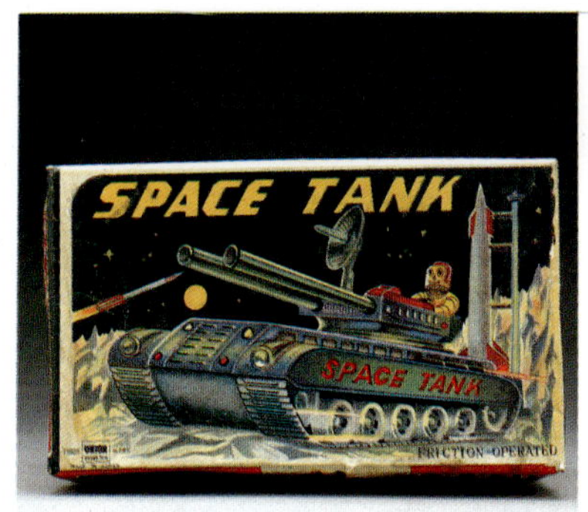

CASE ATTACHED

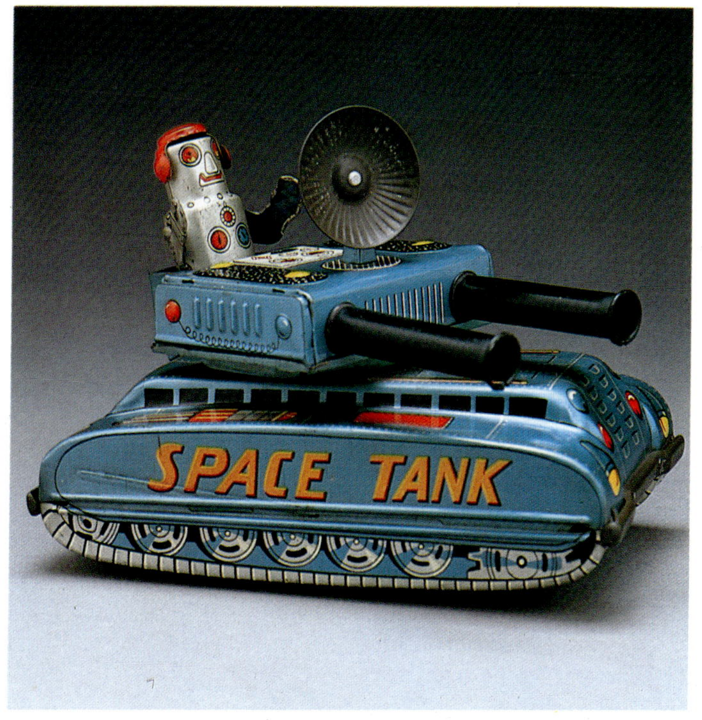

(160) 1950'S／SPACE TANK／UNION／157×90×115

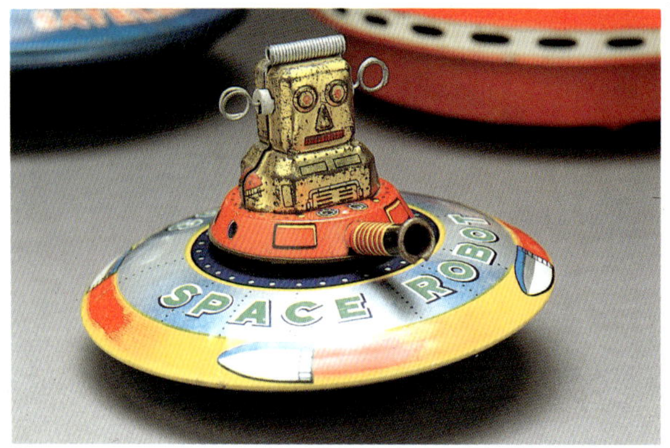

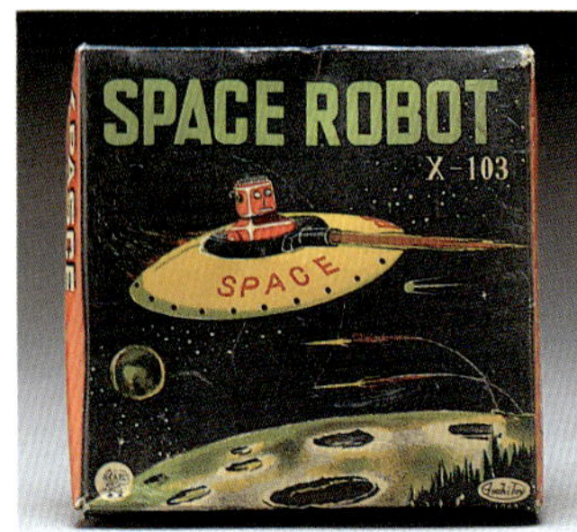

CASE ATTACHED

⑯1 1950'S／SPACE ROBOT／ASAHI TOY／127×127×80

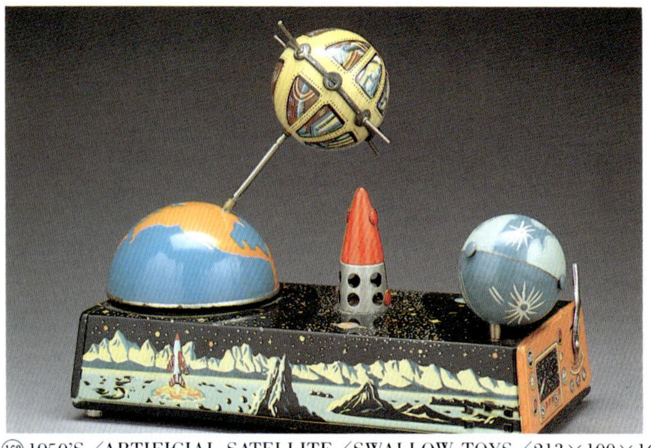

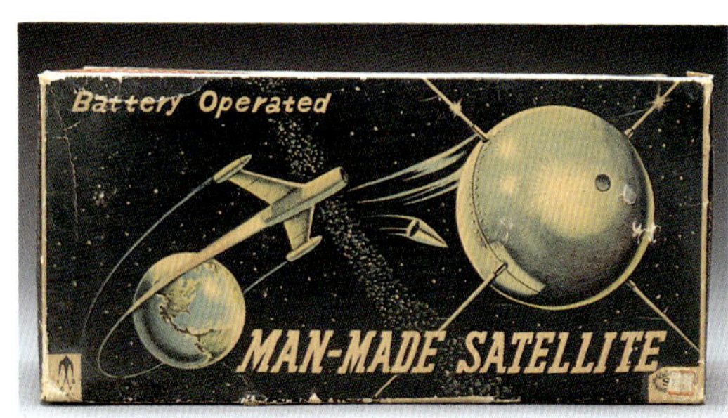

CASE ATTACHED

⑯2 1950'S／ARTIFICIAL SATELLITE／SWALLOW TOYS／213×100×160

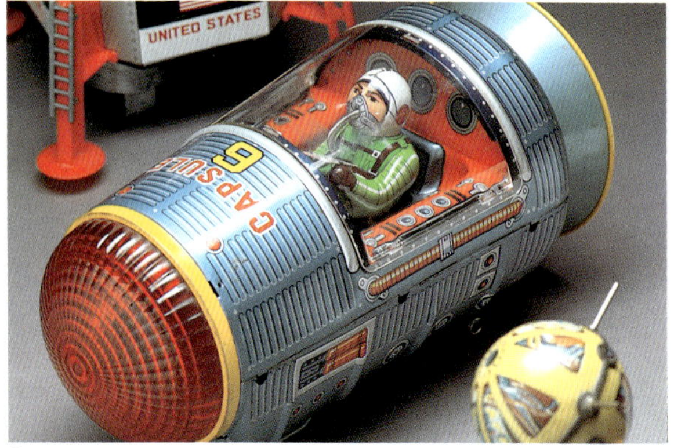

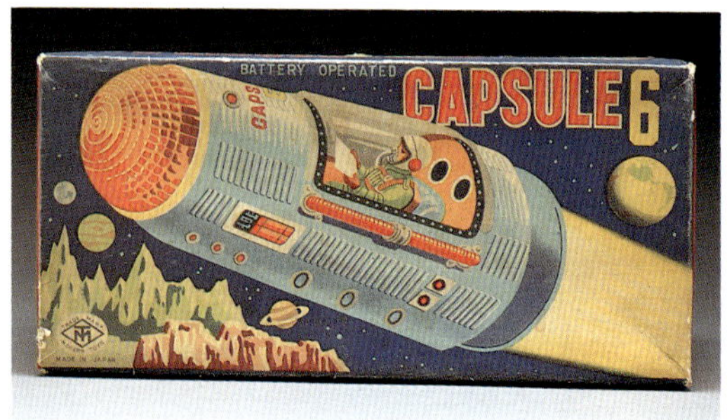

CASE ATTACHED

⑯3 1950'S／CAPSULE 6／MASUDAYA／255×120×130

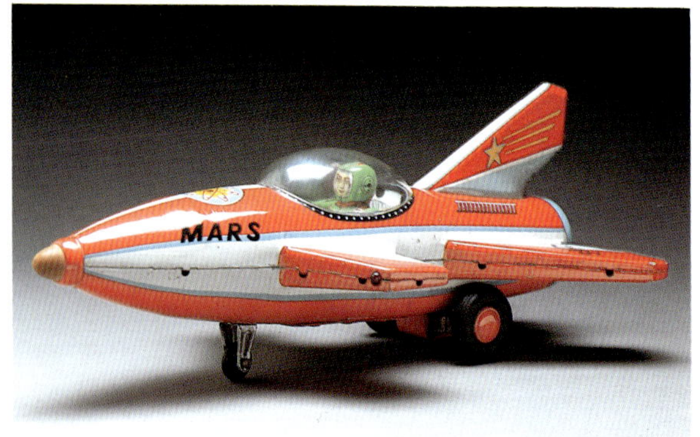

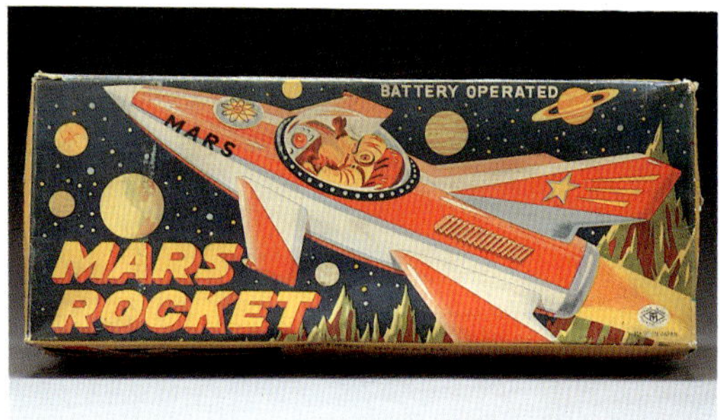

CASE ATTACHED

⑯4 1960'S／MARS ROCKET／MASUDAYA／365×190×140

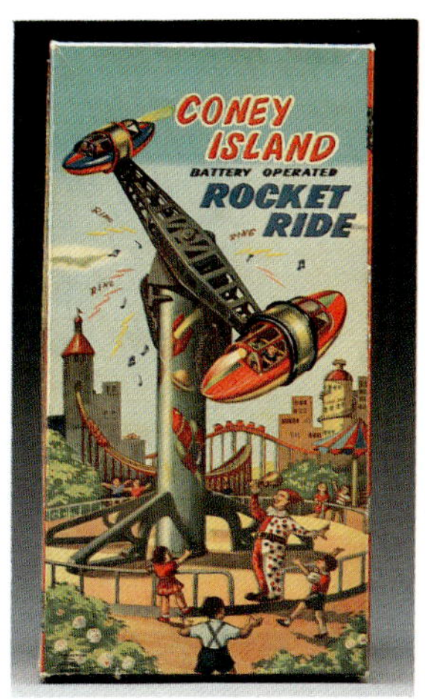

CASE ATTACHED

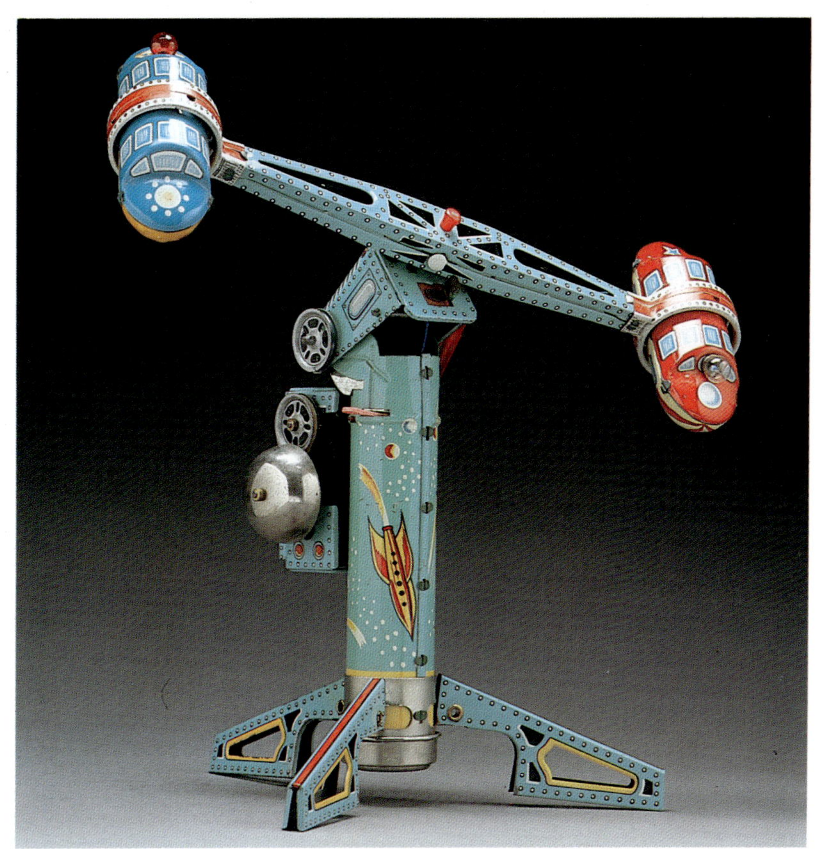
⑯⑤ 1950'S／CONEY ISLAND／ALPS／220×220×340

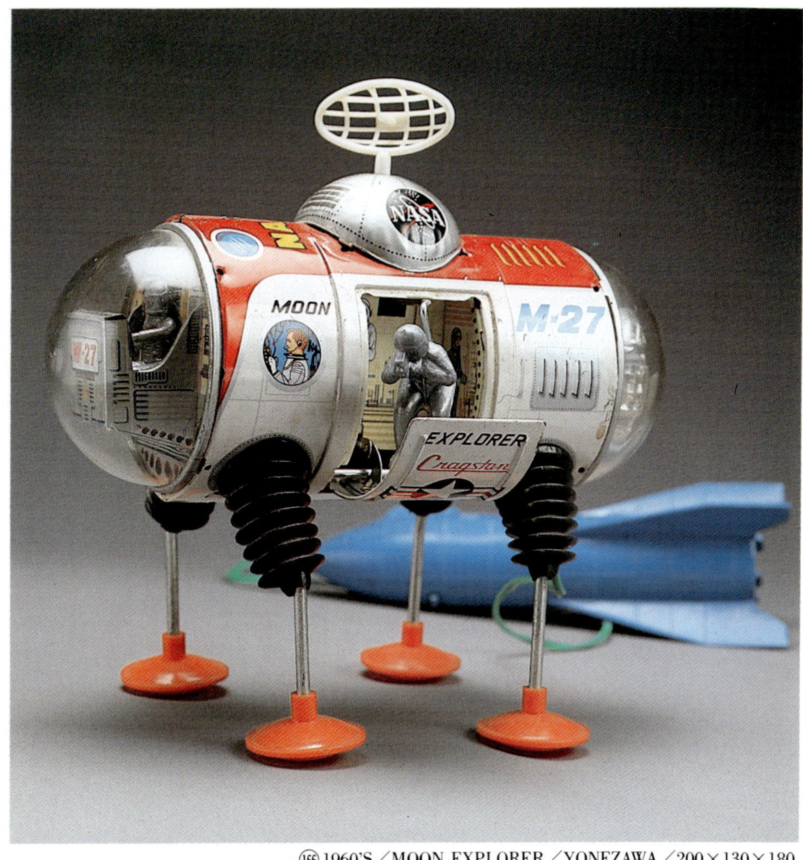

⑯⑥ 1960'S／MOON EXPLORER／YONEZAWA／200×130×180

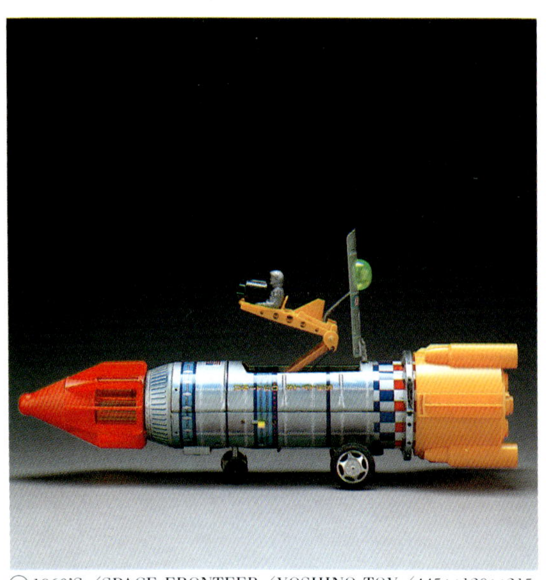

(167) 1960'S／SPACE FRONTEER／YOSHINO TOY／445×120×215

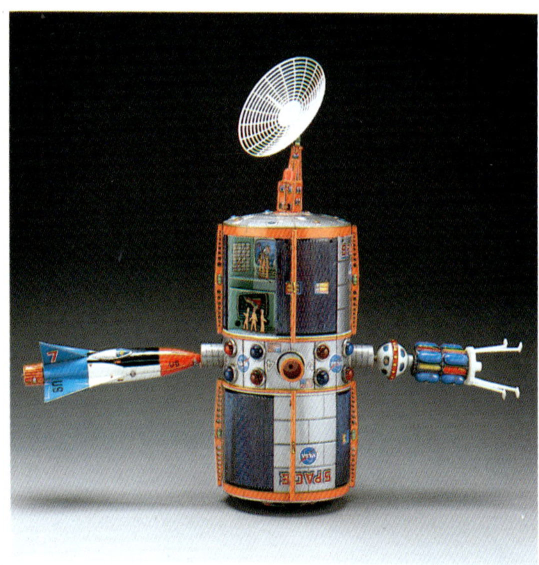

(168) 1950'S／SPACE STATION／WACO／150×445×380

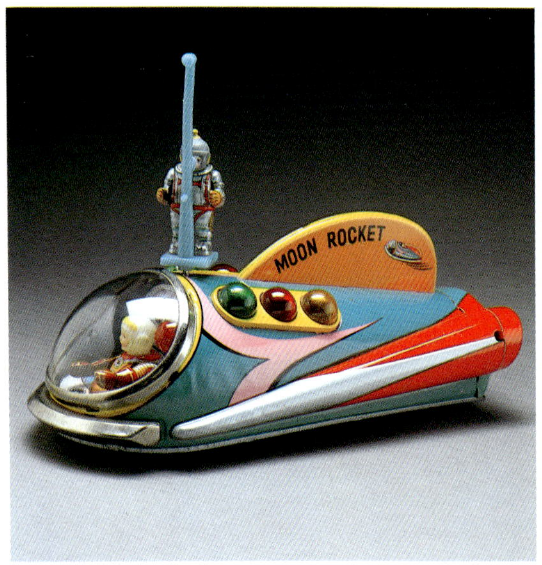

(169) 1960'S／MOON ROCKET／MASUDAYA／235×112×170

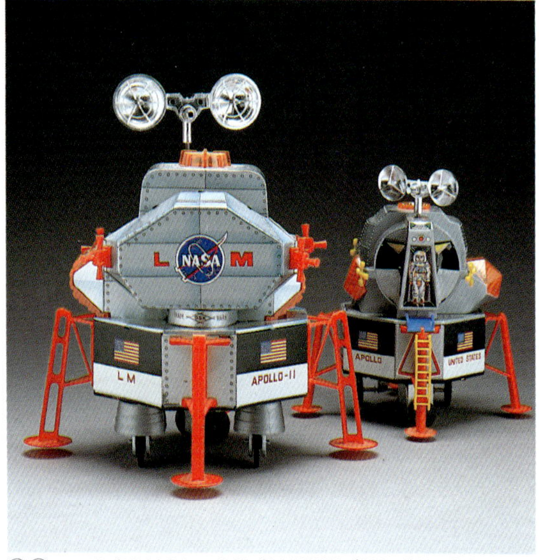

(170)(171) 1960'S／APOLLO-11 LM／DAISHIN／180×180×245, 135×135×183

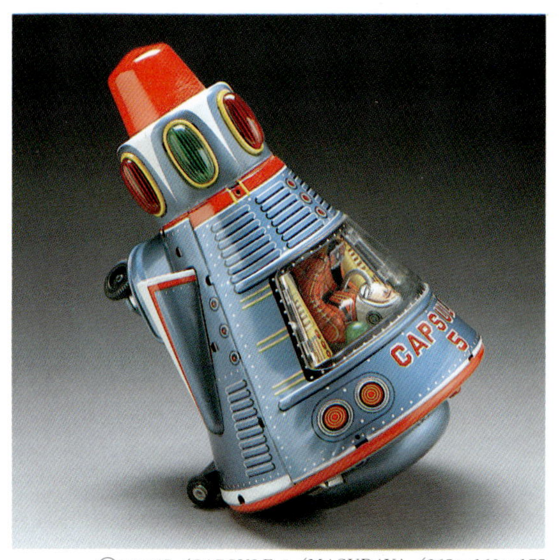

⑰ 1950'S／CAPSULE 5／MASUDAYA／265×160×175

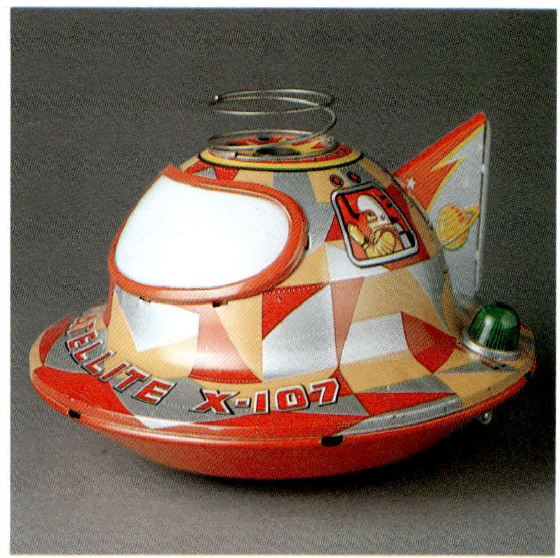

⑰ 1960'S／SATELLITE X-107／MASUDAYA／200×200×128

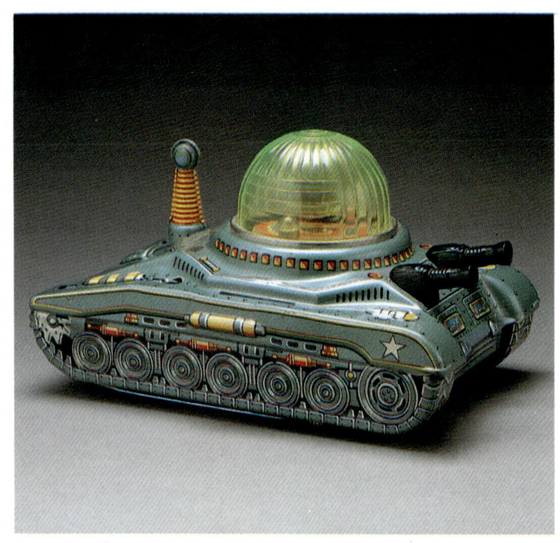

⑰ 1950'S／SPACE TANK／UNKNOWN／203×118×105

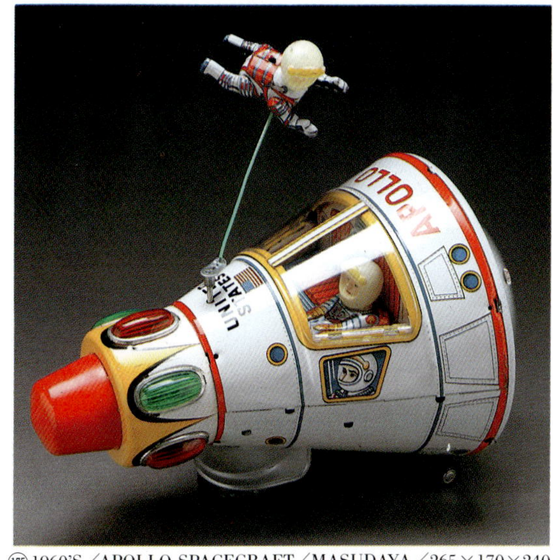

⑰ 1960'S／APOLLO SPACECRAFT／MASUDAYA／265×170×240

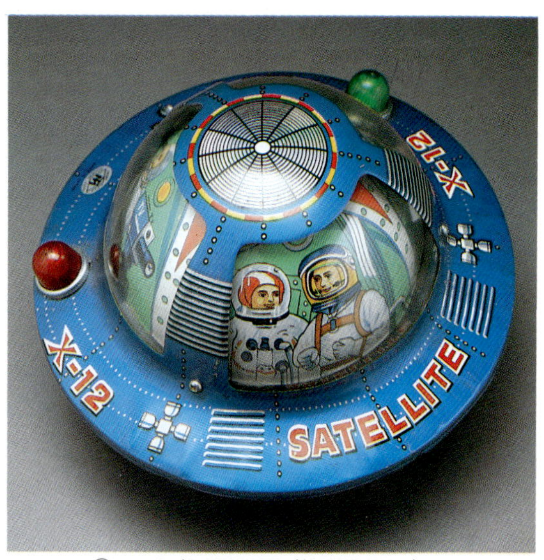

⑰ 1950'S／SATELLITE／MASUDAYA／200×200×110

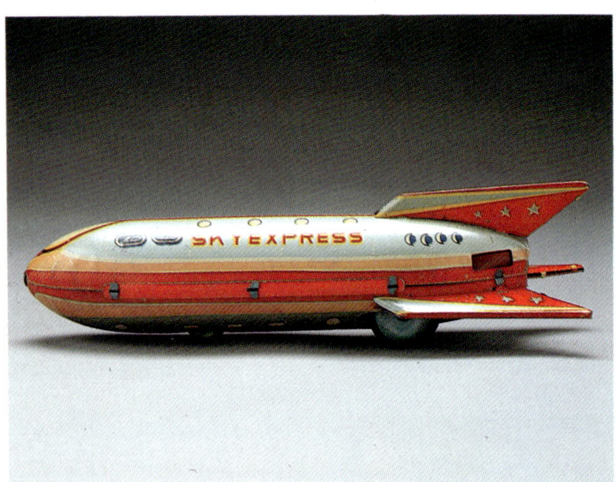

⑰ 1950'S／SKY EXPRESS／USAGIYA／218×58×60

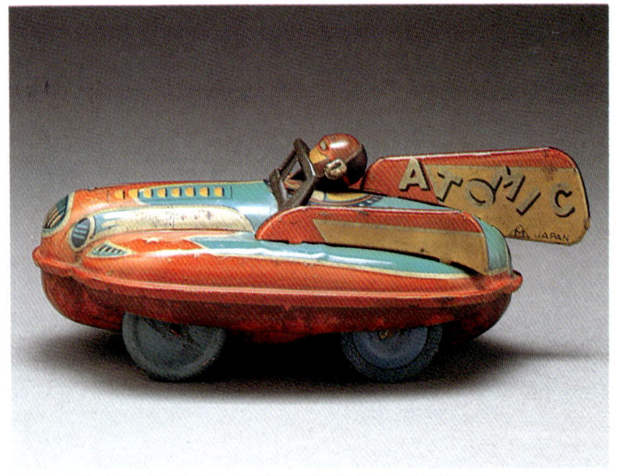

⑱ 1950'S／ATOMIC X-8／MITSUHASHI／145×80×55

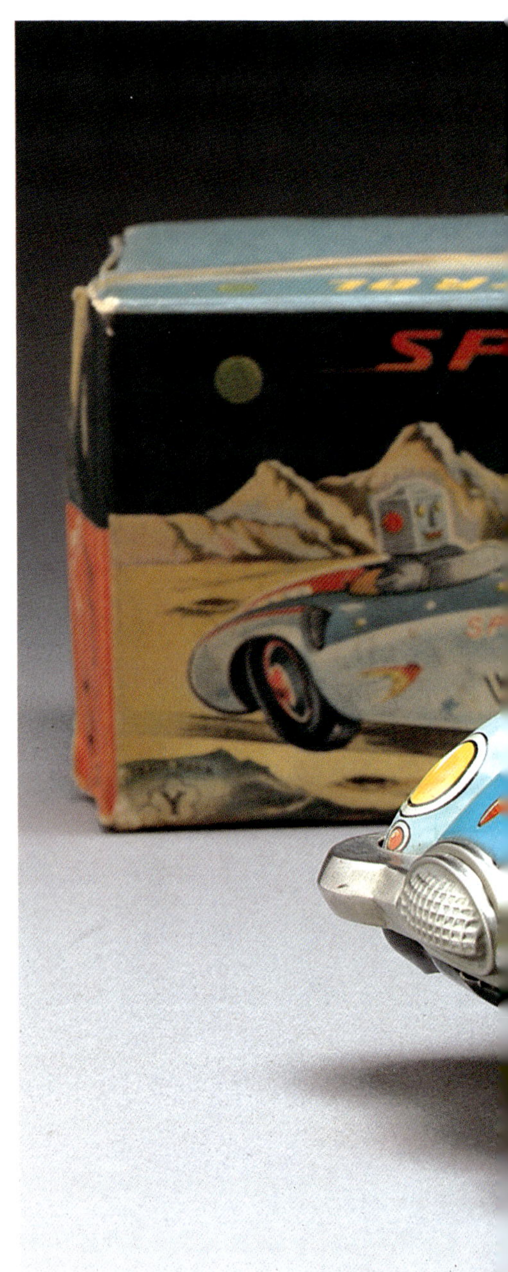

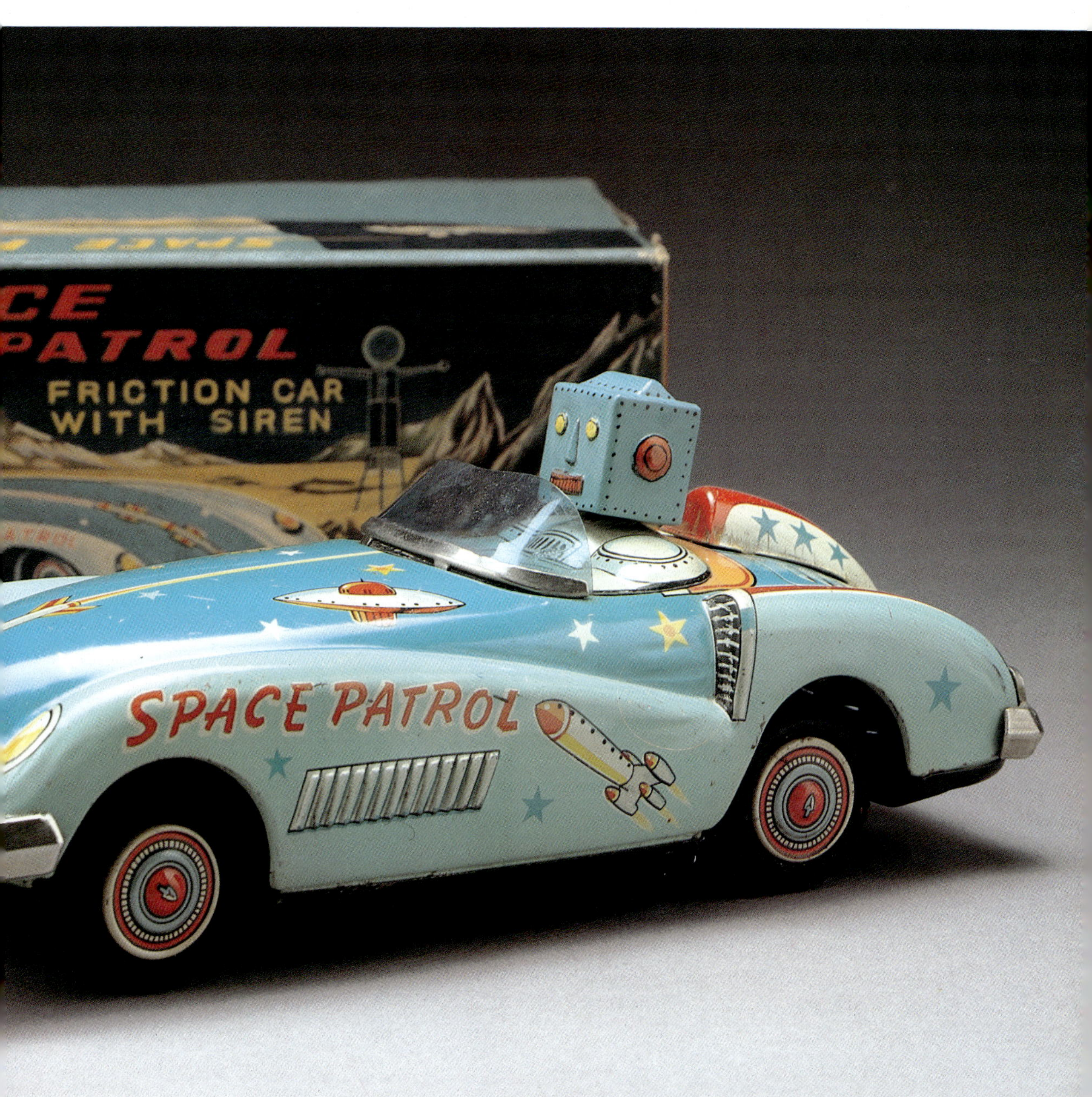

⑰⑨ 1950'S／SPACE PATROL AND CASE／ICHIKO／217×85×82

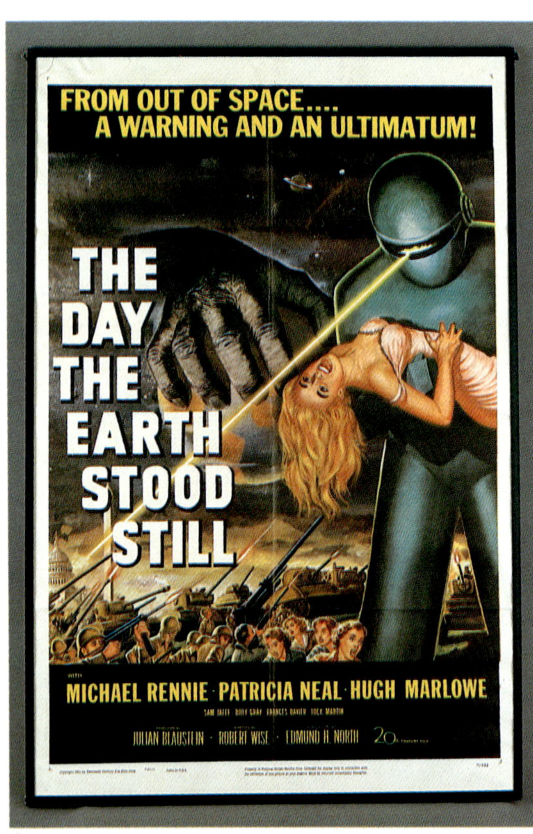

(180) 1951 20TH CENTURY-FOX PRESENTS "THE DAY THE EARTH STOOD STILL ORIGINAL POSTER

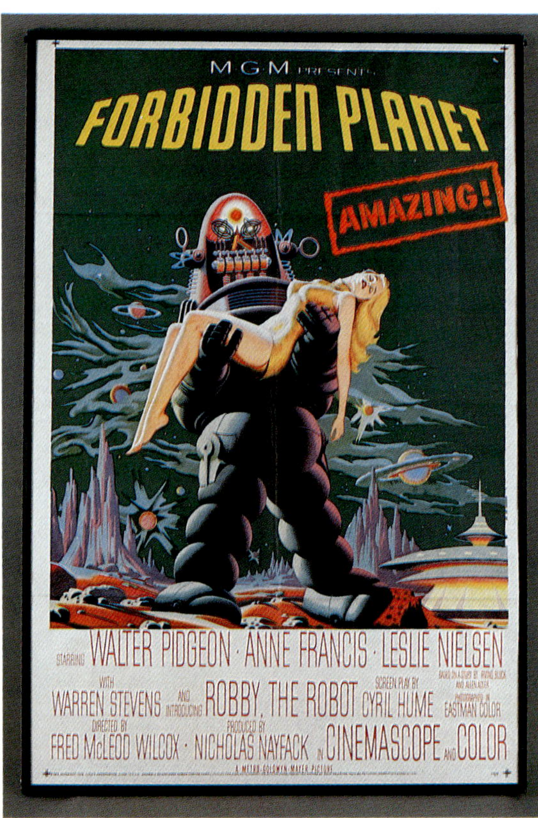

(181) 1956 M.G.M. PRESENTS "FORBIDDEN PLANET" ORIGINAL POSTER

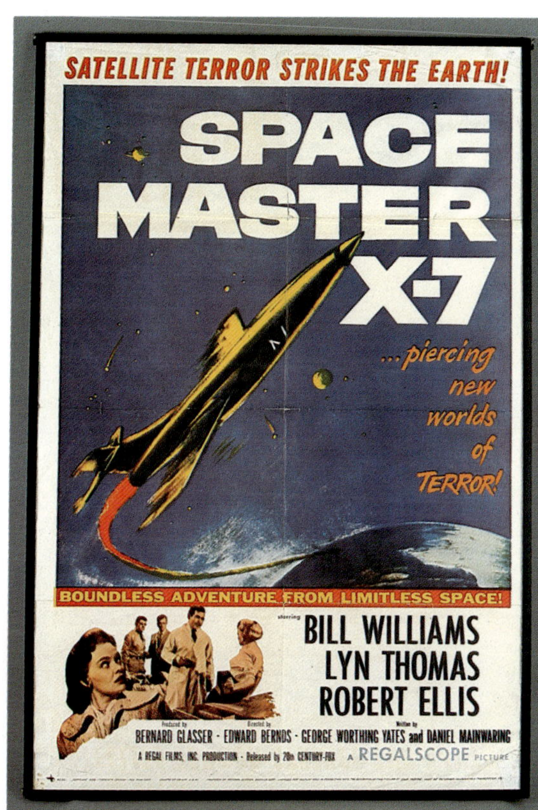

⑱② 1958　20TH CENTURY-FOX PRESENTS　"SPACE MASTER X-7" ORIGINAL POSTER

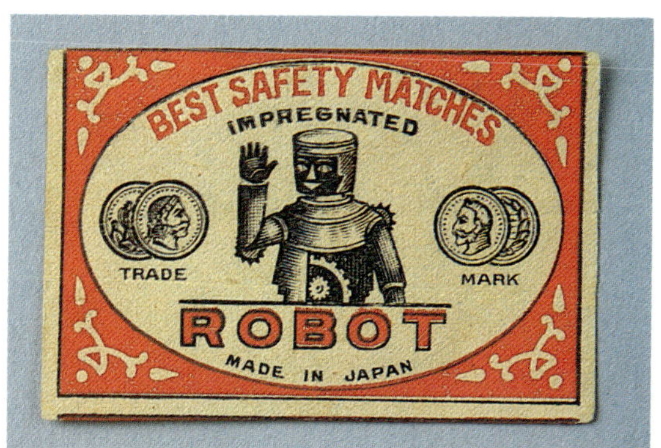

⑱③ 1930'S　MATCH BOX

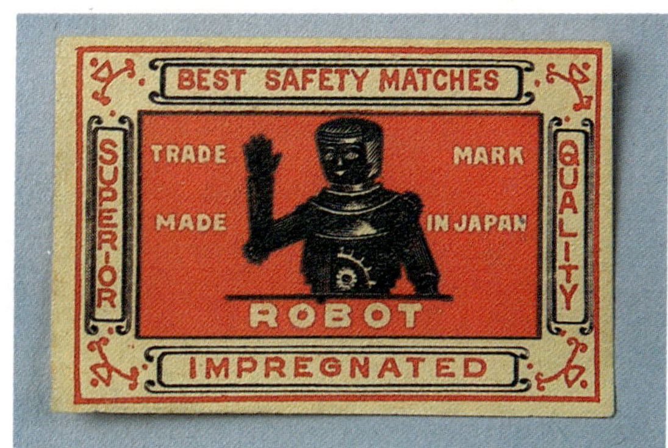

⑱④ 1930'S　MATCH BOX

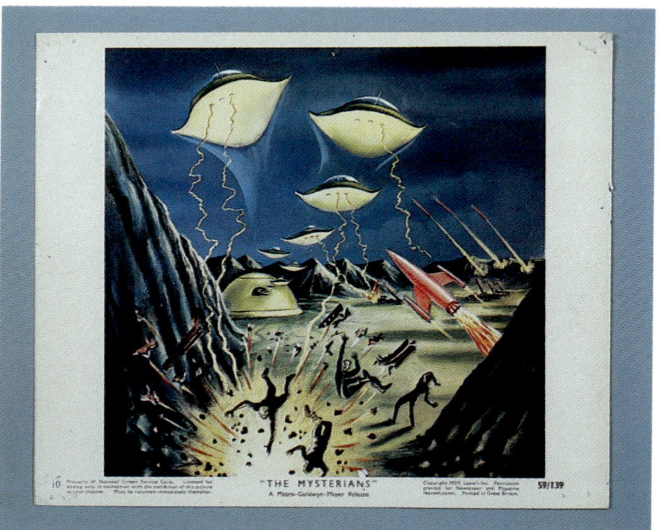

⑱⑤ 1959　A METRO-GOLDWYN-MAYER PRESENTS　"THE MYSTERIANS" POSTER

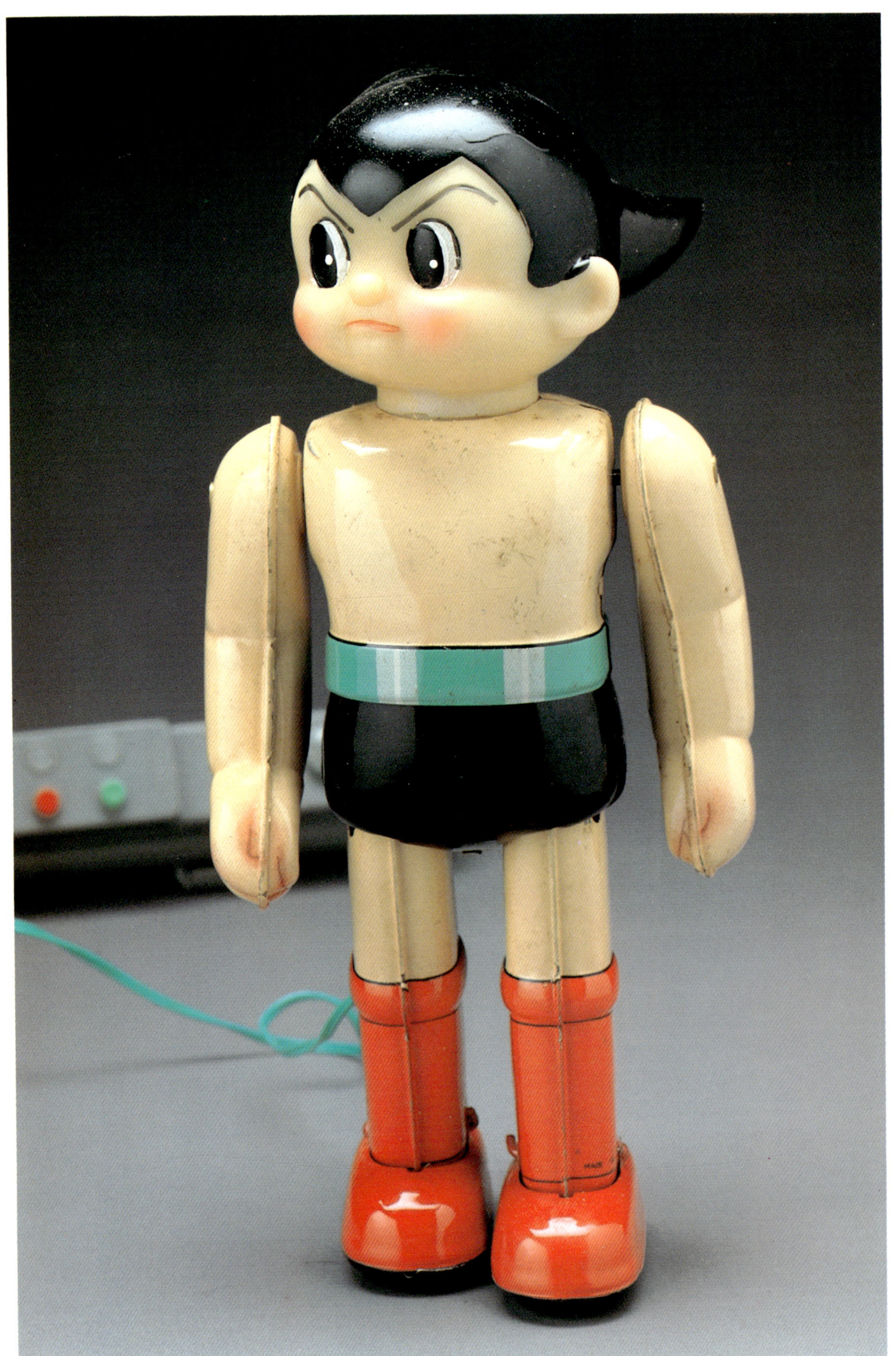

⑱ 1960'S／TETSUWAN ATOM／BANDAI／63×100×220

© TEZUKA PRODUCTION

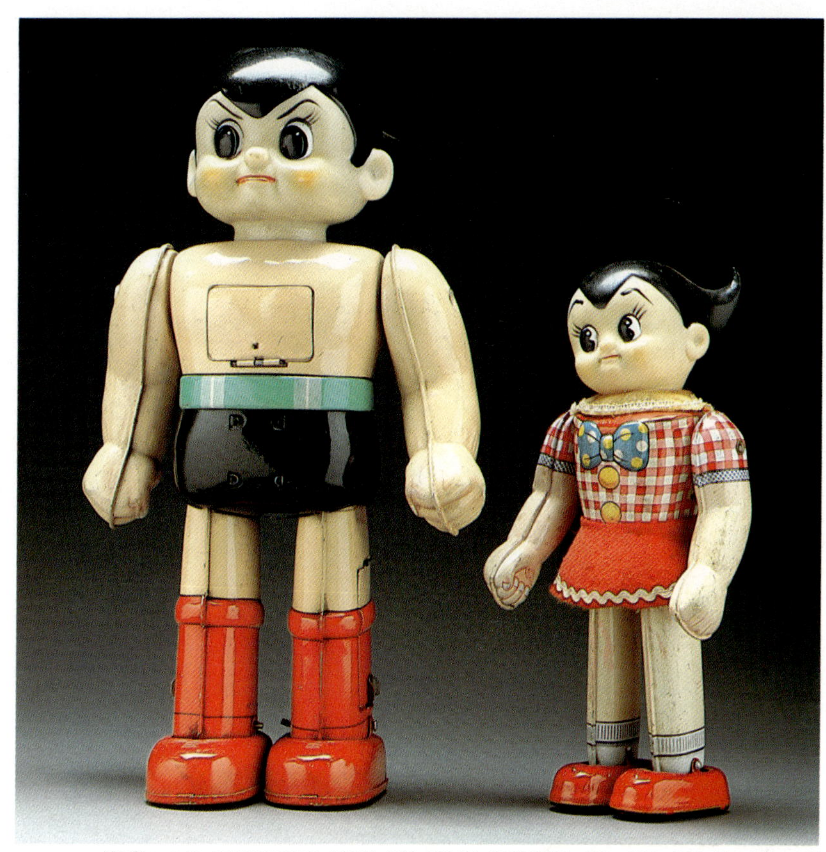

(187)(188) 1960'S／TETSUWAN ATOM AND URAN／NOMURA／85×175×305, 65×110×225

© TEZUKA PRODUCTION

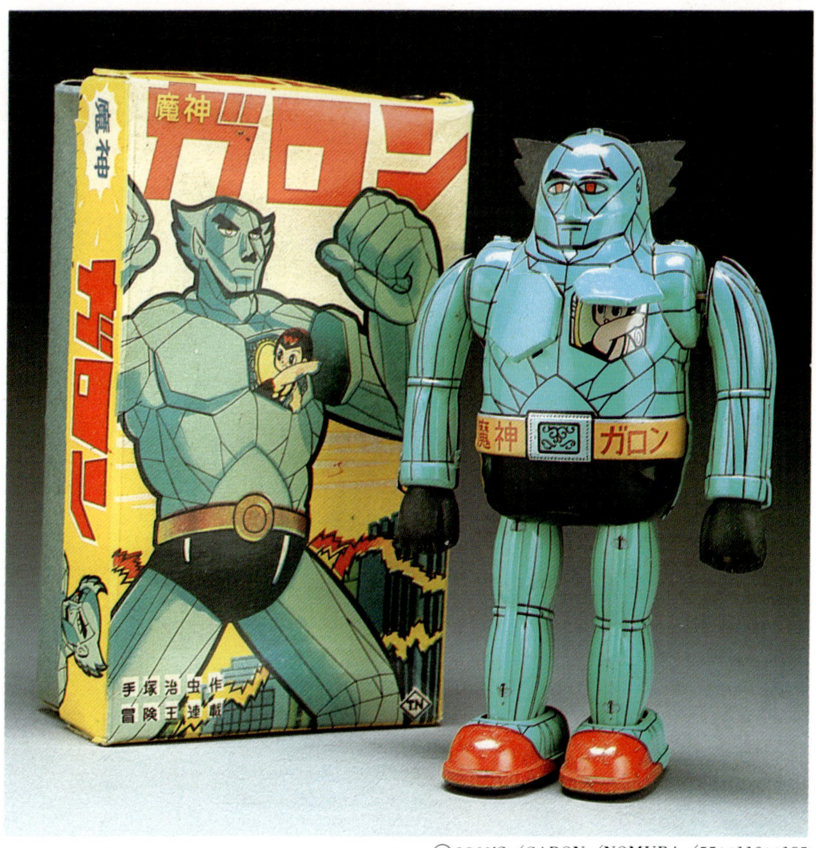

(189) 1960'S／GARON／NOMURA／55×110×185

© TEZUKA PRODUCTION

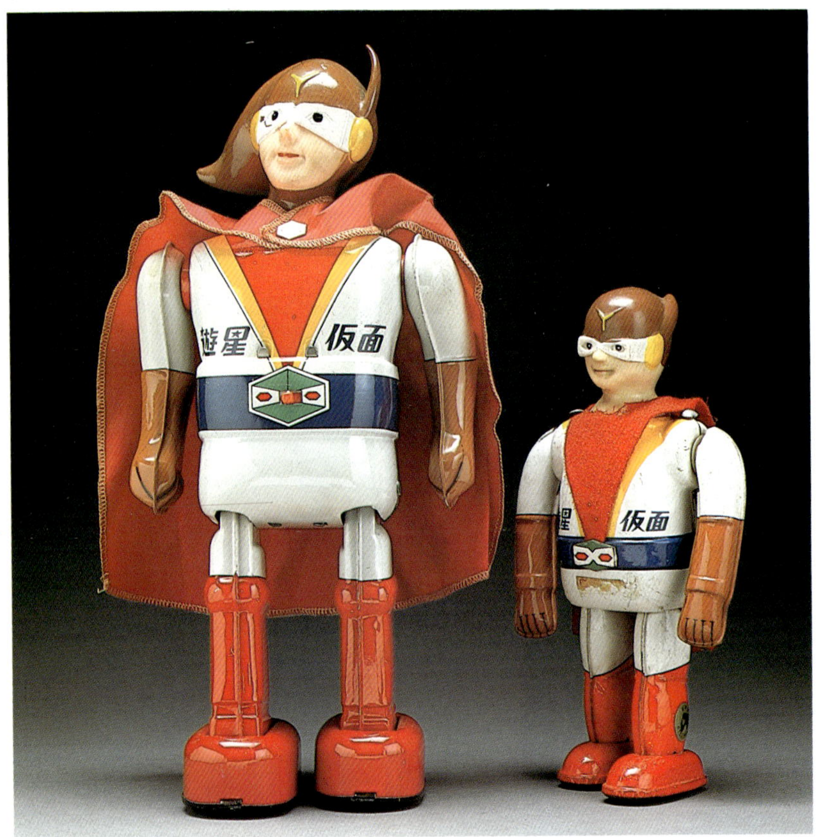

⑲⑲ 1960'S／YUSEI KAMEN／NOMURA／85×135×300, 63×105×205

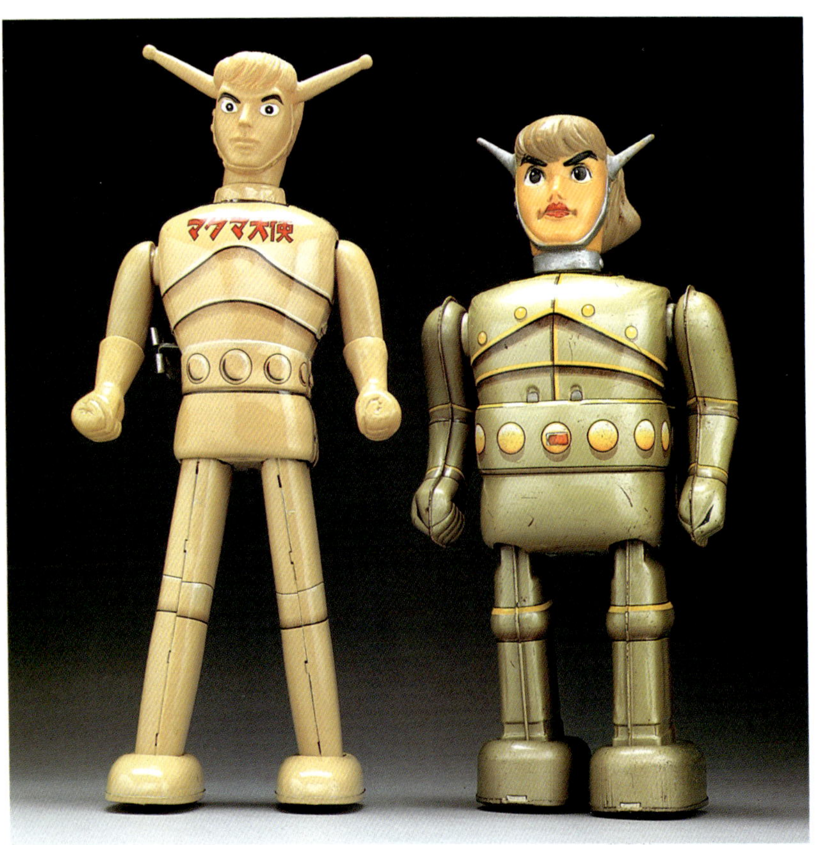

⑲⑲ 1960'S／MAGUMA TAISHI／TADA, NOMURA／82×140×330, 90×135×300

© TEZUKA PRODUCTION

⑲ 1960'S/OHGON BAT/NOMURA/90×135×285

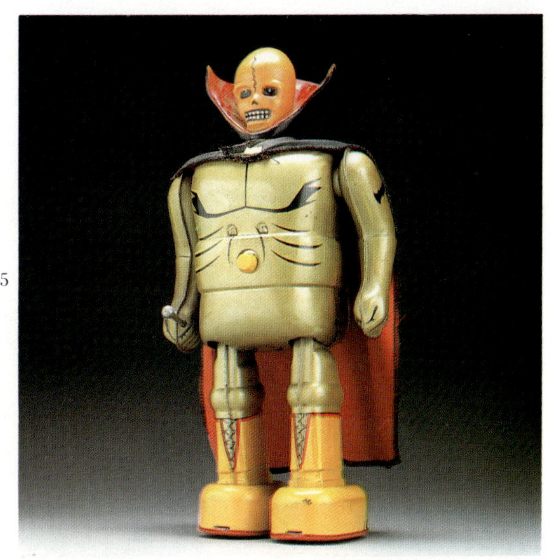

⑲ 1960'S/GETTSUKO KAMEN/BULL MARK/85×165×310

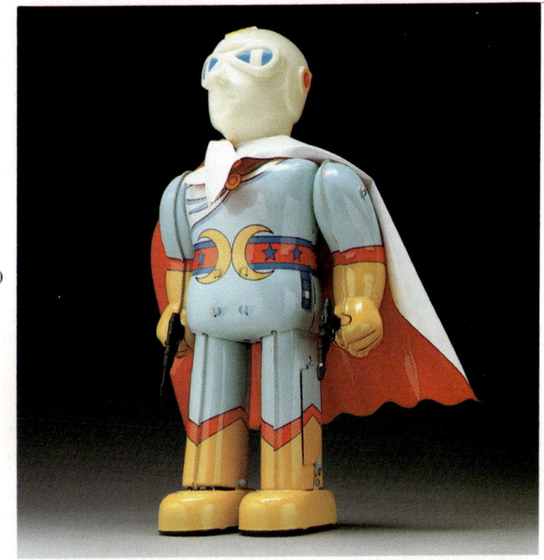

⑲ 1960'S/8 MAN/YONEZAWA/90×195×230

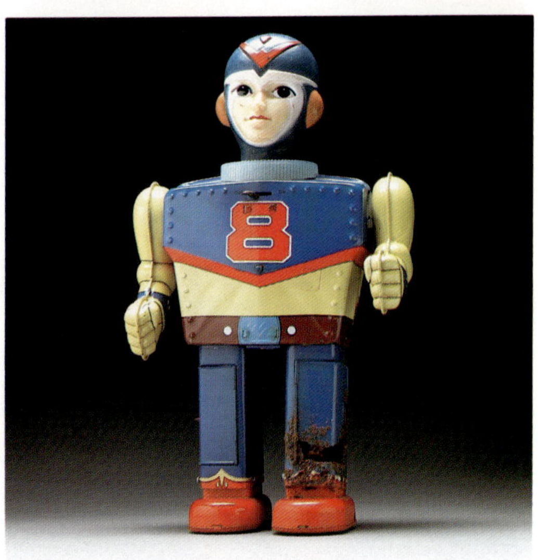

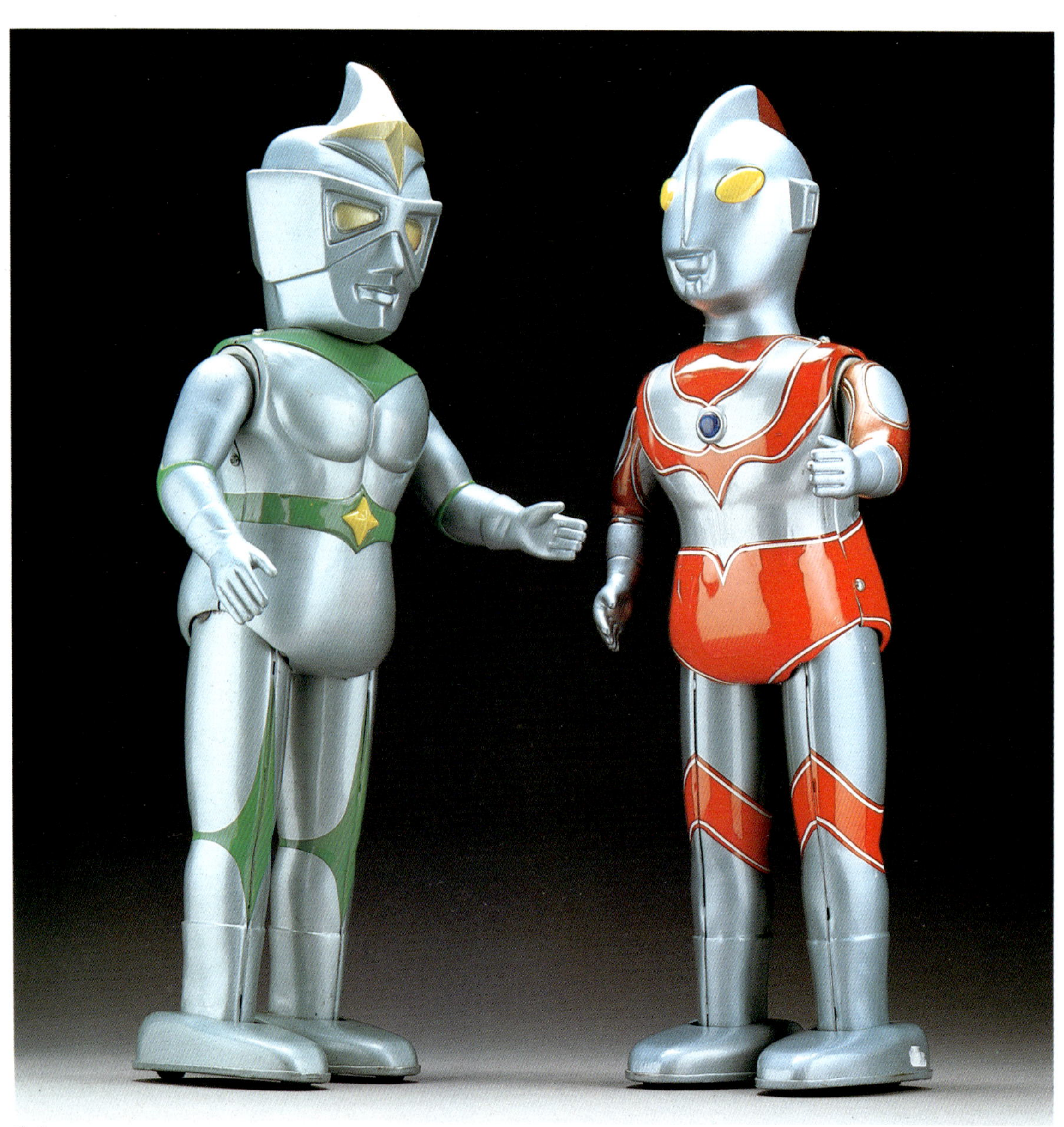

⑲⑲ 1960'S／ULTRA MAN, MIRROR MAN／BULL MARK／100×160×410, 98×160×425

© TSUBURAYA PRODUCTION

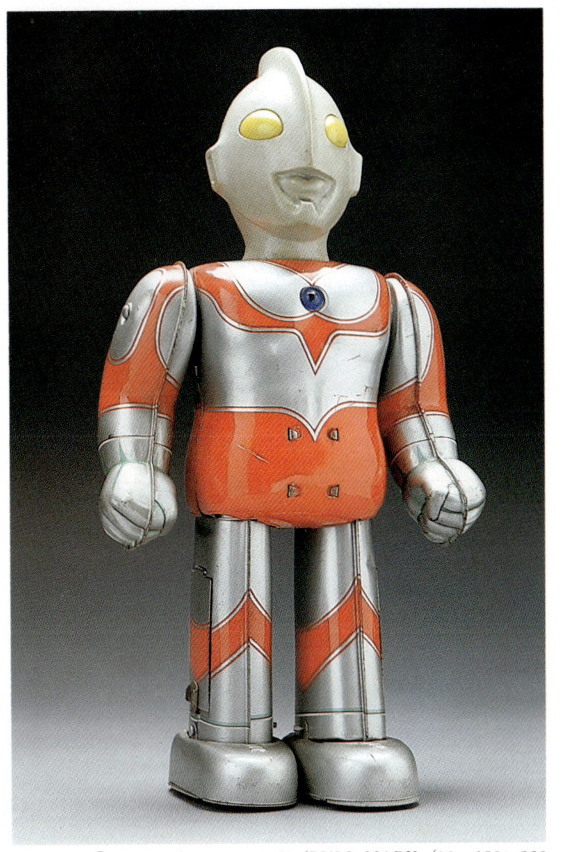

⑲⑨ 1960'S／ULTRA MAN／BULL MARK／90×150×320

© TSUBURAYA PRODUCTION

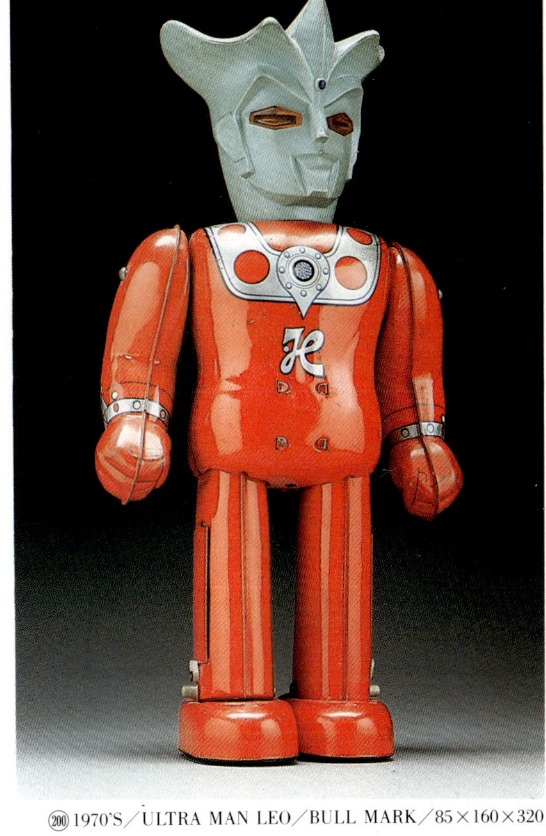

⑳⓪ 1970'S／ULTRA MAN LEO／BULL MARK／85×160×320

© TSUBURAYA PRODUCTION

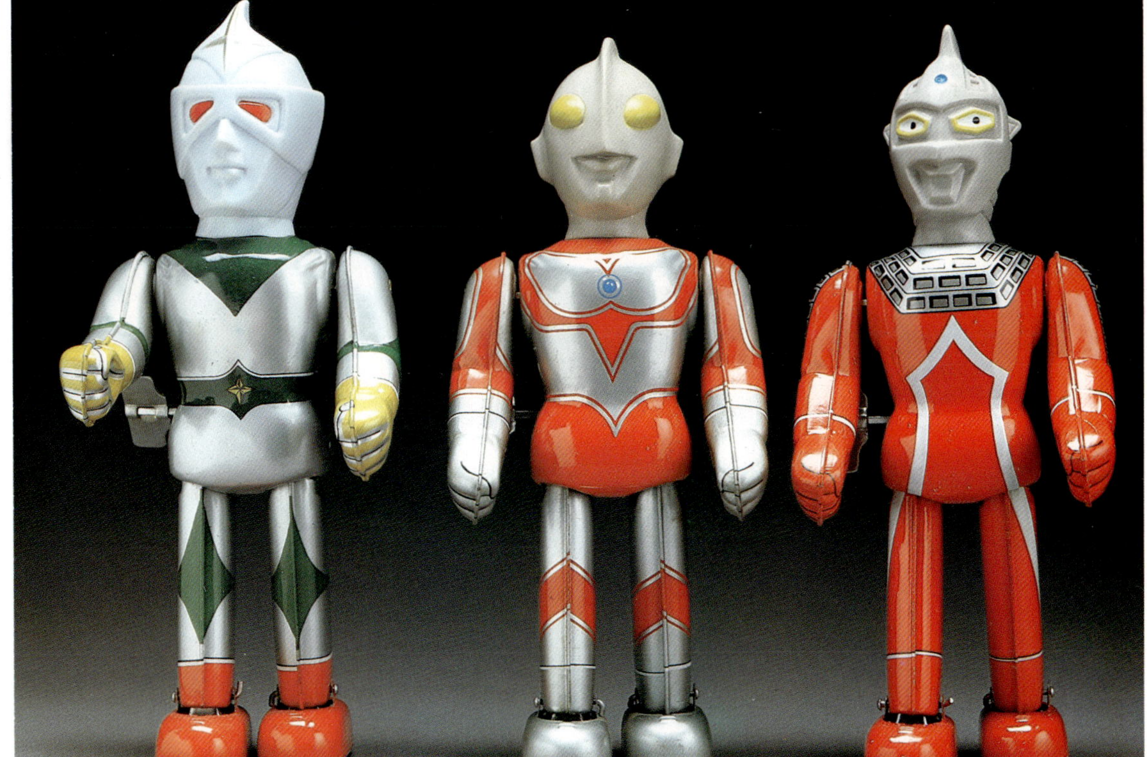

⑳①⑳②⑳③ 1960'S／MIRROR MAN, ULTRA MAN, ULTRA 7／BULL MARK／50×100×235

© TSUBURAYA PRODUCTION

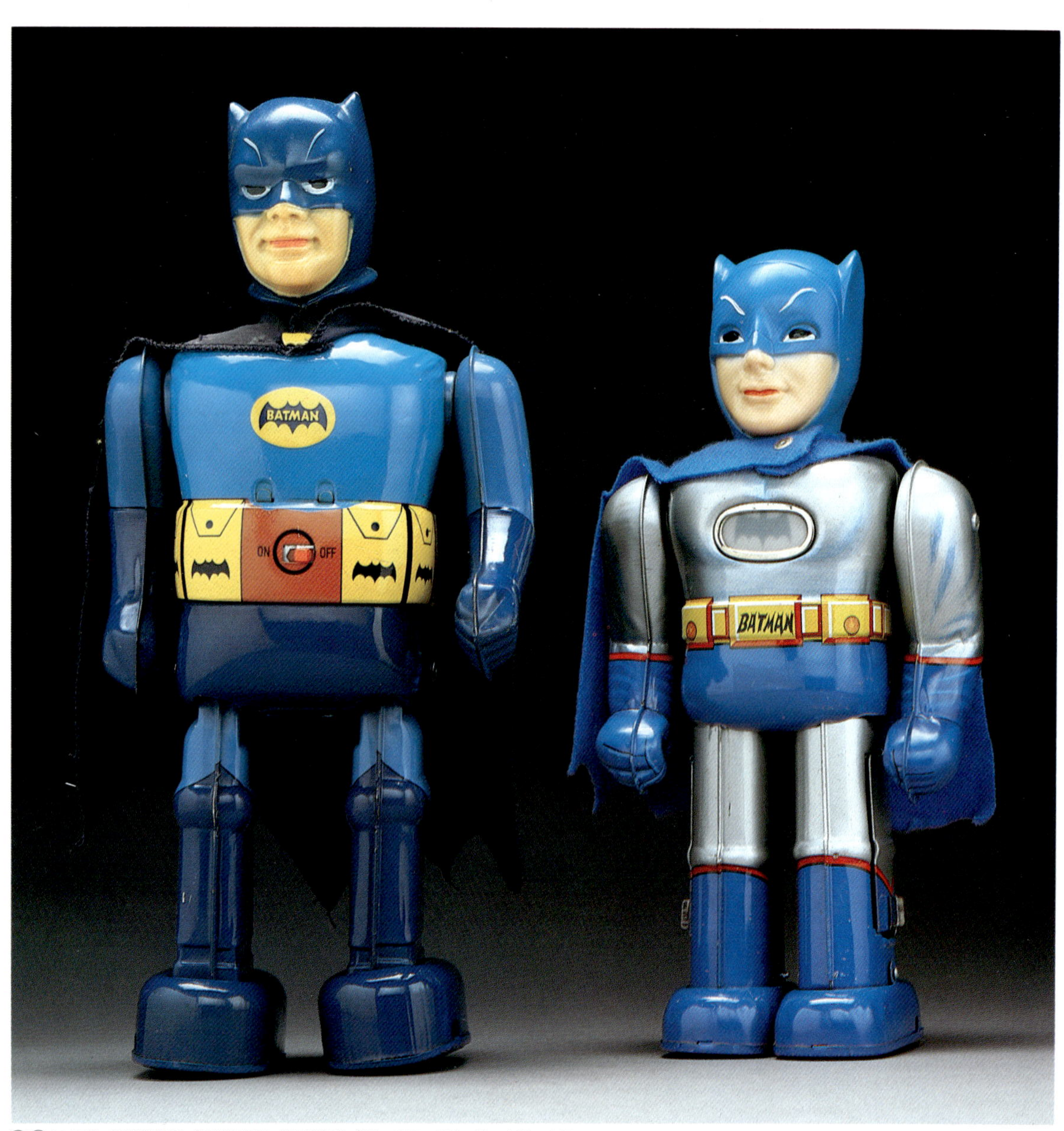

⑳④⑳⑤ 1960'S／BATMAN／NOMURA, BANDAI／90×140×300, 65×120×260

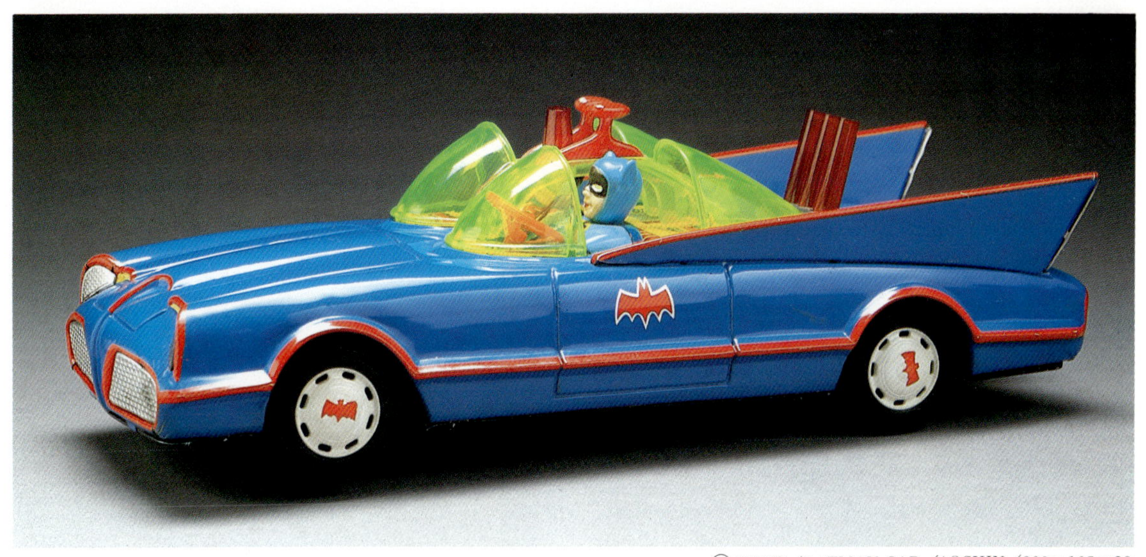

(206) 1960'S／BATMAN CAR／AOSHIN／300×105×90

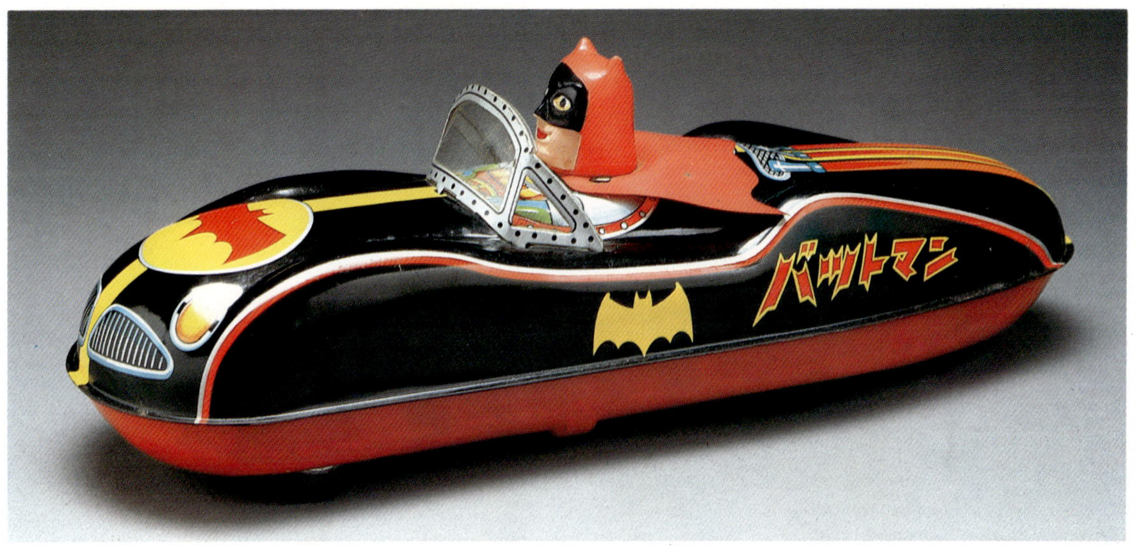

(207) 1960'S／BATMAN CAR／MASUDAYA／310×100×105

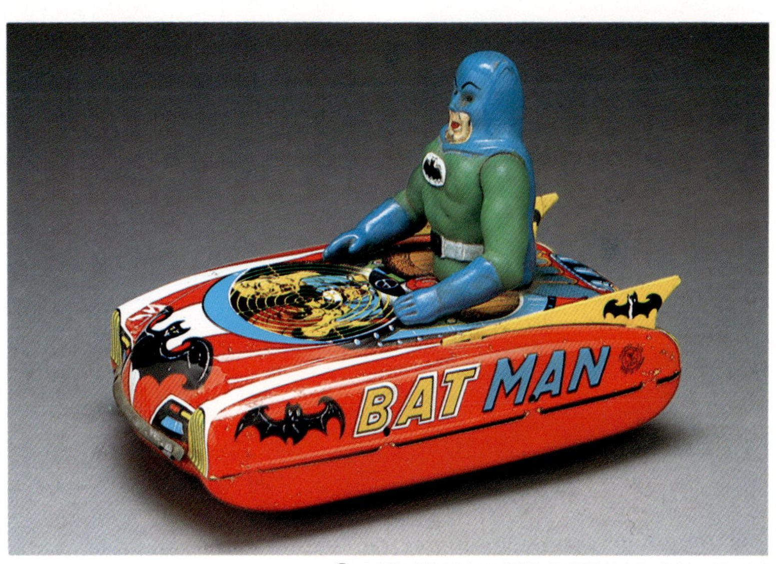

(208) 1960'S／BATMAN CAR／YANOMAN／152×95×103

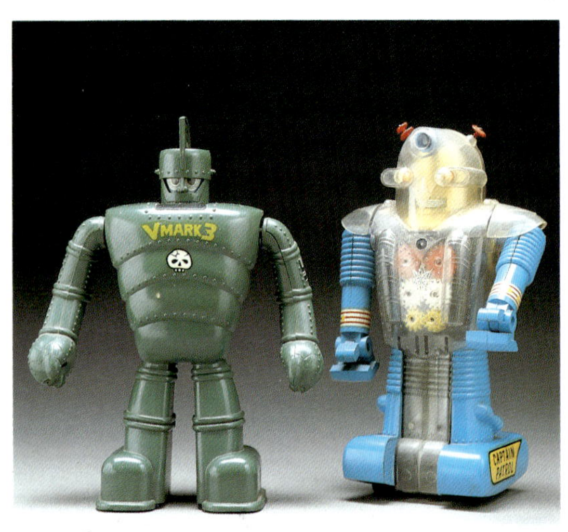

⑳⑩ 1960'S／V MARK 3, CAPTAIN PATROL／UNKNOWN, IMAI／65×118×215, 85×85×215

© TEZUKA PRODUCTION

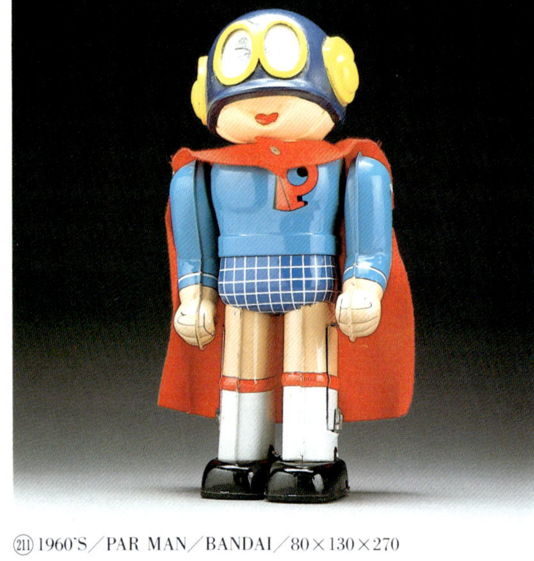

㉑ 1960'S／PAR MAN／BANDAI／80×130×270

© SHOGAKKAN PRODUCTION

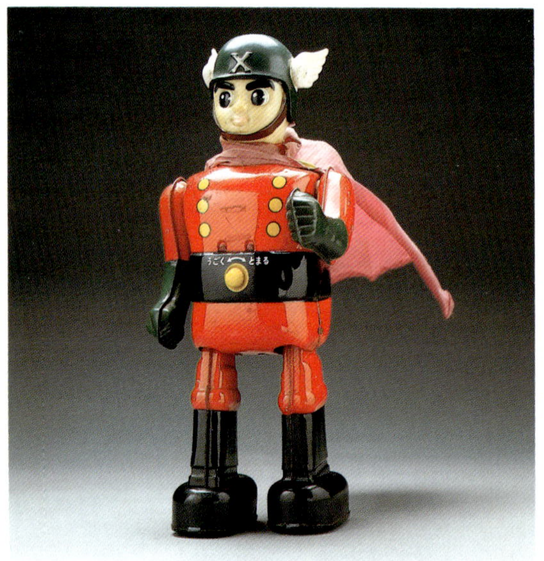

㉒ 1960'S／BIG X／NOMURA／85×135×310

© TEZUKA PRODUCTION

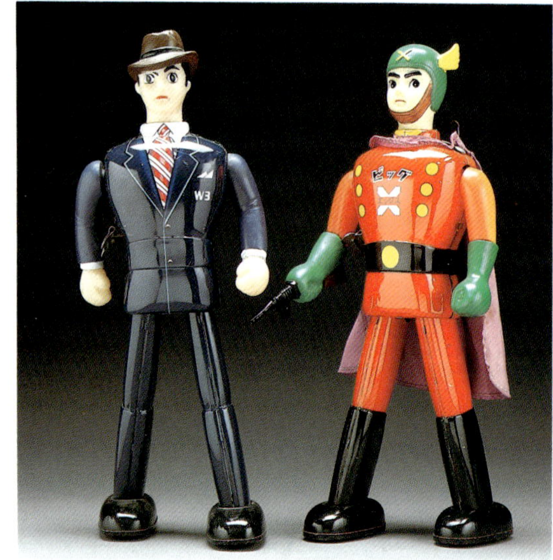

㉓㉔ 1960'S／W-3, BIG X／TADA／83×120×310, 70×120×310

© TEZUKA PRODUCTION

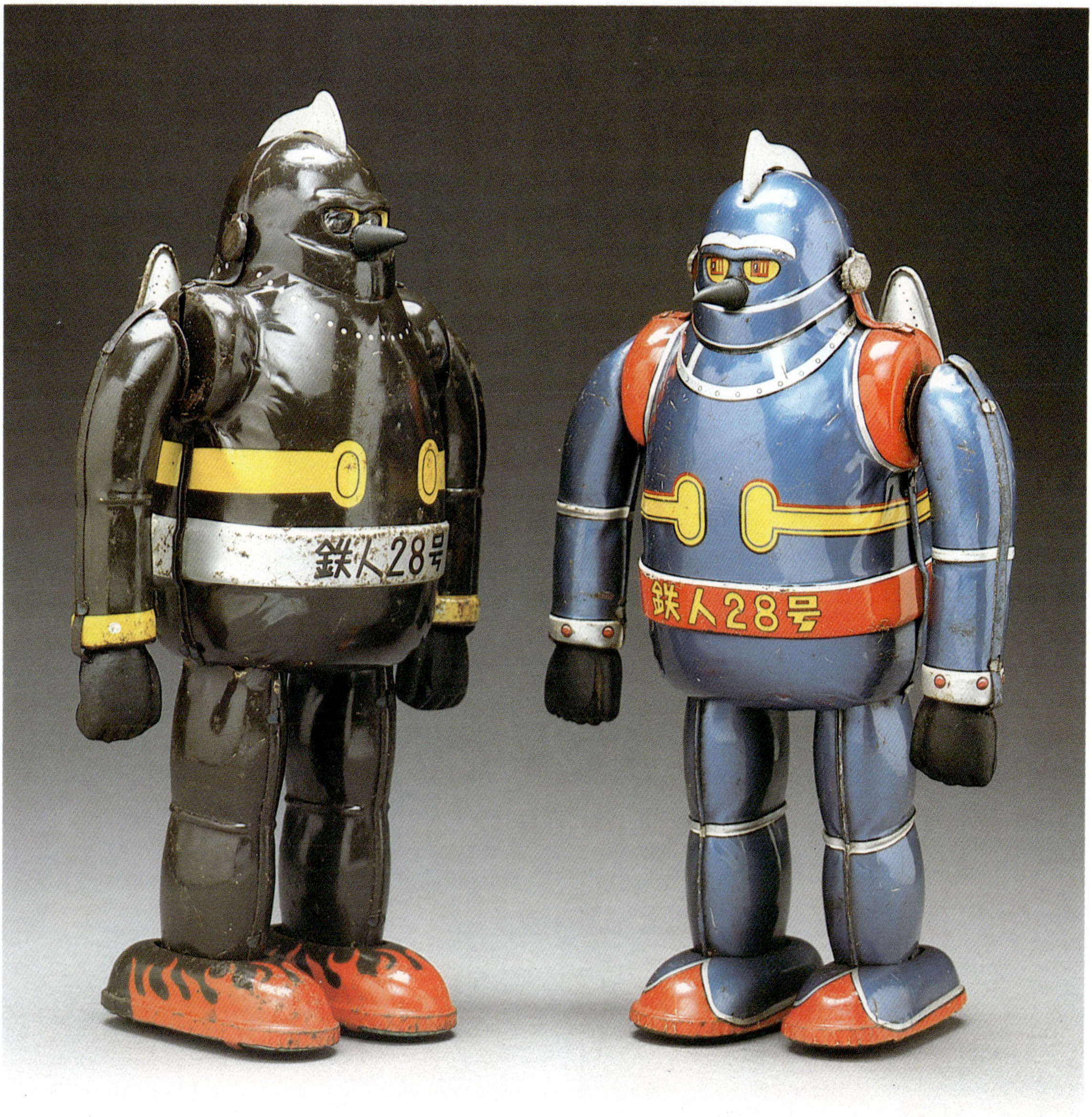

(215)(216) 1960'S／TETSUJIN 28-GO／NOMURA／65×115×195

© HIKARI PRODUCTION

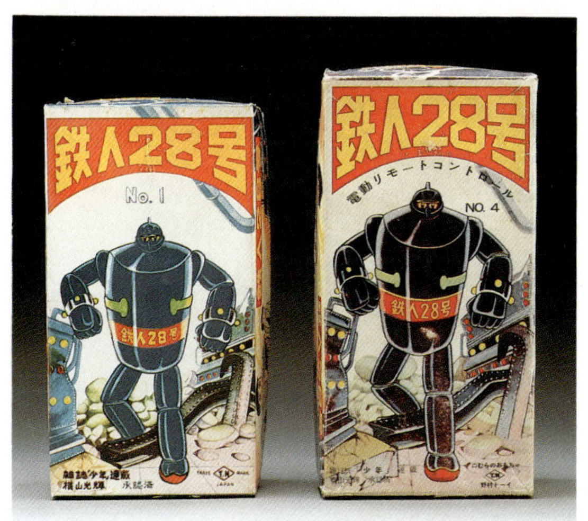

CASE ATTACHED

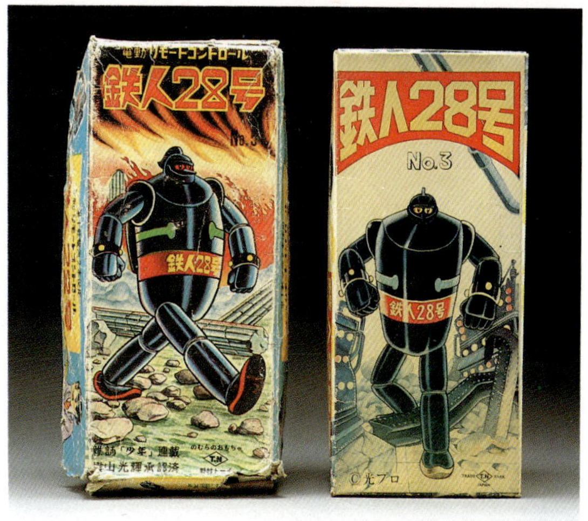

CASE ATTACHED

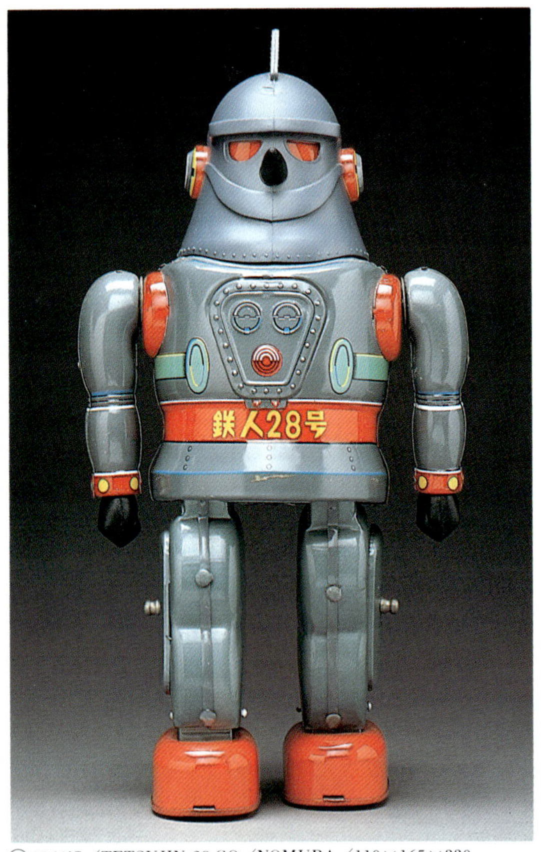

(217) 1960'S／TETSUJIN 28-GO／NOMURA／110×165×330

© HIKARI PRODUCTION

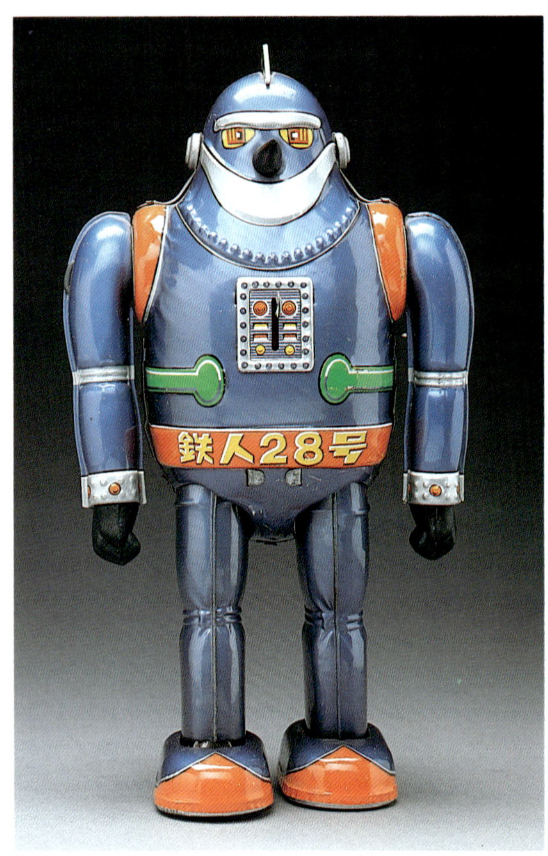

(218) 1950'S／TETSUJIN 28-GO／NOMURA／95×130×240

© HIKARI PRODUCTION

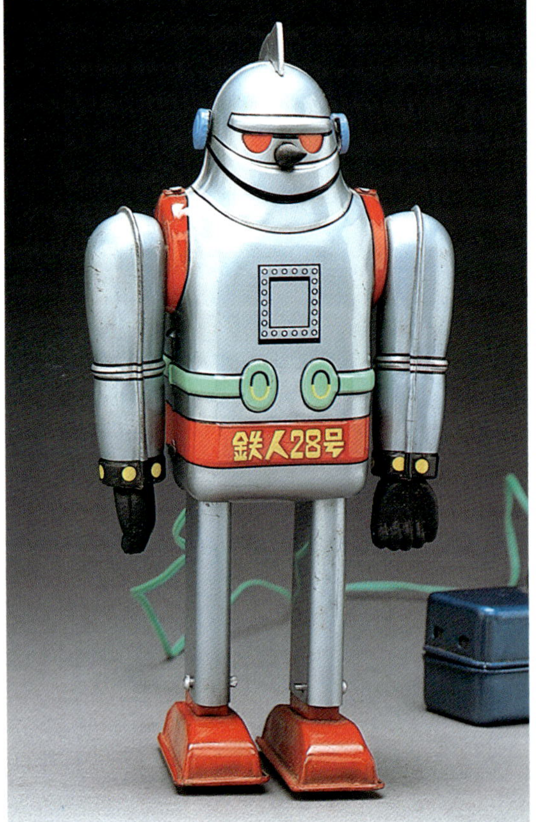

(219) 1960'S／TETSUJIN 28-GO／NOMURA／65×100×200

© HIKARI PRODUCTION

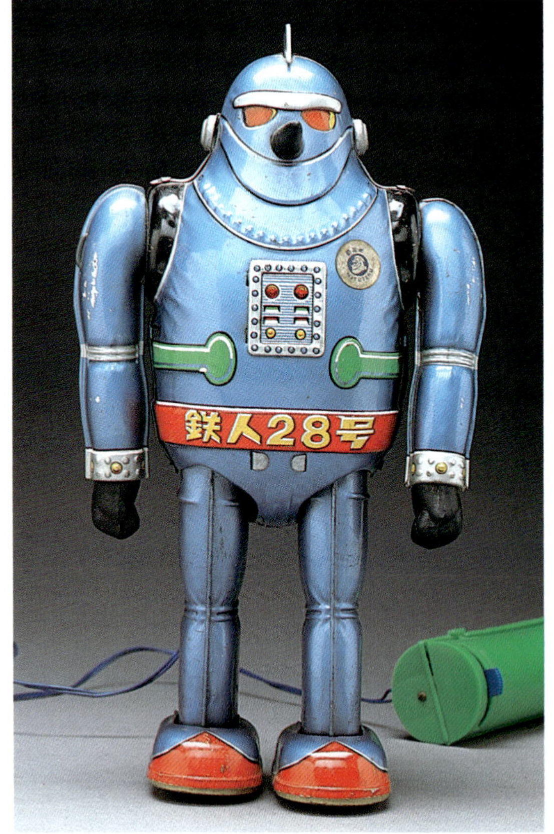

(220) 1950'S／TETSUJIN 28-GO／NOMURA／100×130×240

© HIKARI PRODUCTION

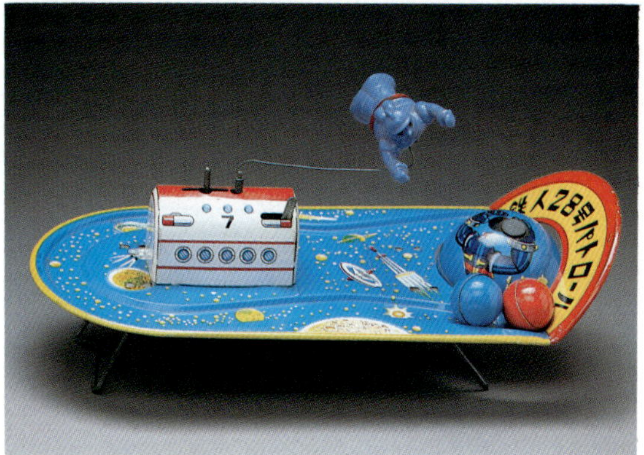

㉑ 1960'S／TETSUJIN 28-GO／UNKNOWN／273×138×150

© HIKARI PRODUCTION

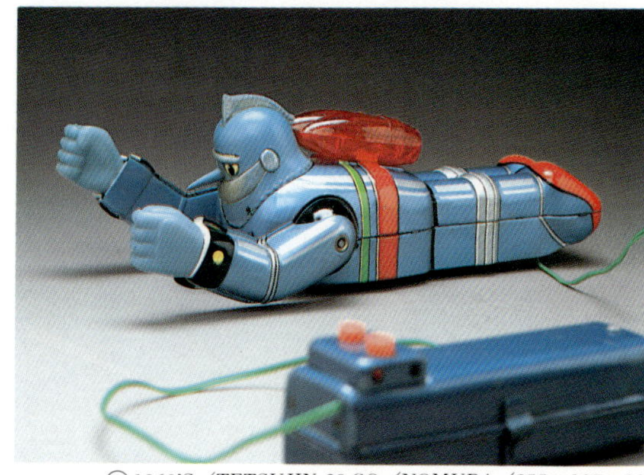

㉒ 1960'S／TETSUJIN 28-GO／NOMURA／255×105×80

© HIKARI PRODUCTION

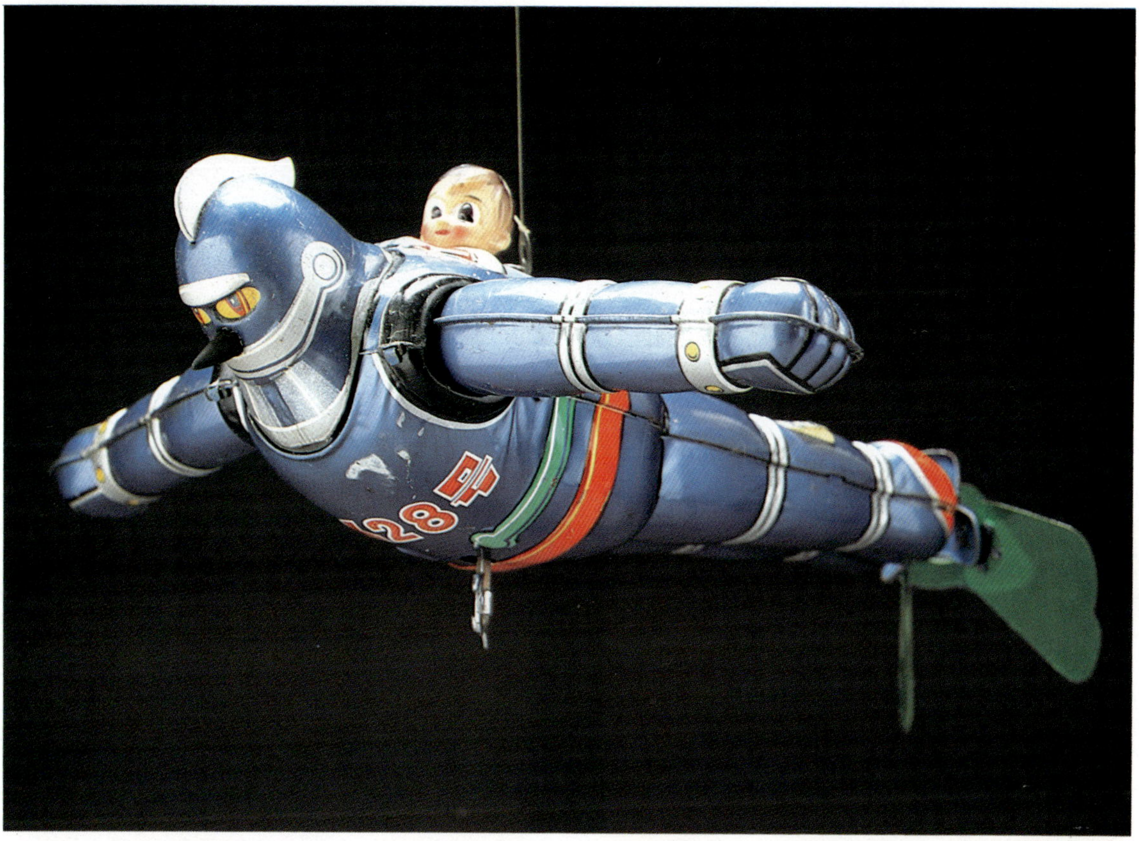

㉓ 1960'S／TETSUJIN 28-GO／NOMURA／230×240×90

© HIKARI PRODUCTION

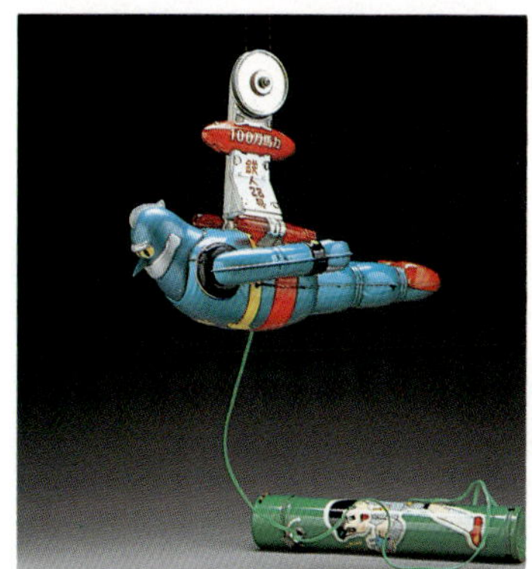

㉔ 1960'S／TETSUJIN 28-GO／BANDAI
／220×115×168

© HIKARI PRODUCTION

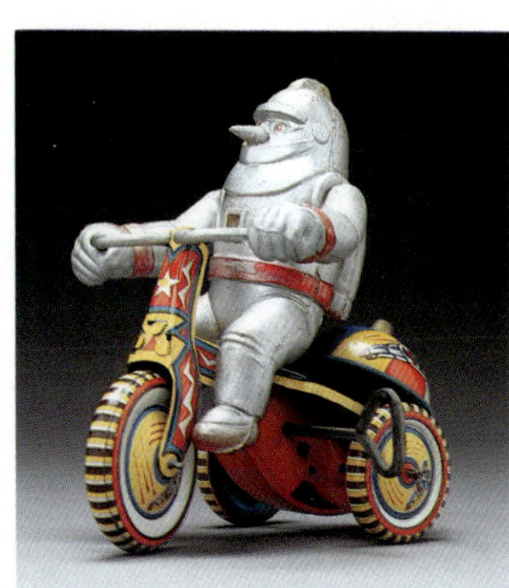

㉕ 1950'S／TETSUJIN 28-GO／MIURA
／112×78×118

© HIKARI PRODUCTION

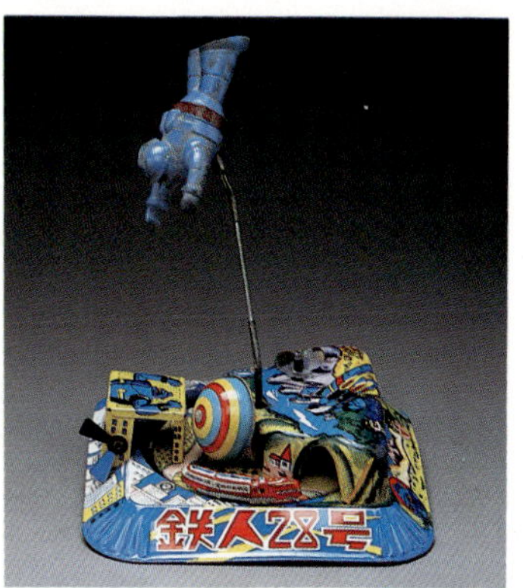

㉖ 1960'S／TETSUJIN 28-GO／YONEZAWA
／140×140×162

© HIKARI PRODUCTION

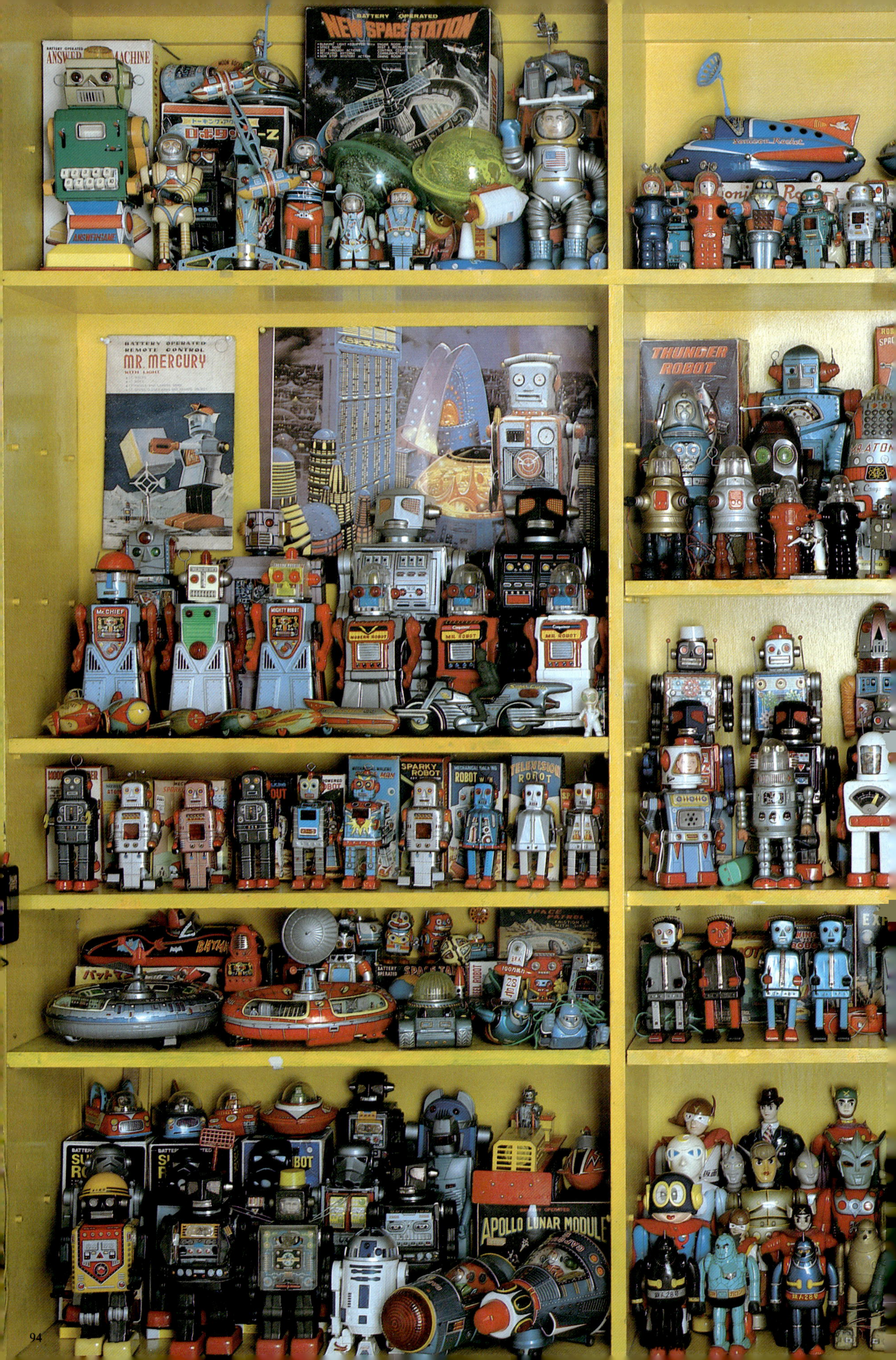
BATTERY OPERATED
NEW SPACE STATION
BATTERY OPERATED
REMOTE CONTROL
MR. MERCURY
WITH LIGHT
THUNDER ROBOT
SPARKY ROBOT
TELEVISION ROBOT
APOLLO LUNAR MODULE

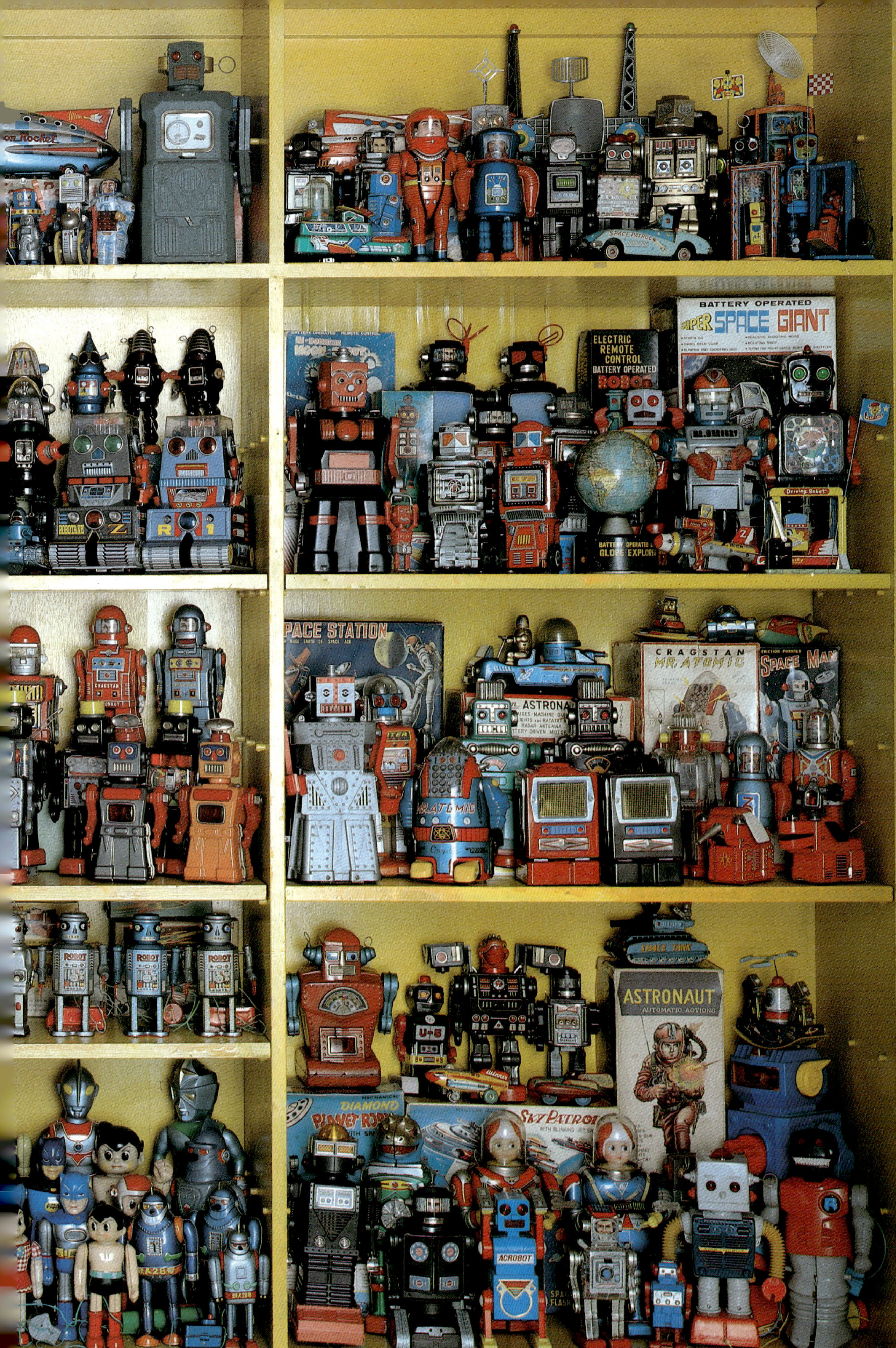
BATTERY OPERATED
SUPER SPACE GIANT
ELECTRIC
REMOTE
CONTROL
BATTERY OPERATED
PACE STATION
CRAGSTAN
MR. ATOMIC
SPACE MAN
ASTRONAUT
AUTOMATIC ACTIONS
SKY PATROL
DIAMOND
ROBOT
ACROBOT

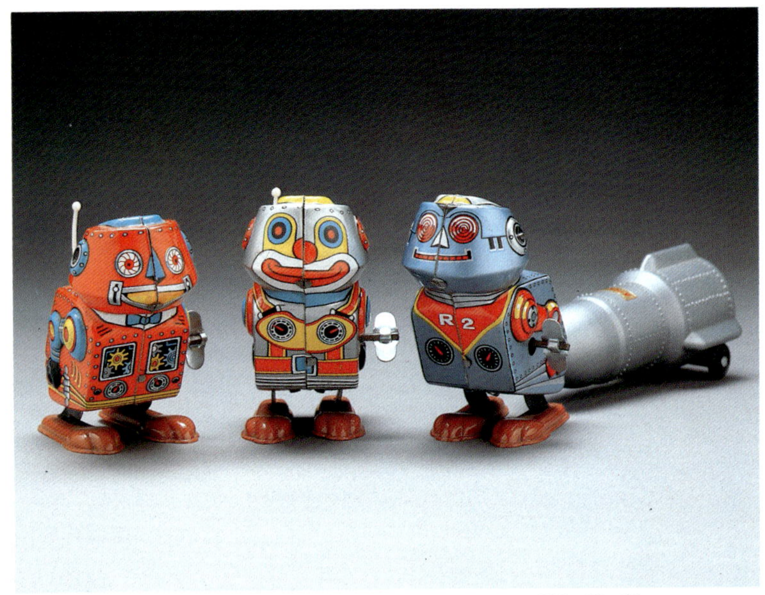

㉒⑦㉒⑧㉒⑨1970'S／ROBOT／YONE TOY／80×55×85、80×55×85、185×55×85

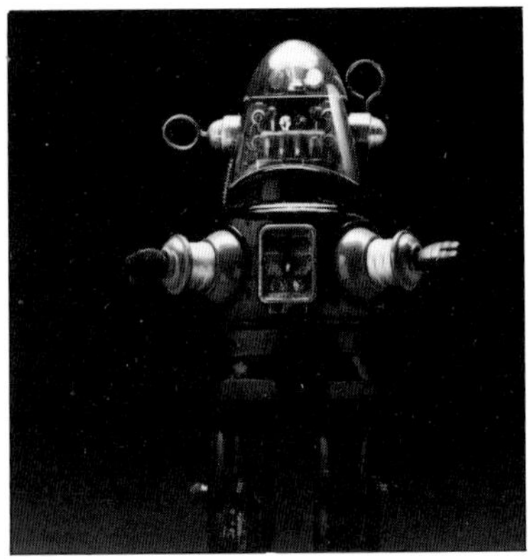

1. **Robby** (Nomura)
Modeled after the robot in MGM's 1956 science fiction thriller, *Forbidden Planet*, the toy runs on two batteries, one inserted in each leg for balance. It walks while pistons move inside the helmet and antennas turn round.

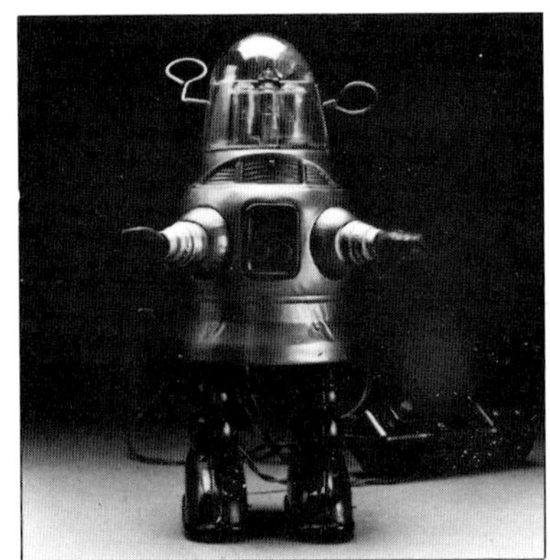

2. **Robby** (Nomura)
This version of Robby operates by remote control. It walks and has the same piston and antenna movement as Robby #1 does. The Robby toys, only one of a number of products to appear after the movie *Forbidden Planet,* easily became as popular as the movie's prototype.

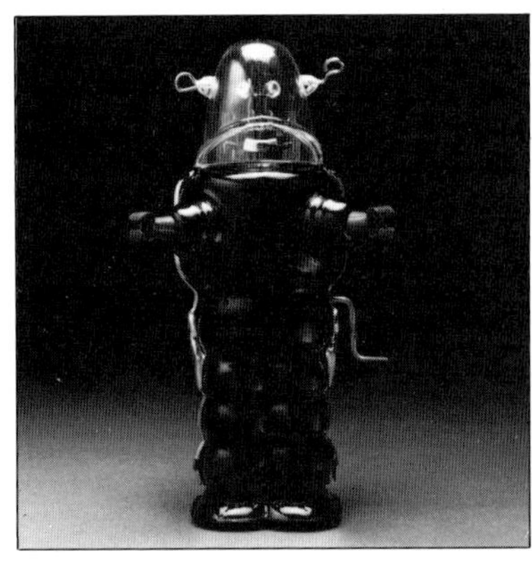

4. **Robby** (Yoshiya)
Keiji Kubo designed this Robby with a friction-type movement wound by a crank on its side. Although it is produced in various colors and sizes, the black version shown here was the original.

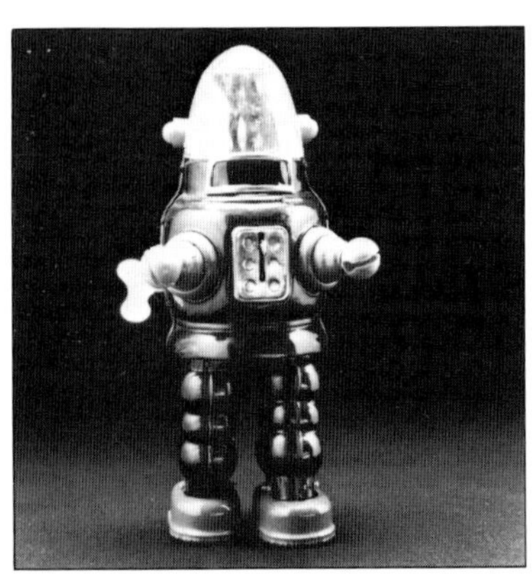

6. **Moon Robot** (Yonezawa)
Spring mechanism. A characteristic detail of all variations of Robby was the transparent helmet. When this tinplate body is set in motion, the twisted metal ribbons inside the helmet turn and sparks appear in the mouthpiece. Hands and ears are made of rubber.

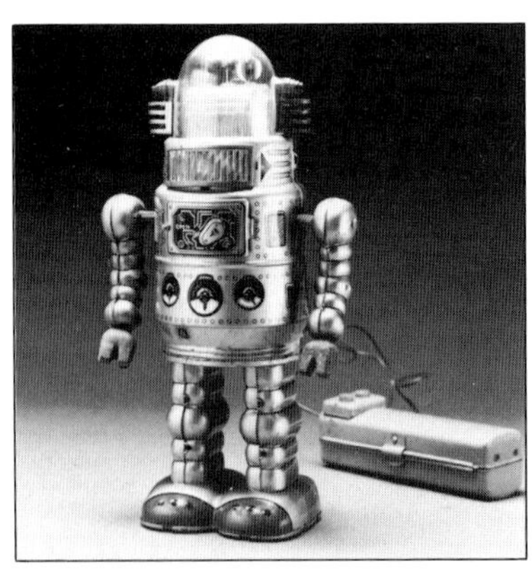

7. **Robot** (Manufacturer unknown)
Battery operated. The hand control has two switches; one switch controls forward motion by moving small pins in and out underneath the feet. The other switch turns the head and antennas and lights up the mouthpiece. This toy has a number of advanced mechanical features.

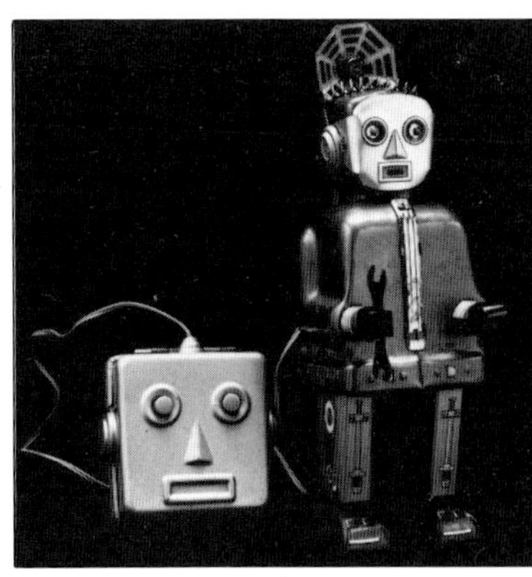

8. **Radar Robot** (Nomura)
Battery operated. Named for the coil and big dish antennas that sit on its head, Radar Robot walks on car-like feet carrying a wrench and flashing its eyes and antennas. The control box has cleverly been given a face with switches for eyes.

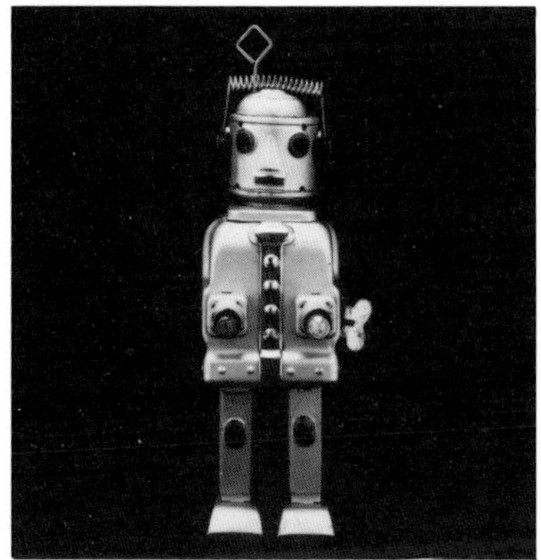

9. **Mr. Robot** (Alps)
An unusual combination of movement: the robot walks by a spring mechanism, and the movement of the legs in turn creates an electrical circuit run on batteries placed in the head. The colored bulbs in the hands flash off and on as the robot walks.

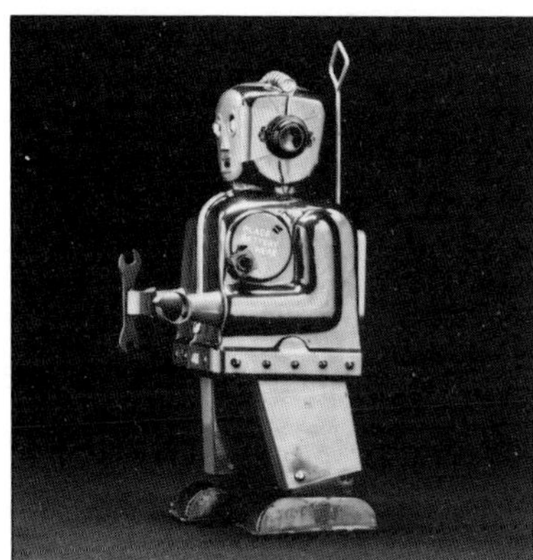

10. **Zoomer the Robot** (Nomura)
Several versions of this robot were manufactured. When the battery is inserted in the chest, the robot walks and the eyes light up. Red and black create a very powerful look.

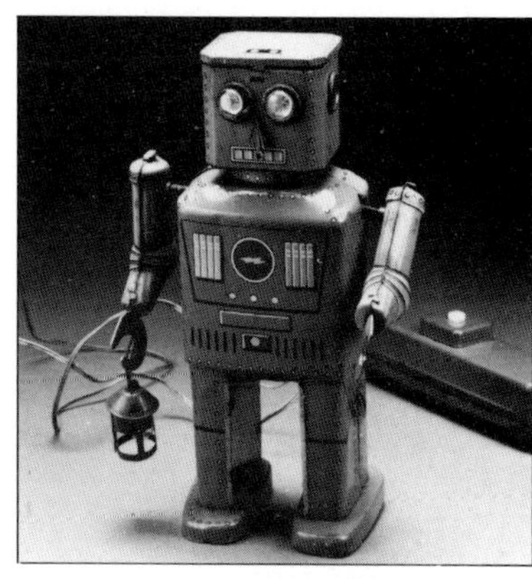

13. **Robot With Lantern** (Line Mar)
Battery operated. As the robot walks, its eyes and lantern light up. It also breathes out real smoke. The bulging eyes and bared teeth create a wonderfully unique expression.

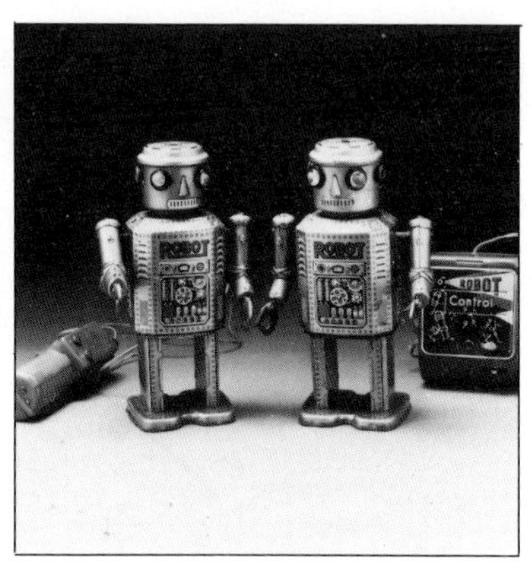

14. 15. **Robot** (Masudaya)
Battery operated. Forward motion is created by pins under the feet that move in and out. The arms swing and the eyes light up. Note the detailed drawing on the body and the control box of the robot on the right; it's probably older than the robot on the left, since that one has a plastic hand control.

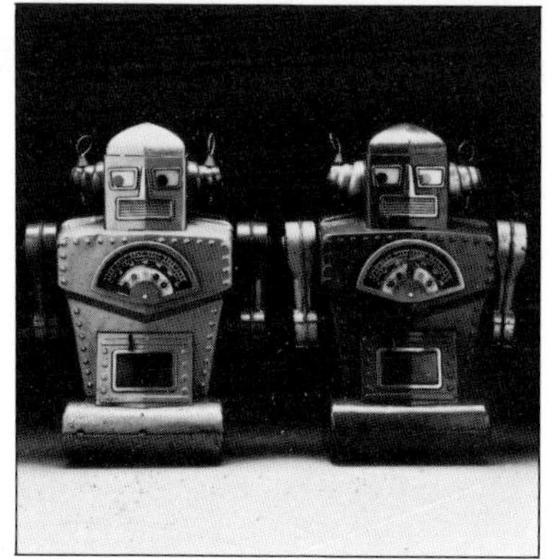

16. 17. **Diamond Planet Robot** (Yonezawa)
Spring mechanism. Masakatsu Tanaka designed this toy which features a small windowed furnace that lights up with sparks and a meter on its chest with fluctuating needle. The tank-shaped bottom is another unique feature with the specific purpose of exploring a rugged planet surface.

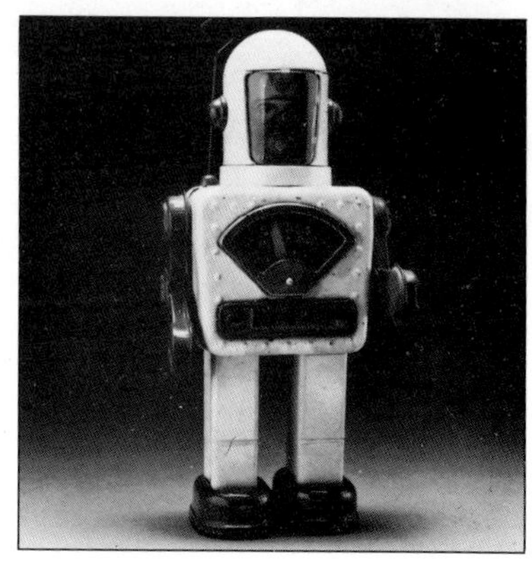

18. **Space Scout** (Yonezawa)
Friction. Once the spring is wound, the astronaut walks and the needle on the chest meter swings. A fairly realistic face is painted inside the helmet; the entire space suit is a very refreshing contrast of red and white.

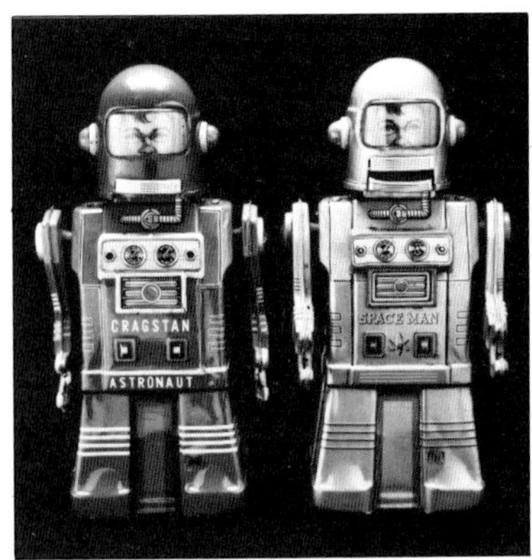

20. 21. **Astronaut, Space Man** (Yonezawa)
Friction. The winding crank is located at the back. Both robots walk, but Space Man (on the right) has a mouth that opens and closes. This wide, bell-shaped body became a distinctive feature for a number of robots, just as the transparent helmet was common to all the Robby-lookalikes.

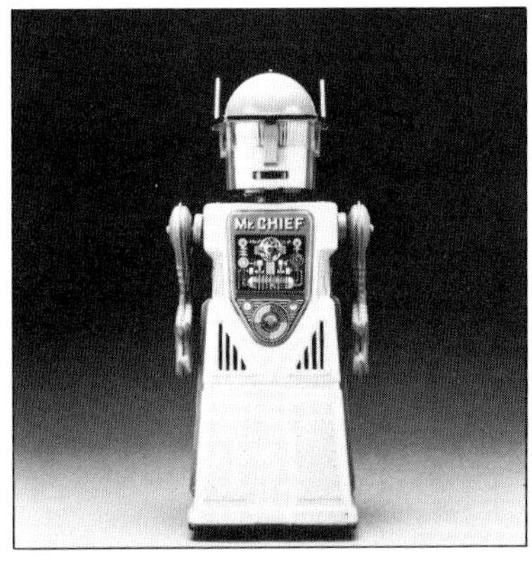

22. **Chief Smoky** (Yoshiya)
Battery operated. Chief Smoky has a bell-shaped body and, as it moves, a head that lights up and smoke spouting from its helmet. This toy features "non-stop action": it automatically changes direction whenever it hits an obstacle and continues to advance.

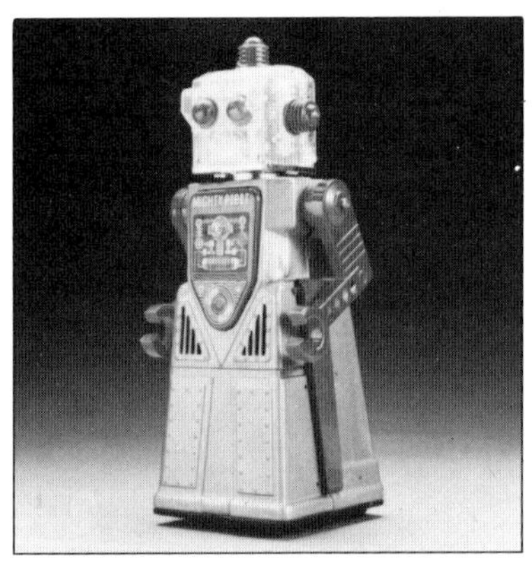

23. **Mighty Robot** (Yoshiya)
Battery operated. The shape and non-stop action feature are similar to those of Chief Smoky (#22). Mighty Robot, however, has a transparent helmet with 16 colorful gears on either side that turn as the toy moves.

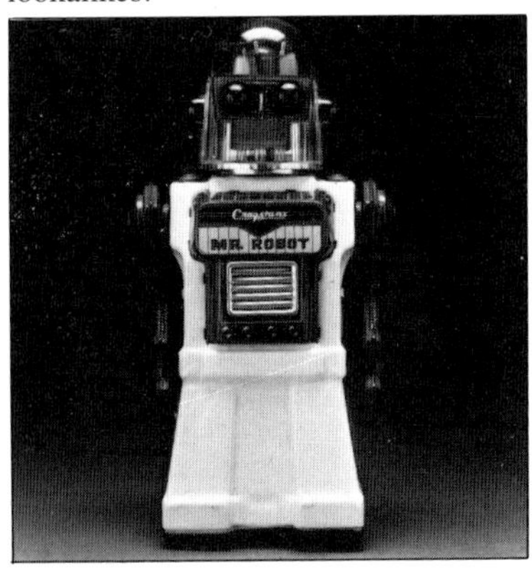

24. **Mr. Robot** (Yonezawa)
Battery operated. With a combination of the transparent Robby-type head and a wide-legged body shape, Mr. Robot is able to move forward, swivel its head and light up. A realistic array of computer-like bulbs and coils are visible inside the helmet. The clean lines and white color are very suggestive of a real robot.

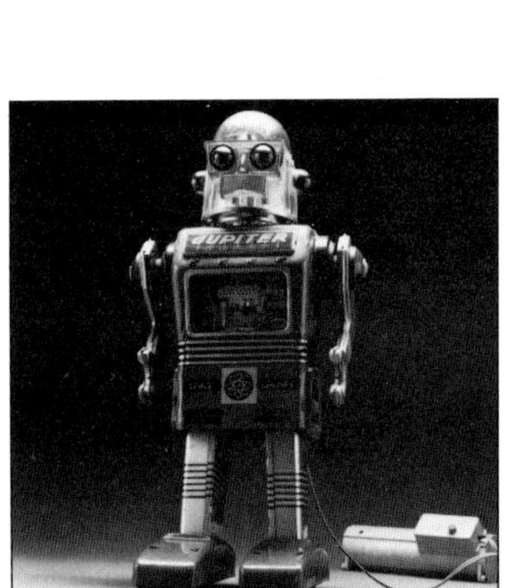

27. **Jupiter Robot** (Yonezawa)
Battery operated. The head is the same as that of #24, but the legs move independently, in a sliding motion. Lights in the head operate and, printed on the chest, is a very realistic rendering of tubes and circuits.

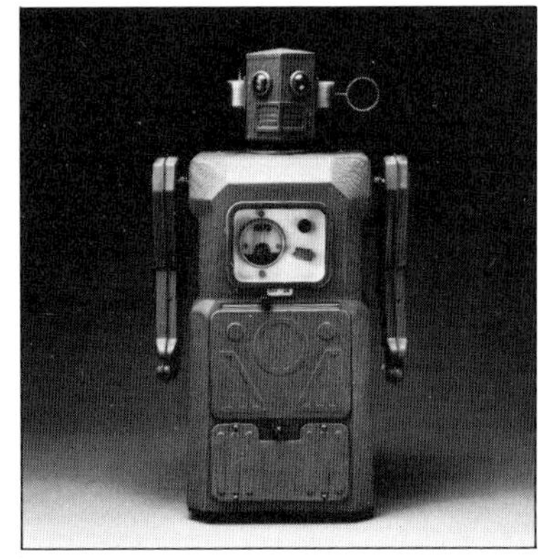

29. **Robot** (Masudaya)
Battery operated. In the late 1950s, Kunihiro Kiso developed this earliest model of a radio-controlled robot. When it walks, its ear antennas turn. A larger than usual robot, its size and expressionless face add to its powerful appearance.

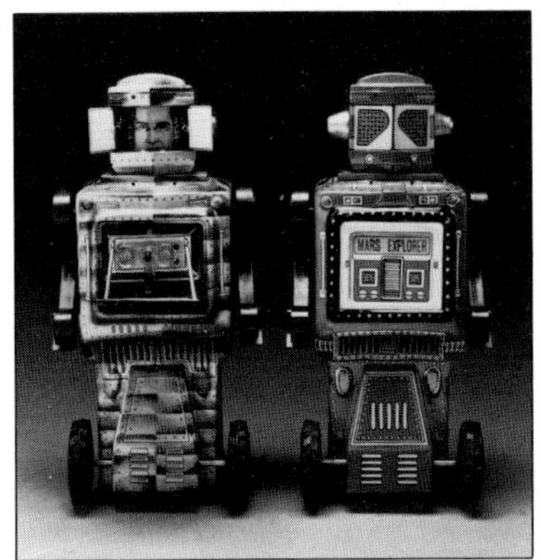

34. 35. **Mars Explorer** (Horikawa)
Battery operated. This robot features a stop-action sequence: it rolls forward on its tires, stops, and face protector doors open, revealing an astronaunt's face. At the same time the front opens and machine guns make a firing noise. The guns stop, both chest and face windows close, and the robot starts forward again. The robot on the left has been painted to look like a tank.

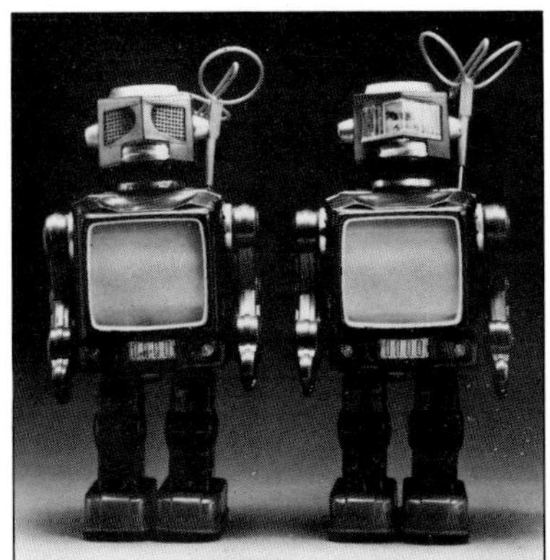

52. 53. **TV Robot** (Horikawa)
Battery operated. This robot walks while pictures appear on the built-in TV; the aerial is attached at the left shoulder. Note the astronaut's face on the robot on the right.

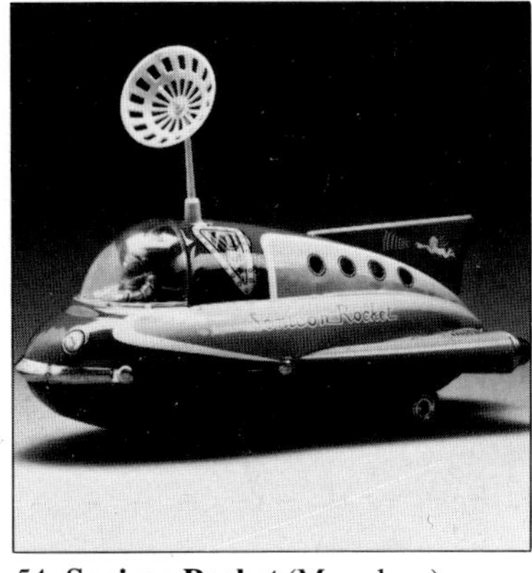

54. **Sonicon Rocket** (Masudaya)
Battery operated. Developed by Kunihiro Kiso, this robot responds to sound: it changes direction at the sound of a human voice or whistle. Its unique shape came from a painting by the late Kiyoshi Yamashita.

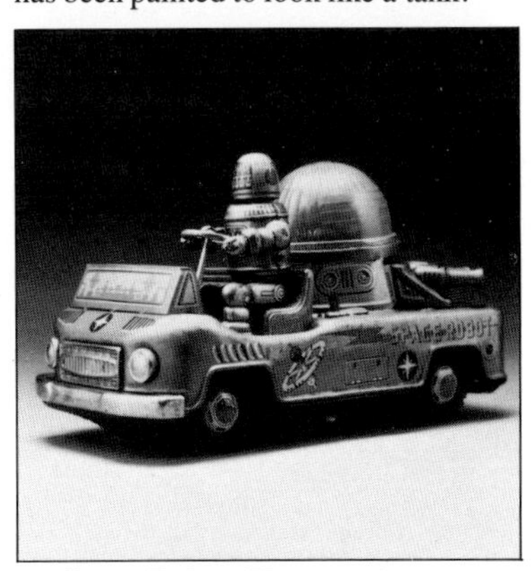

55. **Space Robot** (Yonezawa)
Battery operated. The robot drives the car and looks from side to side, while the dome behind him lights and machine guns fire noisily. This gold-suited robot exudes personality.

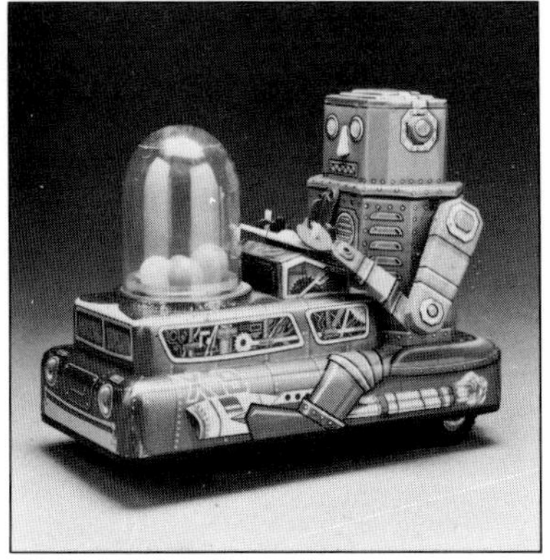

58. **X-9 Robot** (Masudaya)
Battery operated. While the toy moves forward, colorful balls are flipped around the dome by a set of pins underneath. The robot's hands actually grip the steering wheel and its legs are neatly printed on the side of the space car; a colorful and fun toy.

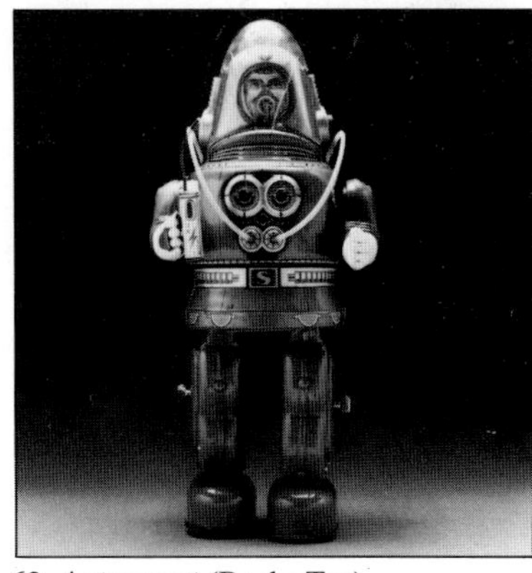

62. **Astronaut** (Rosko Toy)
Batteries placed in both legs enable the robot to walk and "talk" into its walkie talkie. Besides making talking sounds, the robot's head moves, and both helmet and walkie talkie light up with sparks. An oxygen tank is strapped to the astronaut's back.

Explanation

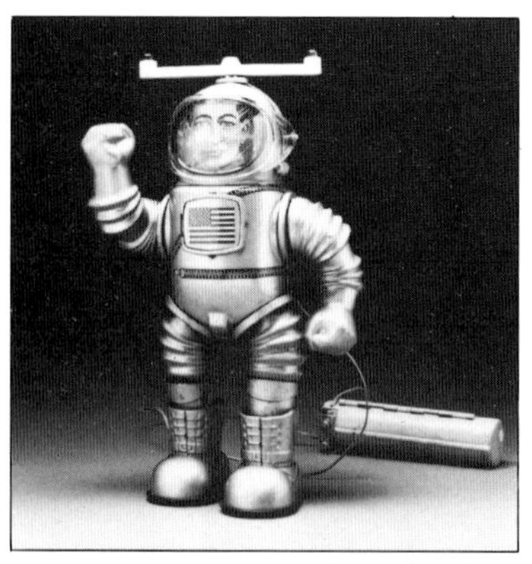

63. **Moon Scout** (Louis Marx)
Battery operated. Two switches on the hand control operate this astronaut as he explores the moon. One switch controls his walking and turns the propeller antenna which flashes in red and green. The other switch opens a flag-decorated compartment on his chest and releases bouncing rubber balls.

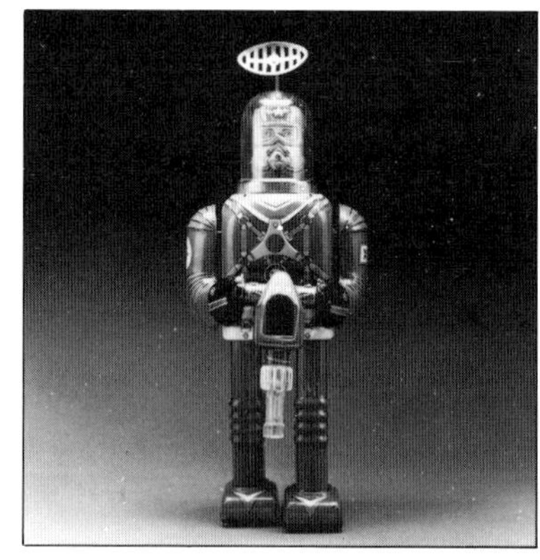

64. **Astronaut** (Daiya)
Battery operated. The battery is housed in the oxygen tank in back. In a stop-action sequence, the robot walks with its dish antenna turning, stops and raises the machine gun while it emits sparks and goes rat-a-tat-tat. Then the gun is lowered and the robot walks forward again.

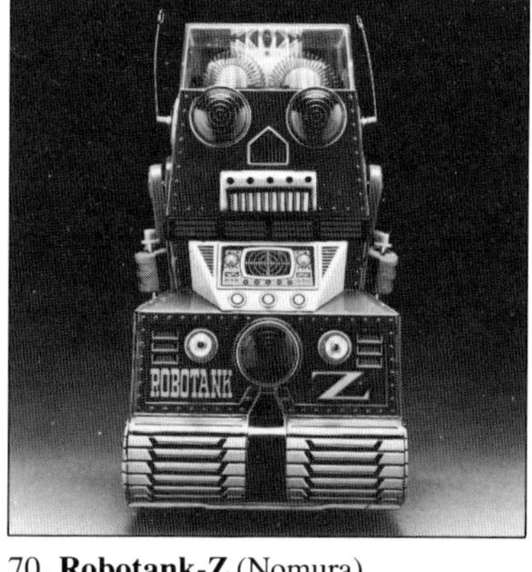

70. **Robotank-Z** (Nomura)
Battery operated. Moves like a tank but speaks like a robot: the tank moves forward, then stops and plays a programmed tape message; the machine gun in front flashes red and sounds gun fire; then the action repeats. The tin-plate toy with plastic arm parts was manufactured in the 1960s, at a time when plastic parts were just being introduced.

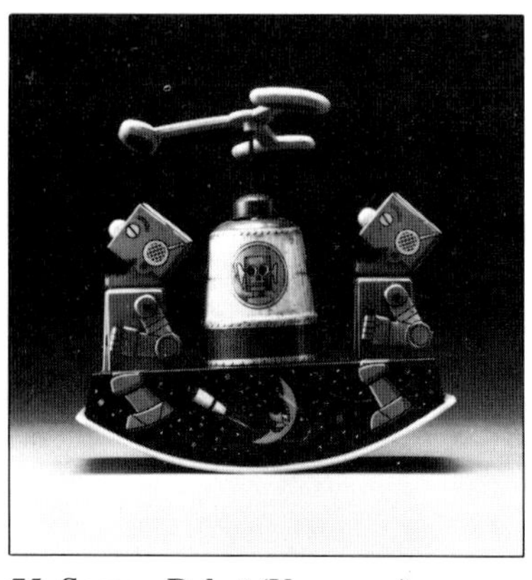

75. **Seesaw Robot** (Yonezawa)
Spring mechanism. The lighter side of robot life. As these two seesaw, their arms swing, antennas turn and mouths open and close. Note the laughing moon detail on this wonderfully fun toy.

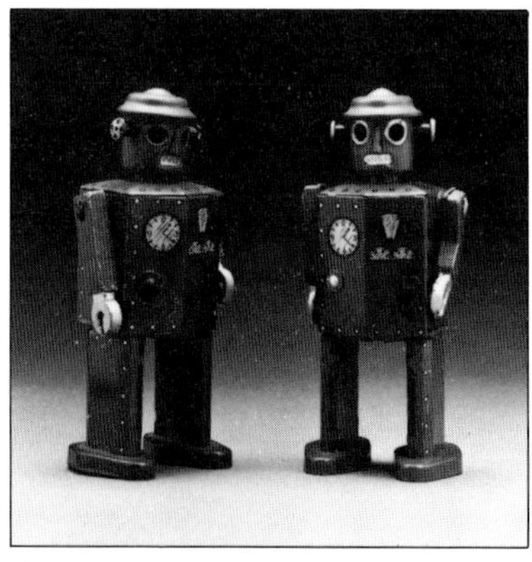

80. 81. **Atomic Robot Man** (unknown)
Spring mechanism. These robots are among the oldest introduced in this book. Manufactured in occupied Japan, they have a very simple but charming design. The one on the right is all tin-plate, but the other has cast-iron hands.

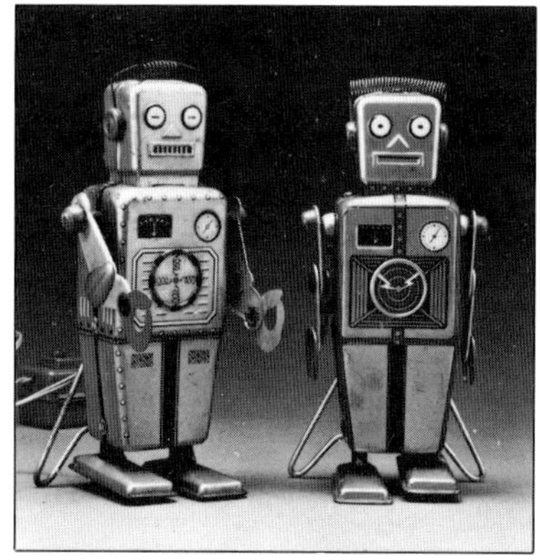

88. 89. **Robot** (Yonezawa)
The robot on the right is battery operated; the one on the left has a spring mechanism. They both walk aided by a wire triangle attached at the back; a coil antenna wraps about the head. Similar robots but with subtly different eyes and expressions.

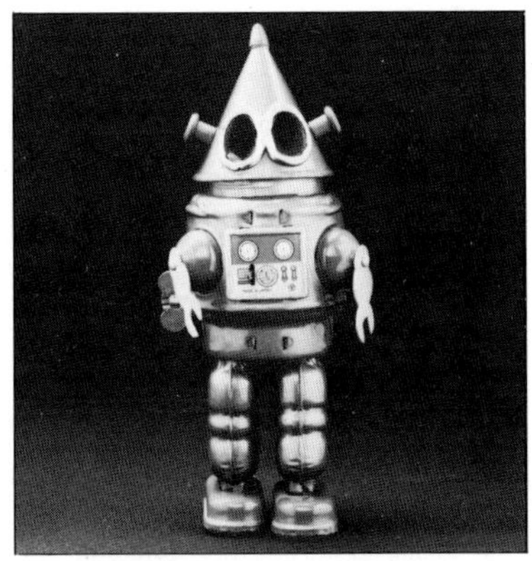

92. **Robot** (Yonezawa)
Spring mechanism. The triangular head, and dangling wrench-shaped arms are the unique features. This robot first appeared in a popular Japanese TV series, "Shonen Jet," in the late 1950s. Designed by Yoshitaka Yonezawa, the robot walks and has eyes that spark.

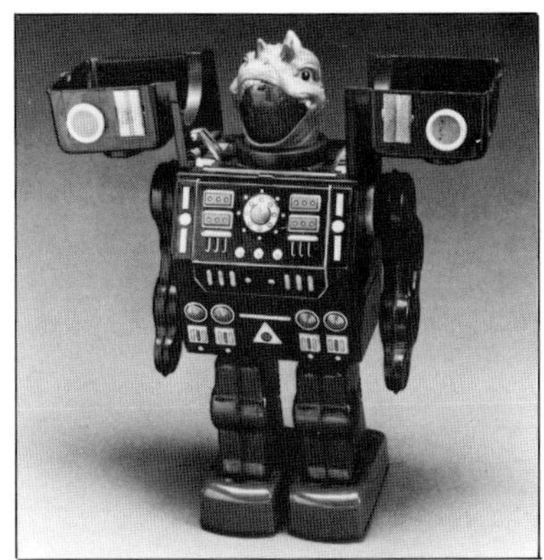

97. **Change Robot** (Horikawa)
Battery operated. A surprise is in store as the robot advances, stops and the head opens up. A monster head pops up, roaring and looking mad (tiny red lights inside flash on and off). Then it returns to a robot shape and repeats the cycle. A unique concept.

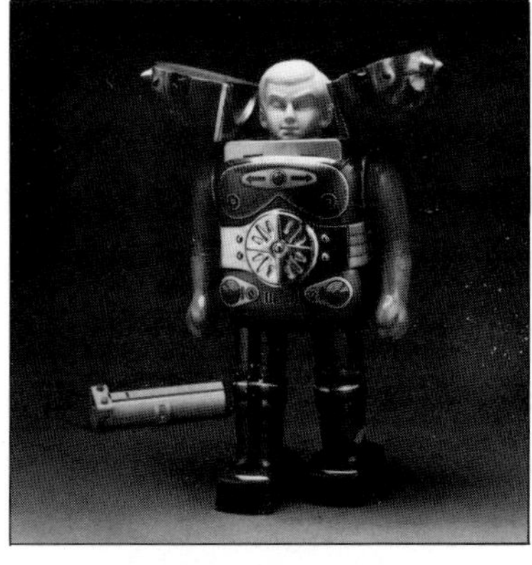

98. **Change Man** (Marumiya)
Battery operated. On a variation of #97, a man's face pops up when the monster's head splits in two. While the body of the robot is painted bright colors, the man's head is an ominous pale green.

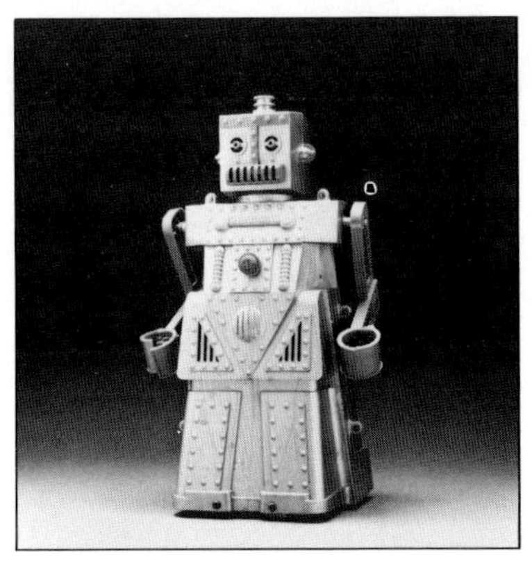

99. **Robert Robot** (unknown)
Friction. When the crank is wound at the back, the robot moves forward and speaks "I am Robert Robot"–in English, which could mean it was manufactured in America. The quiet colors give it personality.

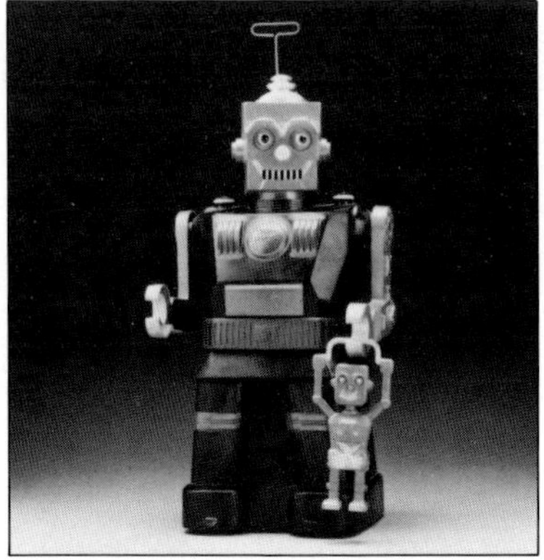

100. **Robot and Son** (Louis Marx)
Battery operated. Made in America in the 1950s this robot, with son in hand, turns its head and blinks its eyes. Baby wears a diaper. The shiny black and red finish is attractive and readily enhances the toy's overall quality.

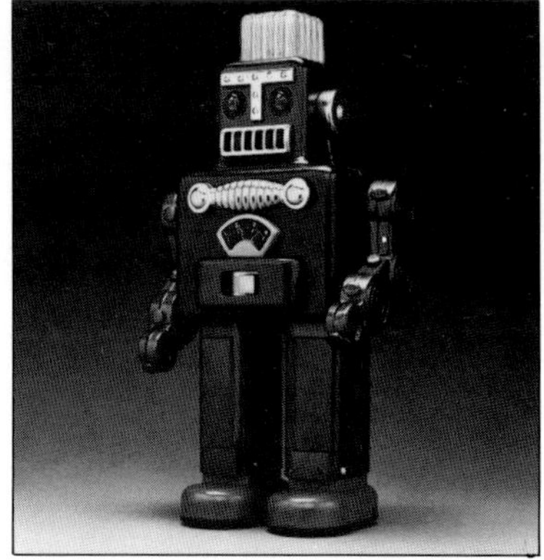

101. **Smoking Robot** (Yonezawa)
Battery operated. This masterful creation is the work of Rikizo Miyazawa. When set in motion, the robot walks forward while throwing off sparks; it stops to breathe out smoke and flash its eyes before walking forward again. The unsophisticated design adds to its robot image, while the facial expression has a human quality.

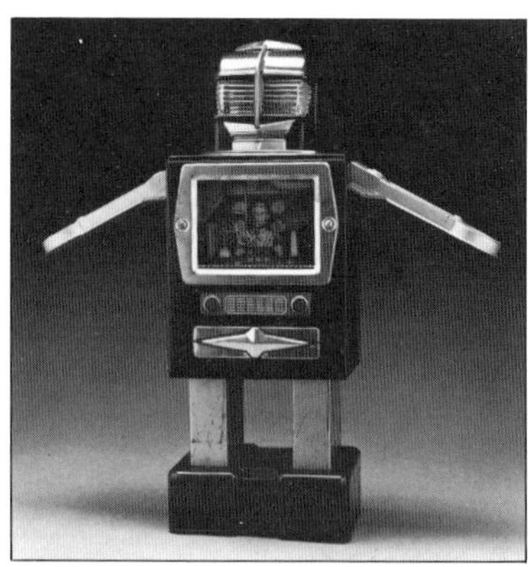

104. **Space Explorer** (Yonezawa)
Battery operated. At first, this toy appears to be a TV set, but once turned on, a robot's arms and legs extend and a picture of a pilot in a cockpit comes on the screen. More turtle-like than robot, it moves forward flashing its green eyes alternately.

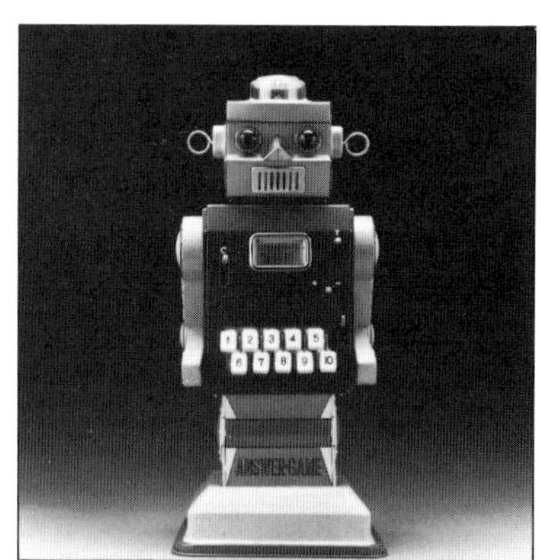

105. **Answer Game Machine** (Ichida)
Battery operated. Designed to compute simple addition and subtraction, this robot resembles a cash register with great use of color and detail. When a problem is keyed in, the answer appears in the small window on the chest while the robot's eyes flash.

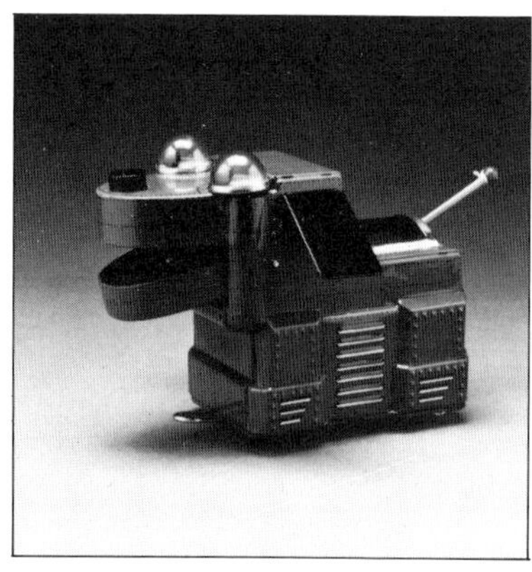

106. **Space Dog** (Yoshiya)
Friction. With a mouth that yaps and tail that waves, this is a very appealing toy, with wonderful details such as the bulging eyes and coiled wire tail.

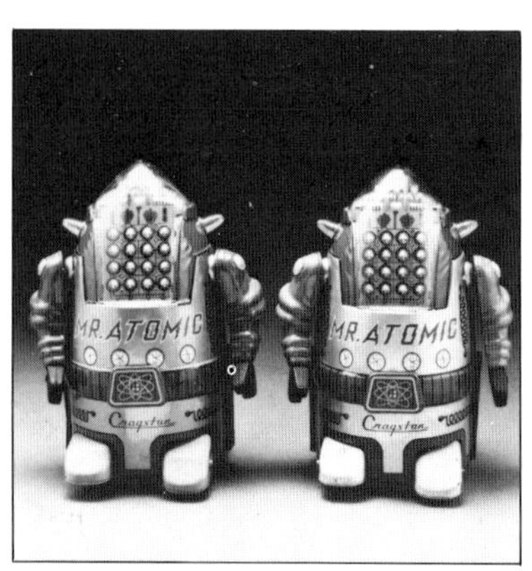

114. 115. **Mr. Atomic** (Yonezawa)
Battery operated. Easily recognized by its humorous rounded shape, "tap-dancing" toe action, and board of lights, Mr. Atomic became a real collector's item because it was manufactured in very small quantities. The matrix of 16 lights flash on and off in 7 different colors.

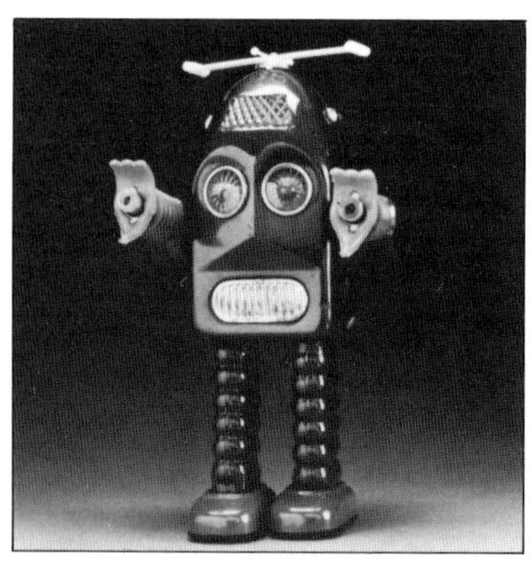

117. **Thunder Robot** (Asakusa Toy)
Battery operated. This strange-looking robot—all head and no body—offers a variety of action. It walks, spins its propeller and lights up a red headlight and green eyes. When it stops walking it raises machine-gun arms and makes sparks and machine-gun noises, then lowers its arms and continues walking.

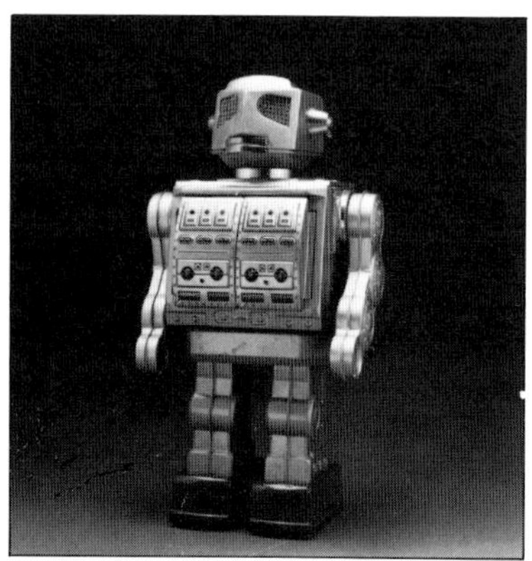

118. **Giant Robot** (Horikawa)
Battery operated. Big and powerful-looking, this robot was one of the all-time bestsellers. Other shapes and sizes were manufactured, all of which could walk and had a chest that rotated and opened to fire a gun. The gun sparks and makes a firing noise.

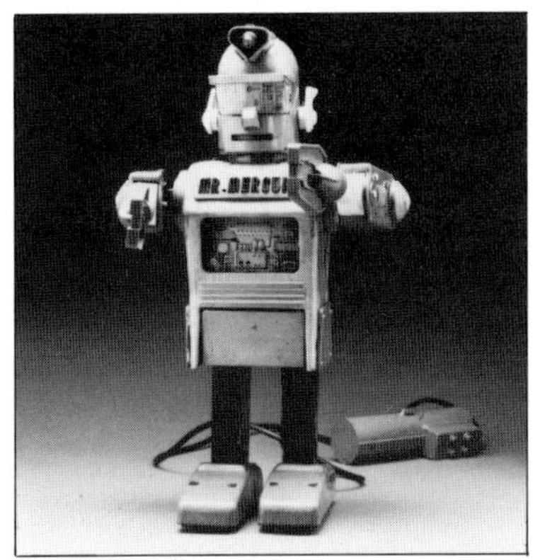

120. **Mr. Mercury** (Yonezawa)
Battery operated. Mr. Mercury has a four-switch control box enabling it to walk, bend forward and pick up objects with its forklift arms. Instead of eyes the robot has a detailed drawing of a control room; more machine parts are printed on its chest.

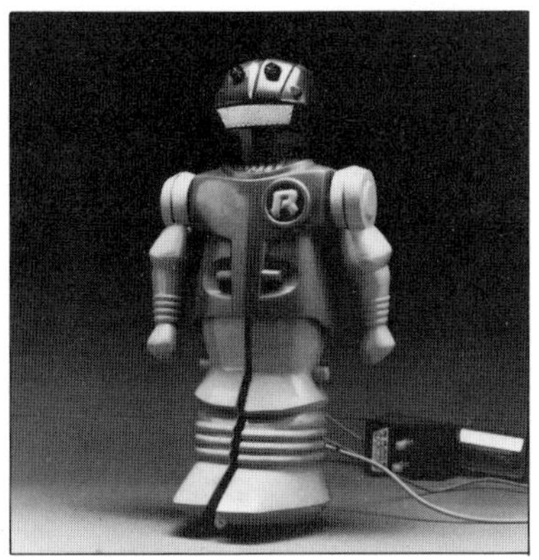

123. **R-Robot** (Bandai)
Battery operated. With a face like a fly and a ski-boot body, this robot was a catalog offering of Sears & Roebuck in the late 1960s. By that time, plastic was a more commonly used material than tin-plate for toys. Action features were arms that swung and shining eyes as it moved forward.

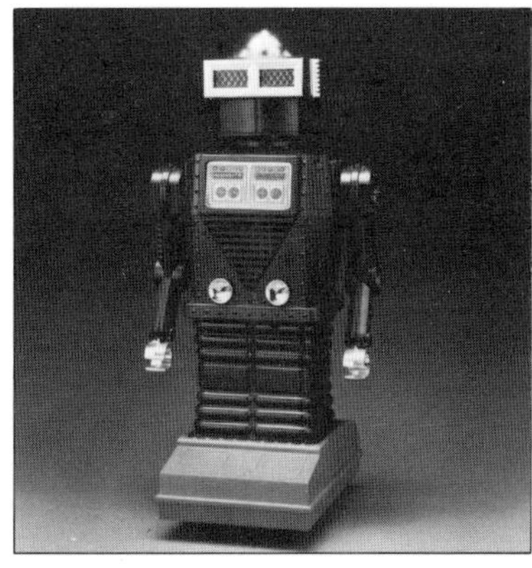

128. **Hysterical Robot** (Unknown)
Battery operated. This robot moves forward, shaking its lighted head. It stops to laugh aloud and reveals a toothy grin while shoulders shake. Chalk up the weird facial expression to the honeycomb eyes and mouth full of teeth.

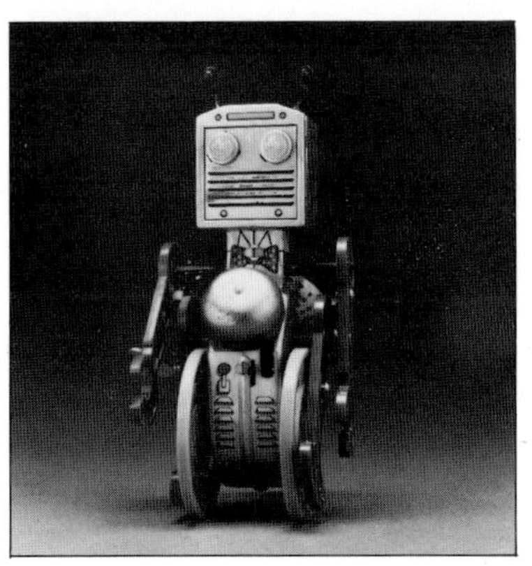

130. **Wheel Robot** (Asahi)
Spring mechanism. Part radio and part bicycle, here's a robot that sports a bow-tie as it runs around, ringing its bell.

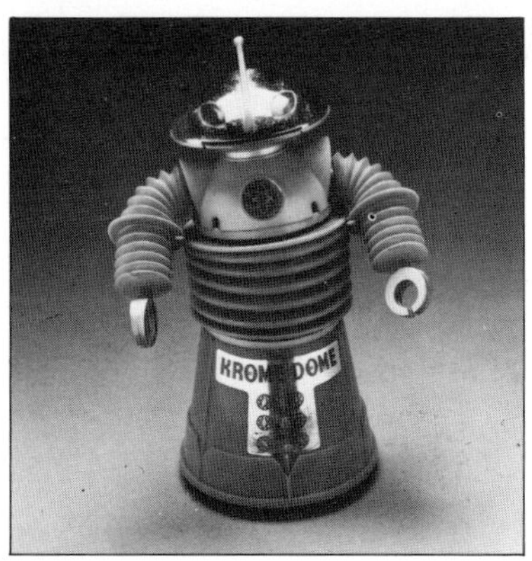

131. **Krome Dome** (Yonezawa)
Battery operated. Like an accordian, the torso stretches and shrinks as the robot's eyes flash. The clam-shaped head also opens and shuts and gives the toy a Martian look. High on the list of most interesting and unusual.

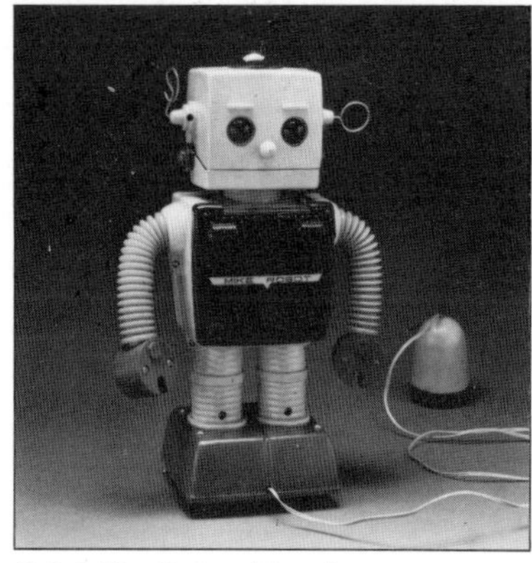

135. **Mike Robot** (Tomy)
Battery operated. The robot responds to the sound of a human voice speaking into the mike on the control piece by moving its mouth and flickering its eyes. This is a very sophisticated toy to have eyes that will light and change intensity as the speaker's voice changes.

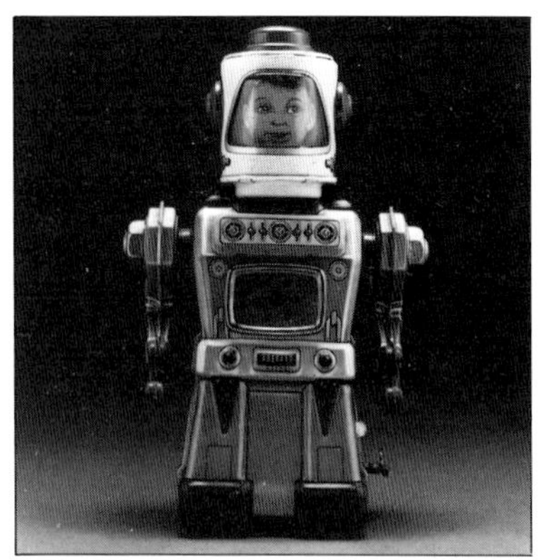

137. **Chime Trooper** (Aoshin)
Spring mechanism. As the bell-shaped astronaut moves, space music plays from a built-in music box. The sturdy body seems mismatched with the little boy face inside the helmet.

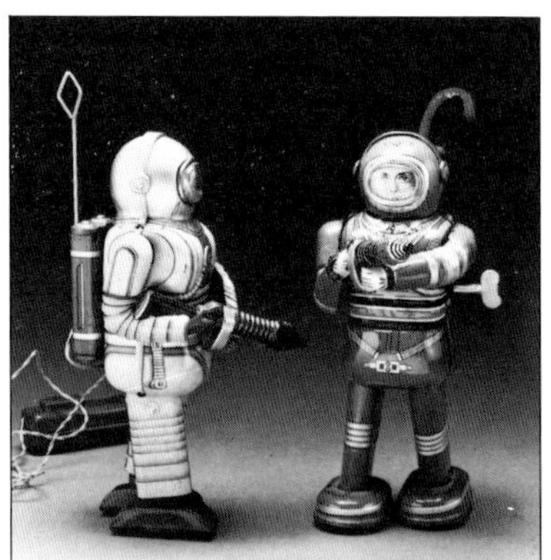

144. 145. **Astronauts** (Nomura, Daiya)
The space explorer on the left is battery operated; the one on the right has a spring mechanism. Both walk and wave their machine guns up and down, but only the one on the left can fire red sparks.

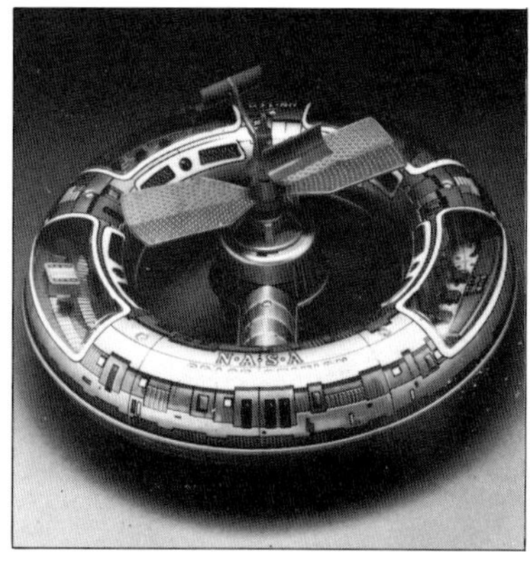

157. **Space Station** (Horikawa)
Battery operated. This doughnut-shaped NASA station is divided into different rooms—engine room, control room, R & R room, and so on—each printed in great detail. With its glowing lights and beeping sound effects, Space Station could transform a dark room into the world of space travel and adventure.

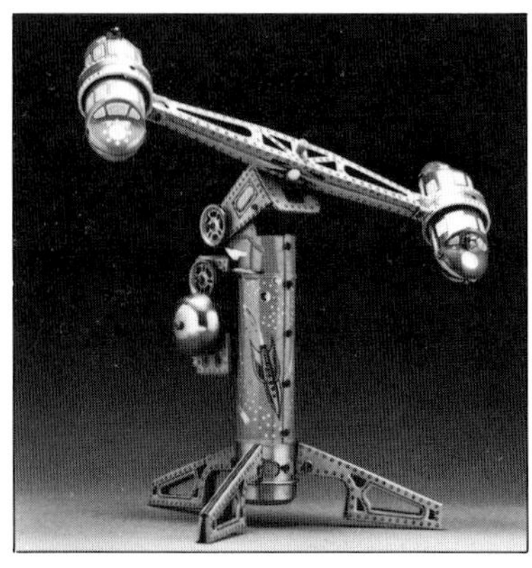

165. **Coney Island** (Alps)
Battery operated. Pictured on the cover of the box is the amusement park ride that was the model for this toy. This was a very popular ride that could satisfy any child's fantasy of being an astronaut. When the toy rockets are set in orbit, the bell rings and lights on the rockets turn on.

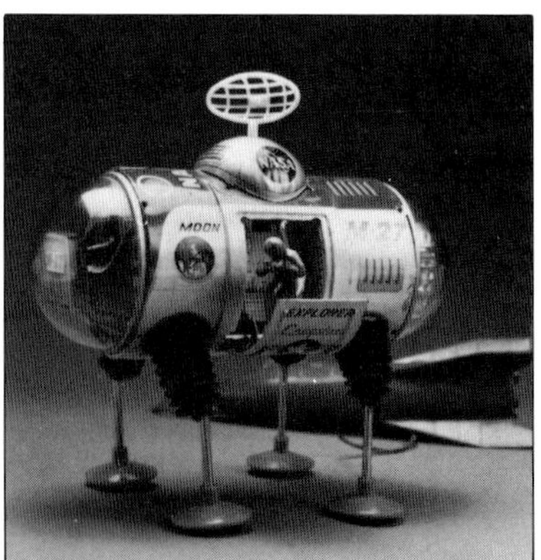

166. **Moon Explorer** (Yonezawa)
Battery operated. The plastic rocket is actually the control box; one of two switches operates the moon craft's walking action. The other opens the hatch where an astronaut pops out intent on taking a picture. The odd-shaped capsule looks a little like a water strider or other long-legged bug.

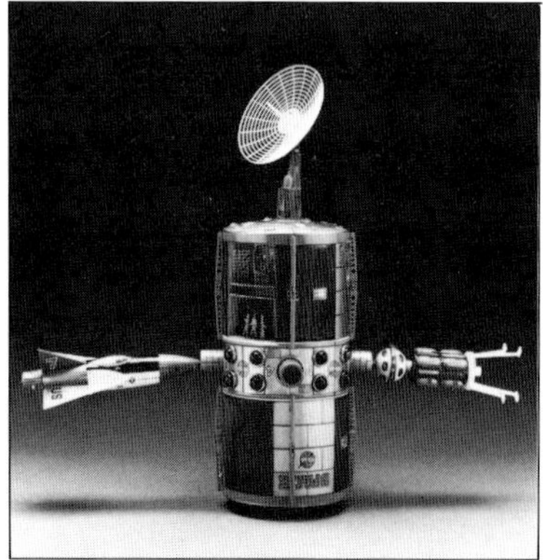

168. **Space Station** (Waco)
Battery operated. This cylindrical space station features an unusual sequence of actions: while blue and red lights flash, tower and antenna turn; this action stops and the upper half rises and spins separately. The side of the space station is decorated with pictures of crew and the control room.

Explanation

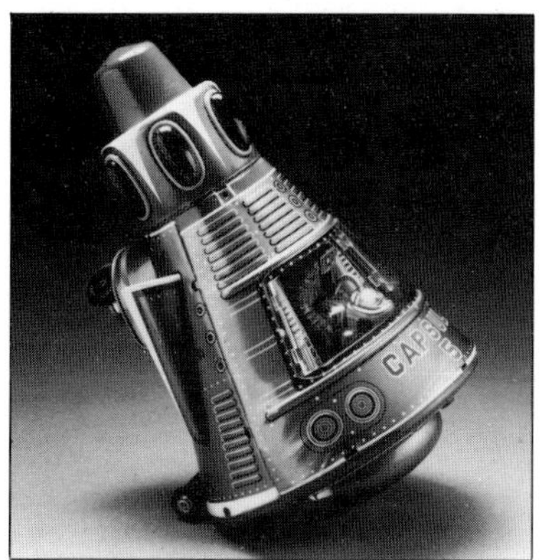

172. **Capsule 5** (Masudaya)
Battery operated. The one-man satellite rocks in an irregular motion while producing sounds and flashing red and blue lights. The astronaut holds a camera. Manufactured in the 1950s at the dawning of the space age, this toy entertained thousands of children and adults mesmerized by the thought of space travel.

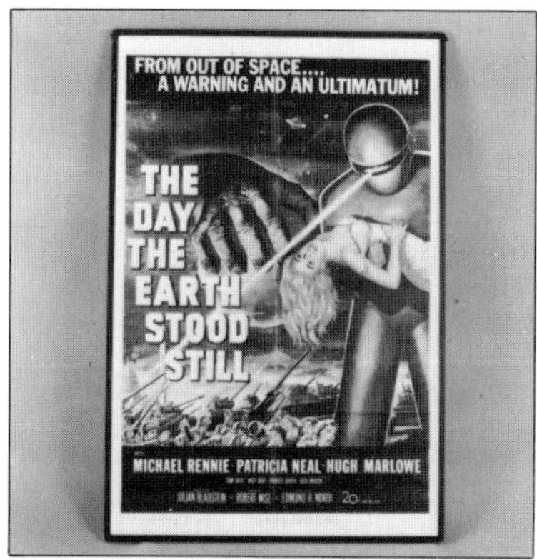

180. **The Day The Earth Stood Still** (original poster)
Twentieth Century Fox produced this science fiction classic in 1951. In the story, an alien from outer space causes all energy on earth to stop in order to bring an end to war. Featured was a robot named Goto who destroyed all the weaponry of the American armed forces with just one look from its powerful eyes.

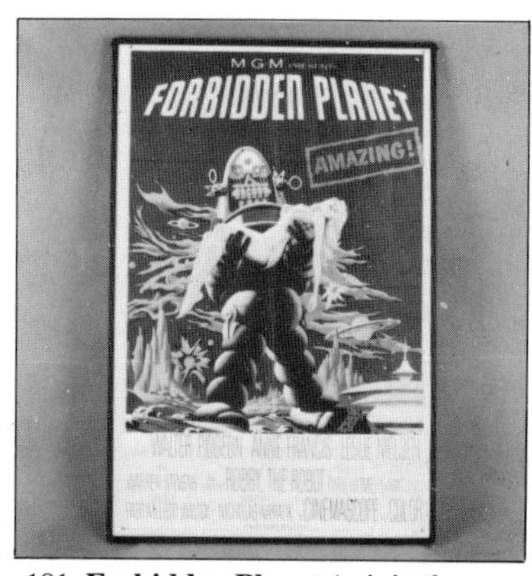

181. **Forbidden Planet** (original poster)
Pictured in the poster is Robby, who debuted in this 1956 MGM movie. One of the world's best known robots, Robby was also one of the friendliest and best at communicating; it also appreciated human emotions. Robby was seen again in a series made for television, "Lost in Space."

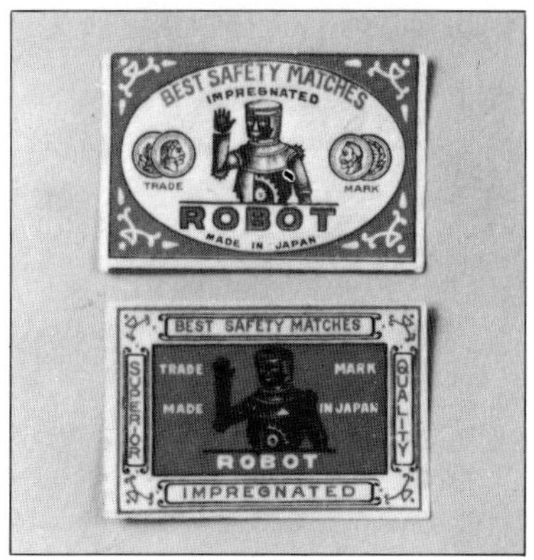

183. 184. **1930s Match Box**
When these match box labels were printed in the 1930s, the word "robot" had just been coined and the whole idea of robots was still pretty fantastical. This particular drawing endows the robot with classical facial features and displays part of the inner gears in a cutaway of the torso.

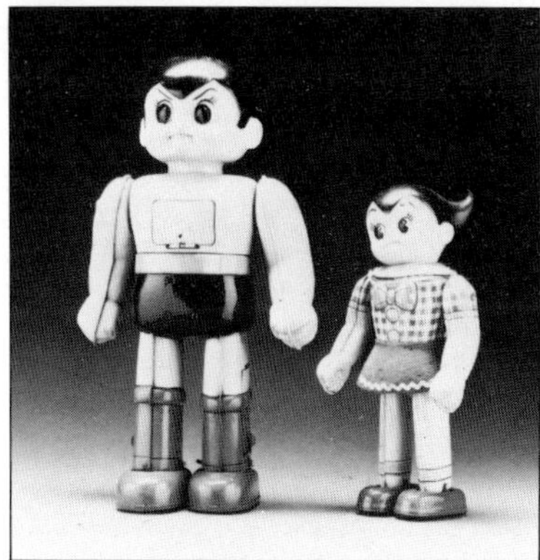

187. 189. **Tetsuwan Atom and Uran** (Nomura)
Tetsuwan Atom is an extremely popular Japanese comic book hero created by Osamu Tetsuka. A variety of Tetsuwan products are still sold. The robot is battery operated and opens at the chest for refueling. On the right is the robot's younger sister, Uran, who works by a spring mechanism.

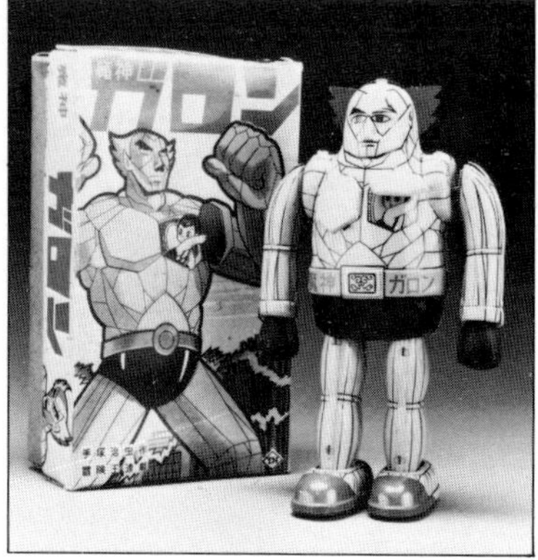

189. **Garon** (Nomura)
Spring mechanism. Garon is another creation of Osamu Tetsuka in the series "Mashin Garon" (Garon the Devil) which appeared in *Boken Oh* (King of Adventure), a Japanese monthly magazine for boys. Garon also appears in some later episodes of "Tetsuwan Atom." The robot advances, then stops as a breast plate opens to reveal the face of a small child. In the story, this child controls all of the robot's actions.

Explanation

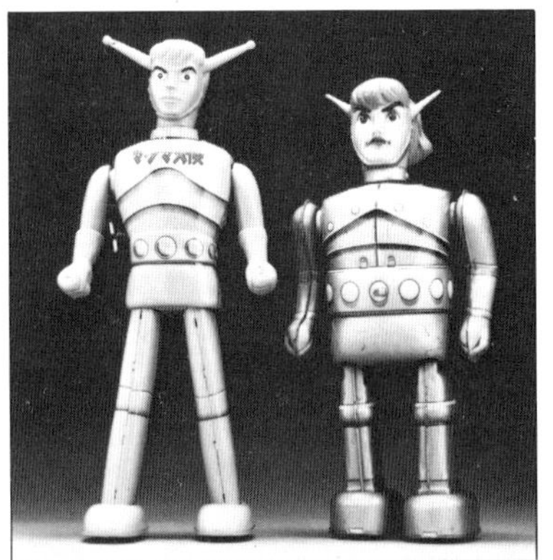

192. 193. **Maguma Taishi** (Tada, Nomura)
Battery operated, friction. "Maguma Taishi" written by Osamu Tetsuka was the first TV series to feature special effects. The hero is an ambassador of justice for earthlings. This series appeared on television at the same time monster movies became popular; most kids who could were glued to the TV set watching their heroes.

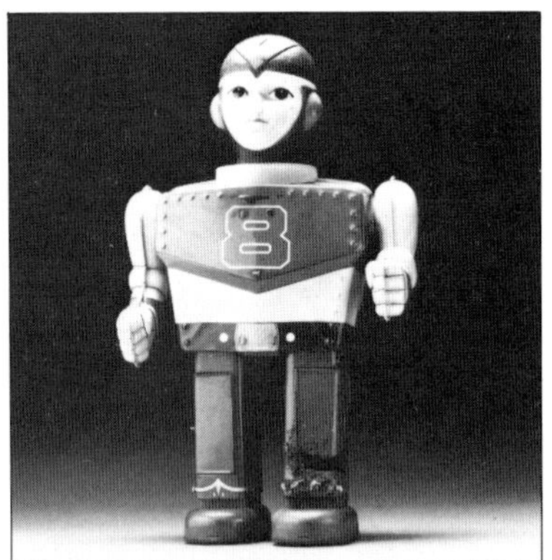

196. **8 Man** (Yonezawa)
Battery operated. 8 Man was the creation of Kazumasa Hirai and Jiro Kuwata for *Shonen Magazine* in Japan. As a protector of justice, 8 Man was more than a mere robot; in scientific terms, 8 Man was a "cyborg" or an artificial human being. Batteries for 8 Man are housed in the legs.

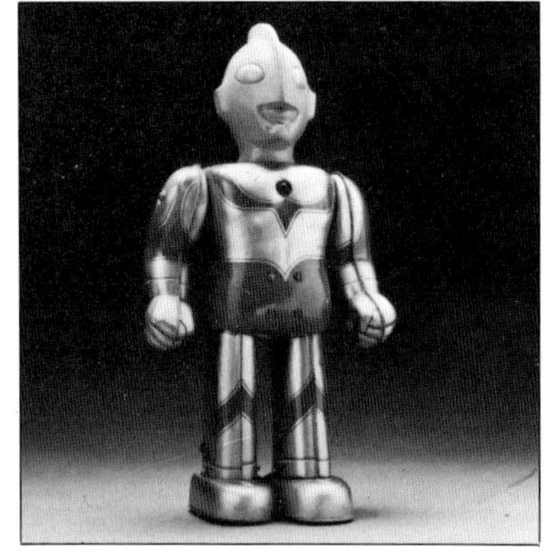

199. **Ultra Man** (Bull Mark)
Battery operated. Ultra Man is the hero of another special effects television series which was produced by Tsuburaya Productions. Ultra Man becomes a hero for children after arriving on earth from the star M-78 on a mission of justice. Sequels to "Ultra Man" were the "Ultra 7" and "Ultra Man Leo" series.

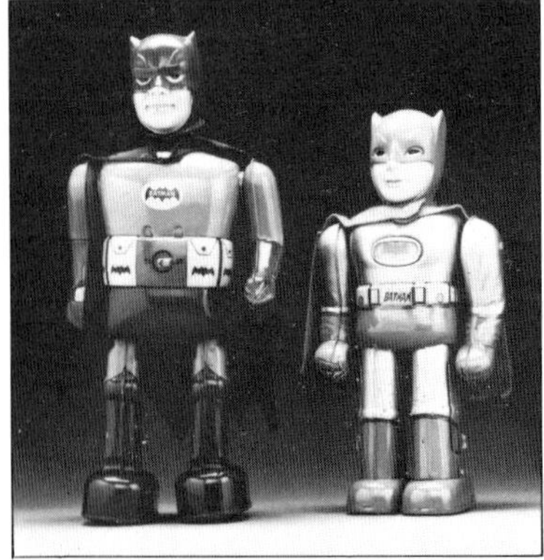

204. 205. **Batman** (Nomura, Bandai)
Battery operated. America's popular TV heroes, Batman and Robin, combine forces to fight evil. Their Batmobile, which could perform all kinds of tricks, was one of the highlights of the show.

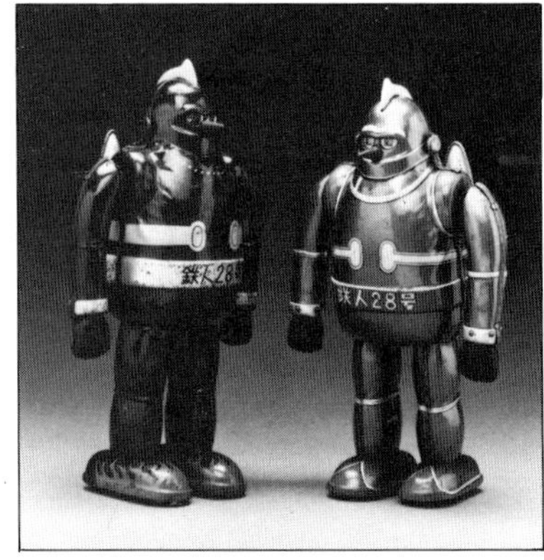

215. 216. **Tetsujin 28-GO** (Nomura)
Spring mechanism. Tetsujin 28-Go became just as popular with comic book fans as Tetsuwan Atom was. Though it didn't have refined, human-like features, this creation of Mitsuteru Yokoyama did have a rough, likable personality. Its sturdy body looks like a coat of armor; even the head resembles the helmet of a medieval knight.

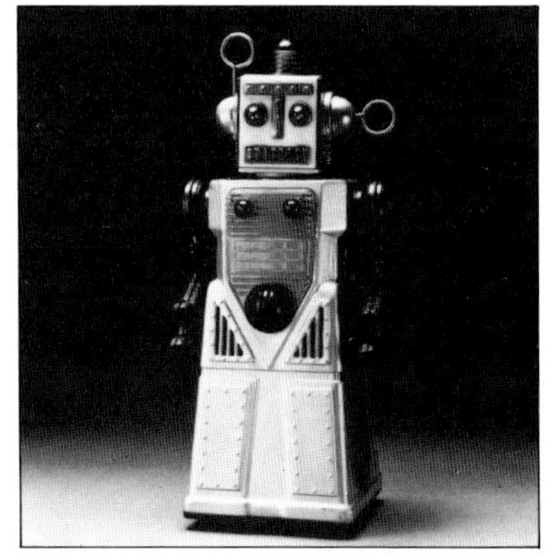

On the Front Cover: **Modern Robot** (Yoshiya)
Battery operated. In a stop action sequence, the robot advances, stops and turns its head while eyes and headlights shine and antennas turn. The head movement stops and the robot advances again. This robot has a nice friendly look.

INDEX

B = Battery operated
S = Spring mechanism
F = Friction

Afterword

Creations of tinplate, flashing lights, and rasping gears, toy robots are the enduring friends from childhood for a generation who grew up in the 1950s. For as little as a flashlight battery and some imagination, they could transform the world into one of fantasy and adventure.

In 1950 the world was just awakening to the possibilities of space exploration and high technology. As Sputnik sailed quietly overhead in 1957, the whole concept of space travel still seemed to belong more to science fiction than the real world. It was a time of new beginnings that inspired a strange mixture of fear and anticipation.

Unquestionably the favorite toy of the fifties was the robot. Robots were strong and capable of practically anything with their fire-shooting chests and X ray eyes. Robby, Mr. Atomic, Mr. Mercury—singlehandedly they fought the forces of evil; the mind boggled at what these mechanical supermen could do. And in no time, the moving picture industry—and TV—were turning their emerging talents to bringing monsters and robots to the screen in such classics as *Forbidden Planet* (1956) and *The Day the Earth Stood Still* (1951).

Less well known are the toy manufacturers. In the 1950s, Japan's major export was not cars or electrical goods, but toys. Most tinplate toys were made in Japan and the variety was tremendous. Inspiration for the toys would come both from real life—a rocket launching, an astronaut in orbit—as well as from science fiction and the toy manufacturer's imagination. Some could be quite whimsical, like a tailwagging robot dog or robots that seesaw.

The parts were all mass-produced, but the assembly still had to be done by hand. Toys were produced this way up to the end of the 1960s when the introduction of plastic spelled the end for tinplate.

The author, who grew up playing with robots in the late fifties in Tokyo, is now 36 and owner of a sporting goods store. Teruhisa Kitahara started to collect the toys of his youth about ten years ago. "I happened into an old toy shop and there, gathering dust in the shop window, were the friends of my childhood—tinplate robots. I'll never forget how elated I felt at seeing them again. It was as if a corner of the shop had been lifted and a part of the past let in." His house now overflows with over 10,000 tinplate toys.

Robots, however, retain a special place in the collection. In this volume there are 229 robots all manufactured in the two decades following World War II. Says Kitahara, "They still inspire the same admiration and fascination they inspired in us as children." •

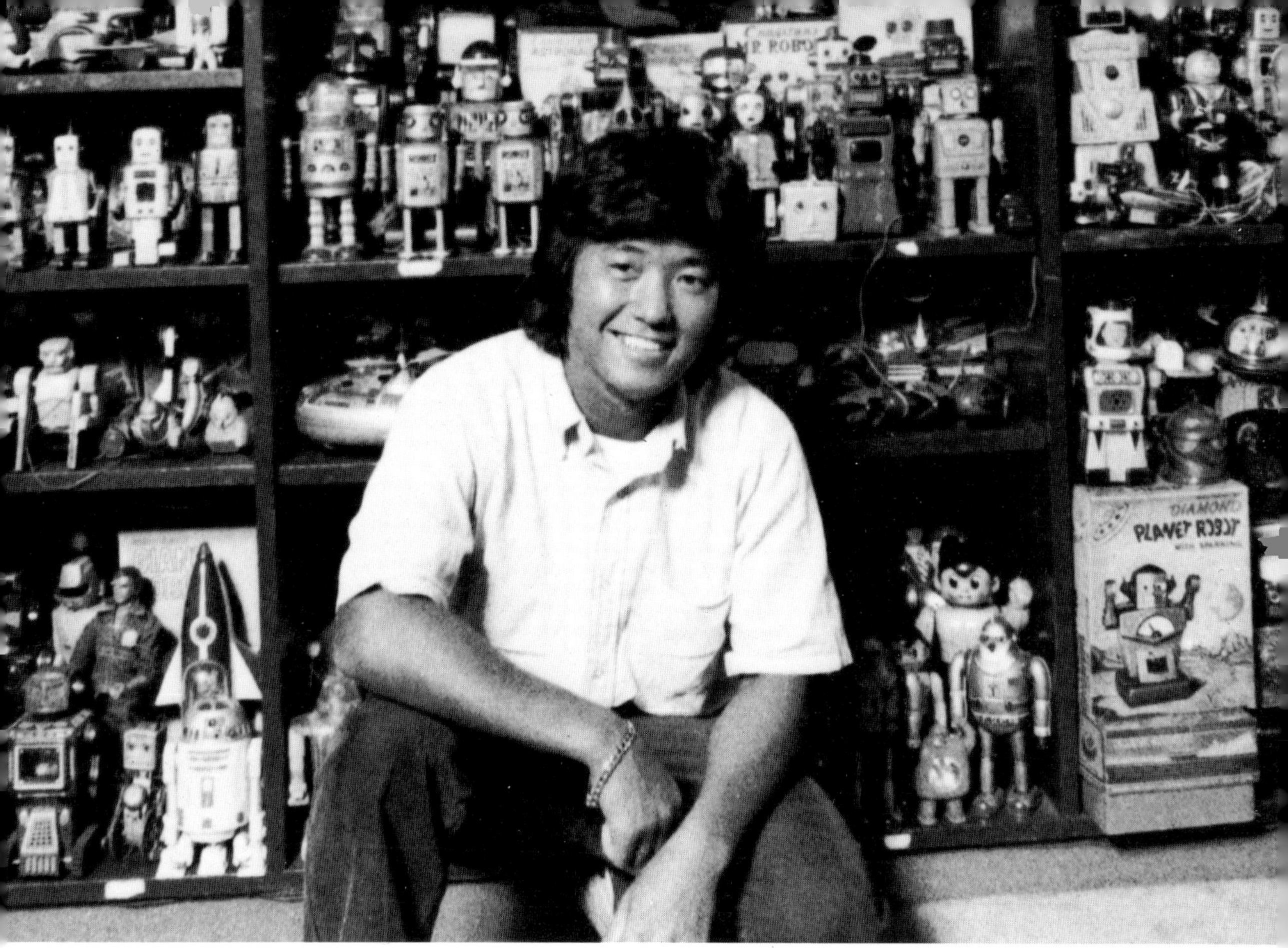

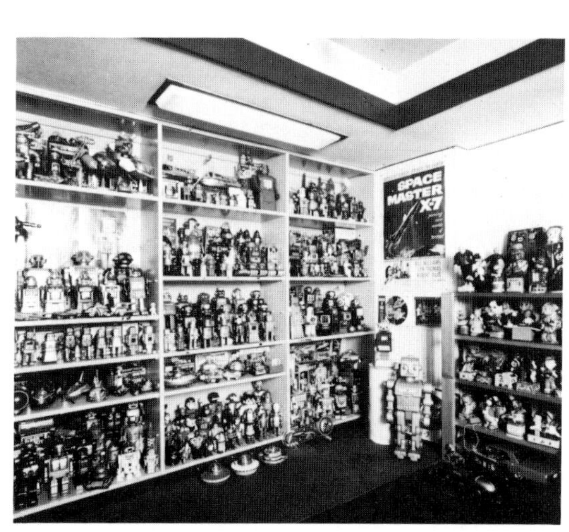
SPACE
MASTER
X-7